THE
PUZZLE
of
NON-WESTERN
DEMOCRACY

RICHARD YOUNGS

CARNEGIE
ENDOWMENT FOR
INTERNATIONAL PEACE

THE

PUZZLE

of

NON-WESTERN

DEMOCRACY

Carnegie Endowment for International Peace
1779 Massachusetts Avenue NW
Washington, DC 20036
P+ 202 483 7600
F+ 202 483 1840
CarnegieEndowment.org

The Carnegie Endowment does not take institutional positions on public policy issues; the views represented here are the author's own and do not necessarily reflect the views of Carnegie, its staff, or its trustees.

To order, contact:
Hopkins Fulfillment Service
P.O. Box 50370
Baltimore, MD 21211-4370
P+ 1 800 537 5487 or 1 410 516 6956
F+ 1 410 516 6998

Cover design by Courtney Griffith
Composition by Zeena Feldman
Printed by United Book Press

Library of Congress Cataloging-in-Publication Data
Youngs, Richard, 1968-
The puzzle of non-western democracy / Richard Youngs.
pages cm
Includes bibliographical references and index.
ISBN 978-0-87003-428-2 (pbk. : alk. paper) – ISBN 978-0-87003-429-9 (cloth : alk. paper) – ISBN 978-0-87003-430-5 (electronic)
1. Democracy–Cross-cultural studies. 2. Democracy–Asia. 3. Democracy–Middle East. 4. Democracy–Africa. 5. Democracy–Latin America. 6. Democratization–International cooperation. I. Title.
JC423.Y696 2015
321.8–dc23   2015011247

CONTENTS

FOREWORD | THOMAS CAROTHERS   vii

PREFACE   ix

CHAPTER 1
INTRODUCTION   I

CHAPTER 2
CALLS FOR NON-WESTERN DEMOCRACY   II

CHAPTER 3
REGIONAL MODELS AND TRENDS   29

CHAPTER 4
**PROBLEMS WITH THE NOTION OF
NON-WESTERN DEMOCRACY**   71

CHAPTER 5
THE DEBATE ON DEMOCRATIC VARIATION   83

CHAPTER 6
A FRAMEWORK FOR DEMOCRATIC VARIATION   101

CHAPTER 7
THE IMPLICATIONS FOR INTERNATIONAL DEMOCRACY SUPPORT   129

CHAPTER 8
THE FUTURE OF DEMOCRATIC VARIATION   157

NOTES   169

SELECTED BIBLIOGRAPHY   187

INDEX   199

ABOUT THE AUTHOR   213

CARNEGIE EUROPE   215

FOREWORD

These are uncertain and challenging times for international democracy support and democratic activism more generally. A daunting, indeed often bewildering array of political developments around the world— such as the startling disintegration of the Arab Spring into a series of civil wars and the rise of "authoritarian capitalism" as a challenge to Western liberal democracy—are prompting democracy supporters to question their foundational assumptions from decades past. The belief, for example, that democracy is on a long-term path of expansion has been replaced by the reality of democratic stagnation or even recession. Confidence that democracy supporters have a clear idea of how democratization happens and how they can best facilitate it has given way to doubts and debates. And the legitimacy of democratic societies working across borders to help other societies become more democratic is under attack from dozens of governments that are striking out harshly against international backing for civil society and other basic elements of democracy support.

In this context it is clear that all of the major assumptions underlying international democracy support must be examined and reformulated in a searching, open-minded way if the enterprise is to chart a course in the new political landscape. One issue that merits particular scrutiny is the model or conception of democracy that Western democracy supporters are trying to help advance in the world. Western policymakers and aid practitioners have for years insisted that they know there is not a single model of democracy and that they do not seek to impose a Western conception on others.

In practice, however, they have not displayed much openness nor devoted much detailed thought to ideas about democracy coming from outside the West. Yet today, calls for alternative, non-Western forms of democracy are proliferating in societies outside the West. And deep-reaching debates over how democracy could or should be renovated are proliferating within established Western democracies.

In this probing, thought-provoking book, Richard Youngs takes a clear-eyed look at this idea of non-Western democracy. He recognizes the need for democratic diversity and renovation—not just outside the West but within the West as well. Yet at the same time, he is profoundly wary of the tendency of some political actors to invoke the appealing but vague notion of non-Western democracy as a cover for antidemocratic ideas and practices. He presses hard on the question of whether non-Western democracy is in fact a viable concept at all, dissecting examples of democratic variation in Asia, Latin America, sub-Saharan Africa, and elsewhere. He works toward a sophisticated synthesis that extracts critical elements of the drive for alternatives to Western liberal democracy and fuses them into a framework for thinking about democratic variation that preserves essential democratic principles. And from this ground he proceeds to consider the practical implications of a greater openness to such variation for international democracy support organizations and activists.

In short, this is a book that embodies the characteristics of Richard Youngs's many writings that have established his reputation as an invaluable thinker on democracy support and democracy itself—a sweeping scope of insights from a notably wide array of cases, the blending of conceptual rigor with practical application, and the pairing of openness to new ideas with tough skepticism about political dogmas and disguises. The book is a significant addition to the work of the Carnegie Endowment's Democracy and Rule of Law Program, which is addressing the changed landscape for international democracy support and seeking to contribute useful ideas that will help democracy activists in all parts of the world effectively address the many challenges they now confront.

> —Thomas Carothers
> Vice President for Studies
> Carnegie Endowment for International Peace

PREFACE

Current global trends in democracy reveal immense complexity. What had appeared to be a somewhat standard path to democratization now looks like the road less traveled and not the way to the future. What had looked like a standard end product of liberal democracy is now challenged as much as it is embraced. And it is challenged not only by autocratic regimes but also by genuine democrats. For analysts, diplomats, aid practitioners, and civil society activists alike, there is a need to rethink—even to go back to basics.

The rich world's democratic challenges no longer look so different from those of emerging or developing nations. The international agenda of extending, protecting, and deepening democracy was one that habitually pointed "out there," to the world beyond the West. Research on this agenda was about the "how" of democratic advancement, not about the "what." The focus was on how different kinds of tactics might dislodge autocrats; and it was on how much political will Western governments really invested behind their prodemocracy rhetoric, especially when it came to confronting authoritarian allies. The agenda was much less about the *form* of democracy that people wanted. Democracy itself was not up for debate in any fundamental way. In the international support agenda, reflection on democracy was object, not subject.

In many regions around the world, politicians, activists, and others struggle to put in place more open government, and many still want international democracy support. Yet the latter is not seen as quite the unquestioningly benign phenomenon that it was. Even if there were always critics offstage—right and left—democracy support did not face the profundity of doubt that afflicts it today. It is now an enterprise that has to make more strenuous efforts to justify itself than it did in the 1990s and at the beginning of this century.

Add all this together and it is clear that democracy supporters must be willing to recast the way they work—and even to critically examine the end goals toward which they work. The Arab Spring opened up possibilities for a new era of democracy support; but in most of the Middle East, this window of opportunity soon slid shut. This experience of (for now) thwarted hope has reinforced the need to open up to scrutiny issues that were previously closed black boxes within the democracy support community. Some assumptions previously held as inviolate must be interrogated with an open mind if support for deeper global democracy is to advance in good health into a new phase.

This book attempts to contribute toward such a rethink. It focuses on one black box that needs prizing open: the question of how different *kinds of democracy* need to be debated, taken seriously, and aided through practical democracy support initiatives. Democracy was never a fixed entity, and many of today's claims that it faces an unprecedented meltdown are overblown. But more searching questions are being asked of democracy's performance than has been the case for many years. In many countries around the world, we see a flourish of deliberation about different models of democracy and about different ways in which democratic accountability needs to be revitalized.

I chose to pursue this line of inquiry because the issue of non-Western democracy has become so much more prominent in recent years. Although not a new issue, it has in the past five years attracted more attention and seeped onto international policy agendas. For someone involved frequently in democracy-related meetings, consultations, workshops, and conferences, it is striking how the question has gradually assumed a higher profile. Certainly in my fifteen years working on democracy support, there have never been so many or such vociferous calls for democracy to be encouraged along paths very different from the Western model. In my many hundreds of interviews and conversations with practitioners, activists, and analysts in Asia, Latin America, the Middle East, and the former Soviet space, it has struck me how much of a recurrent theme this has become.

The same factors that motivated me to write the book also made it analytically taxing. The divisions among various areas of inquiry into democracy cannot now be as absolute as they have sometimes appeared. Today's research agenda needs to bridge a number of areas of inquiry that until recently have been pursued largely in isolation. One such area has traditionally been international democracy promotion; another area has been the analytical exploration of the concept of democracy itself. But the "how" and the "what" of democracy support are now mixed together in a single process of reexamination.

Moreover, not all democracy support comes from the West today; this book examines the emerging role played by non-Western democracies in supporting democracy across national borders. Non-Western democracies are now a provider of democracy support, not an abstract concept debated at the receiving end of Western policies. In this book, I wanted to delve more deeply into this possible globalizing of the democracy agenda—and assess the obstacles that may hinder this incipient trend from extending as far as many would like.

Readers will recognize this book to be more exploratory and more conceptual than most think tank books. It does not seek to make a single policy point. It does not advocate one line of action in one country. Rather, the book takes a step back from immediate day-to-day foreign policy imperatives and suggests ways in which the core conceptual underpinnings of global democracy need to be rethought.

For contributing to this effort, I thank my colleagues in the Democracy and Rule of Law Program at the Carnegie Endowment for International Peace. Thomas Carothers pointed me in the direction of the non-Western topic and provided detailed intellectual guidance throughout the book's preparation. His uniquely sharp questioning and criticism helped immeasurably in bringing greater clarity to the manuscript. Other members of the Carnegie team, Saskia Brechenmacher, Sarah Chayes, Mahroh Jahangiri, and Rachel Kleinfeld, all took considerable time to offer extensive input too; I am extremely grateful to them. Carnegie's publications team, especially Ilonka Oszvald and Jocelyn Soly, ably oversaw the production of the book. Three highly respected external reviewers, Peter Burnell, Ivan Krastev, and Roland Rich, gave detailed and expert feedback. I was also able to draw from the Carnegie Rising Democracies Network, which groups together analysts from non-Western democracies and has been meeting on a regular basis over the past two years. From this group, Andreas Feldmann and Tsveta Petrova gave particularly detailed advice and suggestions. Support for Carnegie's Democracy and Rule of Law Program from the Robert Bosch Stiftung, the Ford Foundation, the John D. and Catherine T. MacArthur Foundation, and the UK Department for International Development helped make the research and writing of this book possible. I am very grateful for this support. Of course, the opinions herein are my responsibility, and do not necessarily reflect the views of those institutions that have helped support the research and writing that went into it.

—Richard Youngs
May 2015

CHAPTER 1

INTRODUCTION

As global power shifts away from the West, democracy is under the spotlight. Many articles and books express pessimism about the future of Western, liberal democracy. They often suggest that Western-style democracy must give way to other forms of democracy. Many experts, politicians, and policymakers feel that if democracy is to prosper in the future, it must do so through non-Western templates. While citizens in all regions of the world want more open forms of governance, many think democracy's current problems stem from its narrow, Western straitjacket.

Calls for non-Western democracy are not new. They have served as a background critique of the West's democracy-support policies since the end of the Cold War. Still, these calls have gained momentum in the past five years and are today at the forefront of debates about the type of politics that is likely to prevail in a post-Western world order. Western liberal democracy in North America and Europe is beset by problems and less able to stand as an unblemished beacon to the world. Meanwhile, the rest of the world is increasingly self-confident and keen to contribute ideas to twenty-first-century politics.

The plea for variation in democratic forms holds strong intuitive appeal. Many Western governments themselves express sympathy with the view that alternative routes to democracy need to be explored. As Western democracy-support strategies have struggled to gain traction, these governments have cast around for new ideas and come to agree that local ownership of such initiatives is important. Few involved in democracy and human rights support programs today question the need for customized policies that conform to "local values" rather than Western templates. In fact, the latter are habitually damned as unsuited to non-Western countries —not only by anti-Western strands of opinion but also by most practitioners and analysts engaged in democracy issues within the West itself. After all, who could possibly be against variety, when this is part of democracy's very ethos?

It is common for participants in international meetings and conferences on democracy to excoriate the evils of Western or liberal democracy and to call passionately for non-Western democracy. "You must stop imposing a Western form of democracy!" they cry. Or, "We must be more supportive of local forms of democracy." Such calls elicit approving applause. Speaking out in favor of non-Western democracy is one of the surest ways to win broad appreciation among democracy experts.

But just as assuredly, the conversation stops there, without anyone asking what is meant by non-Western democracy. Imprecision reigns. Do citizens in other parts of the world want a political order that is really different from the Western model? Is the call for non-Western democracy about maintaining tradition or fast-forwarding to a different type of political modernity? Talk of traditional forms of politics goes on as developing states rush toward modernization. Are these two things compatible? Is non-Western democracy the same thing as a less liberal form of democracy?

The twenty-first century might see democracy not only spread but also become more varied. If successful, such divergence might help to head off a resurgence of authoritarianism. If misconceived, it could usher in the ills of illiberalism. How the quest for less Western-specific democracy turns out will be crucial for the new global order.

At a moment when liberal norms are challenged by rising powers, this question matters: If democracy is to fare well in the twenty-first century, must its global reach look less Western? And if so, what are the implications for Western foreign policies, especially initiatives that aim to foster democracy?

IN FAVOR OF MODERATE VARIATION

In this book, I do four things. First, I outline where the calls for different models of democracy have come from and what lies behind them. Second,

I point to problems with the concept of non-Western democracy. Third, I suggest alternative ways to think about democratic variation. And fourth, I explore how this analysis should inform the policies of organizations involved in international democracy support.

My overarching argument holds that the search for variety in democratic forms is valid. The need to revitalize democracy is essential. The increasingly prominent non-Western democracy discourse cannot be dismissed as an entirely disingenuous pretext for illiberal politics. However, when it comes to improving the quality of democracy worldwide, there are limits to the usefulness of the non-Western concept.

Although variation in democratic templates merits support, I question the assumption that there is a well-defined and wholesale dichotomy between Western and non-Western models of democracy. Variation can and should incorporate local elements of culture, authenticity, and historical tradition. But it is less clear that there exists a non-Western variety with structural features that deviate from the core, standard version of democracy. A more nuanced approach to democratic variety is warranted.

The advocates of non-Western democracy raise a straw man. These proponents contend that Western liberal democracy is of limited appeal in other regions of the world because it is hopelessly minimalistic—it does not deliver economic justice, protect community identities, or empower citizens. The advocates of non-Western democracy also accuse Western powers of supporting a narrow, rigid form of Western democracy internationally. Although the call for variation is justified, we must be cautious about such breezy assertions in order to have a more productive debate—and one that is less theoretical and more forward looking in its relevance to policymakers concerned with international democracy support.

There are two somewhat different debates in play. One is about the idea of non-Western alternatives to Western liberal democracy. The other is about variations in democracy more broadly. These two debates unfold in parallel but are often conflated. It is vital, however, to understand that they have quite different implications. The former often leads to advocacy for political features or practices that stand directly at odds with the core democratic standards that exist in the West. The latter is more about searching for ways to improve democracy in a more general sense—across non-Western and Western regions.

The book explores both debates, but it leans toward the latter as the more vital ground. Non-Western countries might legitimately develop democracy differently from the West, but many of today's challenges outside the West are similar to those within it. The book unpacks specific areas in which non-Western countries might introduce legitimate and innovative variations to forms of democratic accountability. But the book also drives home the point that calls for non-Western democracy are frequently inspired by concerns that animate the reimagining of politics in North America and Europe as much as they do in non-Western countries. If the West tends to misunderstand others' perspectives on democracy, others tend equally to caricature Western democracy.

Some readers will feel the book goes too far in the direction of advocating democratic variation. Others will feel it restricts itself too much to a core liberal-democratic framework. In expectation of slings and arrows from both sides, I appeal for flexibility. Debates on democratic regeneration—and better international support for democracy—are currently hampered. On one side, there are those who are overly defensive of a singular and somewhat beleaguered Western template. On the other side, there are those who let their broad antipathy to the West distort clear thinking on how demands for core universal values can be better met.

I believe that democratic variation must flow from exploratory openness. There are undoubtedly lines to be drawn in order to preserve core democratic principles; concepts such as "traditional justice" might hide deeply undemocratic dynamics. The notion of "authenticity" can be taken too far; listening to non-Western perspectives is not axiomatically a route to uncontested truths in other societies. However, the West does need to cooperate with non-Western reformers in genuinely exploring promising means for ensuring that democracy gains local legitimacy. This represents an extremely difficult and delicate balance to strike, but it is a puzzle that must urgently be addressed.

THE BOOK'S STRUCTURE

The book is organized into eight chapters. The next one, chapter 2, offers an account of how the focus on different models of democracy has intensified in recent years. It highlights how leaders, politicians, and diplomats both inside and outside the West now talk about the concept of non-Western democracy. And it explains why they do so.

Chapter 3 examines the debates over regional models of democracy. It looks at the state of current arguments in favor of distinctive Middle Eastern, Latin American, African, and Asian forms of democracy. The longevity of calls for regionally specific models of democracy suggests there is real weight to this localized focus. At the same time, analysts and politicians struggle to define with precision what such regional models should look like. And although some of the calls for Arab, Latin American, African, or Asian democracy are rooted in genuine impulses for democratic variation, some are espousals of soft authoritarianism.

Chapter 4 examines the reasons why arguments for a distinctive concept of non-Western democracy are not fully convincing. A lack of clarity characterizes calls for non-Western democracy. They fail to articulate the distinctive elements that would constitute a non-Western template of democratic politics. And the calls aim at quite different objectives. Some critiques object to Western democracy per se; others suggest that democracy's institutional forms need more modest tweaking to fit national specificities. And in other cases, the calls are for different sets of *policies* that do not in fact seem to entail a different model of democracy. It is the outcomes of neoliberal economic or social policies—more than the institutional structures of Western politics—that many critics object to.

Chapter 5 moves the analysis toward a broader set of debates about democratic variation, summarizing important ideas for improving democratic quality that have taken shape in recent years. These ideas are not framed explicitly in terms of non-Western democracy; many are just as concerned with the state of Western democracy as they are with the developing world. Yet these ideas offer ways of usefully thinking about variety in different types of democracy. This chapter lays the analytical foundations for connecting the rather vague calls for non-Western democracy with a more concrete and targeted exploration of democratic variation.

Chapter 6 identifies legitimate elements of distinctiveness in democratic forms and practices. Non-Western preferences may be meaningfully different, even if they are not extensive enough to constitute entirely distinctive models. It is possible and important to distinguish between the benign and the bogus in calls for non-Western democracy. While it is right to be alert for authoritarian tendencies hiding within some calls for non-Western templates, there are potentially helpful variations from what is normally thought of as Western democracy. This chapter draws out the issues where the advocates of democratic variation are on solid ground.

To this end, the chapter advocates a guiding principle of "liberalism plus." This idea is meant to suggest that democratic variation should be pursued through innovations that add to the core template of liberal democracy rather than subtract from it. Liberalism plus categorically does *not* mean simply more of the same kind of politics that already exists in Western countries. Rather, it is meant to convey the need to look seriously at non-Western ideas that give greater meaning to political liberalism's core spirit of tolerance, pluralism, and popular accountability over the powerful.

The chapter lays out *five axes for thinking about democratic variation*: individual rights, economic justice, communitarian identity, new forms of civic action and representation, and legal pluralism. Variation along these axes offers genuine potential for positive innovation to democracy. I do not argue that regimes generally defined as "not democratic" but that attend in some positive ways to these areas should be categorized as "democratic." Rather, I seek to identify variation in the ways in which democratic quality might genuinely be improved.

Chapter 7 explores implications for international democracy-support policies. Western donors have begun to address the issue of democratic variation more than is generally realized. Moreover, rising non-Western democracies are themselves beginning to support democracy beyond their borders and making use of new types of democratic variation as they do so. I argue that all democracy supporters need to develop their policies further in this direction. They need to match their initiatives to the suggested five axes of democratic variation. These axes should not be seen as the building blocks of non-Western democracy support, but rather as issues that democracy supporters should explore as they develop and implement their programs and initiatives.

Chapter 8 concludes the book by exploring the broader significance of the non-Western democracy debate. Essential to the renewal of global democracy will be finding the right kind and degree of political variation. It will also be necessary if international democracy-support policies are to retain any integrity and legitimacy. The quest for democratic variation springs from the extremely fluid and indeterminate trends that shape today's global politics. And it is a search whose outcome will have an increasingly strong bearing on democracy's future prospects.

A NOTE ON CONCEPTS

As noted earlier, the book is framed as an exploration of the debates over non-Western democracy. Many readers may feel that this non-Western lens requires a firm definitional justification. Some will be skeptical about the "Western" and "non-Western" terminology. However, the exploration is posed in these terms because—as will become apparent—this is how so many political actors and analysts today frame the debate. This makes it necessary to explore the question of whether there are varieties of democracy that are non-Western. My argument is explicitly that no such clear-cut definitions of Western and non-Western democracy exist. To adhere to fixed definitions of these terms would be subversive of the book's rationale.

Another distinction is made between democratic *values* and democratic *institutions*. Some Western observers insist that people outside the West support the same basic democratic principles as those in the West but that non-Westerners want these principles expressed through different institutional forms and practices. This book argues that this "norms versus institutions" division is indeed helpful, but it does not fully capture the way we should think about democratic variation. When politicians and diplomats claim that people everywhere subscribe to the same core democratic values but simply want these guaranteed through different institutional configurations, they are partly right—but they also oversimplify the nature of global political debates. Aspects of non-Western calls for variation are about values, not institutional forms. There are genuine and necessary debates to be had about how democratic values should now be defined. In some ways the situation has been inverted: many countries today contest some core norms, while accepting most of the basic Western institutional template.

Differentiating between the definitions of "Western" and "liberal" democracy is trickier. Although these terms tend to be used interchangeably, a theme running through the book is that there is a complex relationship between the notions of "Western democracy" and "liberal democracy." A lot of what follows revolves around debates over the concepts of liberalism and illiberalism. Table 1.1. gives a breakdown of the main varieties of democracy that analysts have traditionally identified. Liberal democracy is defined as the combination of open political competition and the protection of individual rights. Illiberal democracy is where some degree of political competition exists, but individual rights are constricted or not fully protected. One of the most important questions to answer is whether calls for non-Western democracy are in essence calls for illiberal democracy. This has become one of today's most sensitive questions both analytically and politically. Many trends point toward rising illiberalism—understood as opposition to the notion of largely unfettered individual rights.

At least some variations of what is most commonly advocated as non-Western democracy are, in essence, democracy with abridged liberal rights. But the Western-versus-non-Western democracy debate is not synonymous with the liberal-versus-illiberal democracy debate. Many of the calls for non-Western democracy do amount to forms of illiberal democracy. But some non-Western variations do not necessarily attack the protection of individual rights. This is where a more positive attitude toward democratic variation is desirable. Although some non-Western proposals are about subtracting from liberalism, others seek to add to it and render liberal democracy's core spirit more effective.

Where alternative models are essentially less liberal models, the question is whether these should be seen simply as having a lower degree of democratic quality. It is also necessary to inquire how much populations outside the West want such templates. This is the thorniest of the high-level questions surrounding the non-Western democracy conundrum. Should international democracy supporters accept or challenge nonliberal models of democracy? Although there are no easy, singularly applicable answers to this puzzle, I argue against being too tolerant of illiberalism. I point out that in most places, large numbers of citizens reject the claim that an illiberal form of democracy is locally "authentic" and desired. At the same time, I suggest that it is important to genuinely and openly explore the way that personal rights relate to a society's broad set of values and identities.

As will become clear, these definitional points assume political meaning. The way that liberalism is defined affects how far democratic variation can be extended beyond its Western templates. This is set to be an increasingly important question for global politics in the post-Western order.

TABLE 1.1. PRINCIPLES OF DEMOCRACY

1. ELECTORAL (AKA ELITE, MINIMAL, REALIST, SCHUMPETERIAN)		
IDEALS contestation; competition	QUESTION Are important government offices filled by free and fair multiparty elections?	INSTITUTIONS elections; political parties; competitiveness; voting; turnover
2. LIBERAL		
IDEALS limited government; horizontal accountability; individual rights; civil liberties; transparency	QUESTION Is power constrained and individual rights guaranteed?	INSTITUTIONS independent media, interest groups, and judiciary; written constitution with explicit guarantees
3. MAJORITARIAN (AKA RESPONSIBLE PARTY GOVERNMENT)		
IDEALS majority rule; centralization; vertical accountability	QUESTION Does the majority (or plurality) rule?	INSTITUTIONS consolidated and centralized, with special focus on the role of political parties
4. CONSENSUAL (AKA PLURALIST)		
IDEALS power sharing; multiple veto-points	QUESTION How numerous, independent, and diverse are the groups and institutions that participate in policymaking?	INSTITUTIONS multiparty system; proportional electoral laws; supermajorities; oversized cabinets; federalism
5. PARTICIPATORY		
IDEAL direct, active participation in decisionmaking by the people	QUESTION Do ordinary citizens participate in, or actively affect, political decisionmaking beyond voting?	INSTITUTIONS consultations; civil society; local government; direct democracy
6. DELIBERATIVE		
IDEAL government by reason	QUESTION Are political decisions the product of public deliberation?	INSTITUTIONS media; hearings; panels; other deliberative bodies
7. EGALITARIAN		
IDEAL political equality	QUESTION Are all citizens equally empowered?	INSTITUTIONS socioeconomic and political factors that generate conditions for political equality

Source: Based on V-Dem, "Varieties of Democracy, Methodology," March 31, 2014, v-dem.net/media/filer_public/e2/6d/e26d8ffe-283c-4323-8bb9-37d388415d87/v-dem_methodology_v1.pdf

CHAPTER 2

CALLS FOR NON-WESTERN DEMOCRACY

C alls in countries outside the West for alternatives to Western democracy have been heard ever since Western powers began exporting their political models to Africa, Asia, the Middle East, and Latin America. Alexis de Tocqueville long ago expressed skepticism over institutional models being transferred from one country to another, arguing that customs—or "habits of the heart"—would resist such imitation. Though not new, arguments in favor of finding and adopting non-Western forms of democracy are made more volubly and more widely than ever before. This chapter shows how politicians and policymakers from around the world have supported these arguments and outlines the debates that have nourished such views.

BACK ON THE AGENDA

From the 1960s through the 1980s, political activists and scholars in the developing world as well as many Western scholars of comparative politics often discussed the question of alternatives to Western democracy. As the newly decolonized states of Africa moved away from the West and its political systems, the dialogue shifted to creating authentic African democracies. In Latin America, talk in the 1970s of "Latin American democracy" was part of a broader conversation about anti-Western activism. In East Asia in the 1980s, there was considerable focus on Asian democracy and Asian values.

These different alternative ideas had somewhat different emphases. Proponents of "African democracy" often focused on raising to the national level the solidarity that existed at the village level. Forming robust and solid nations was the central political concern of decolonized Africa. Democratization was a part of the larger cause of forging viable nation-states. The ideas of popular sovereignty, national sovereignty, and political empowerment became intertwined with each other.

Latin Americans calling for "Latin American democracy" highlighted mass participation and economic justice as key elements of the systems they desired as alternatives to "northern" models of democracy. These preferences reflected the fact that Latin America had a long tradition of elitist politics, high levels of economic inequality, and high numbers of marginalized people, both indigenous populations and poor people generally. The Cuban model was influential, with its successes in poverty reduction, economic equality, and social policy.

The Asian model was different still. It was more about meritocracy, order, and discipline. It reflected a sense that some societies had certain core traditional, social strengths that needed to be preserved and combined with the arrival of democratic thinking.

With the onset of the Third Wave of democracy in the second half of the 1980s and first half of the 1990s, the idea of alternative, non-Western democracy lost considerable steam. The Western model seemed triumphant. Suddenly, instead of people in developing countries saying that it was insulting to make them follow Western paths, they started insisting that it was offensive not to expect them to achieve the same political outcomes as Western democracies.

Countries moved beyond collapsing authoritarian regimes and appeared to follow a standardized path of setting up multiparty systems, holding elections, and rewriting constitutions. This transition paradigm was mostly about moving toward the Western political model. Noted expert Jack Donnelly was able to write in 1999 that,

> the particular, contingent conjunction of democracy, development, and human rights gives the liberal democratic welfare state its hegemonic appeal. . . . Only the particular combination of democracy, development, and human rights achieved

in the liberal democratic welfare state is worthy of our highest praise and sustained effort. . . . [We must] keep human rights, and thus the substantive commitment to human dignity, explicitly central in our political language.[1]

But the momentum of the Third Wave stalled as it moved into the twenty-first century. Many countries in transition failed to achieve democratic consolidation and have since moved into a political grey zone, hovering between authoritarianism and liberal democracy. Data show that forms of democracy curtailing personal and civil liberties have spread.[2] Illiberal regimes appear less of a mutant form and more of a prevalent regime type that does not fit easily on a linear spectrum between democratic and authoritarian ones.

In addition, talk of alternative models has gone hand in hand with rising powers' bolder assertion of their national sovereignty. Indeed, David Clark notes that the pushback against Western democracy has almost become conflated—and confused—with the defense of sovereignty.[3] The calls for non-Western democracy are a product of changes within states and of shifts in the power balances between them.

A separate problem is that Western-style democracy is suffering ill health. In many Western countries, populist parties are rising. Citizens complain that they lack meaningful policy alternatives. During the Cold War, liberal democracy gained legitimacy by being better than totalitarianism. But citizens hold Western-style democracy to much tougher account since it has become the most prevalent form of government. Protests reflect public disillusionment with corruption, conflict, elite fecklessness, and poor economic performance.

All this feeds into the rising interest, once again, in non-Western democracy. Journalist Anne Applebaum, for example, suggests that developing countries currently beset by tensions over possible reform paths should not look to the problem-stricken West: "If they want long-term stability, Egyptians need pluralism, power-sharing and institutions that can resolve conflict, not suppress it. But they need not look to Europe or North America for examples: The developing world has many such institutions, if only they make the effort to find them."[4]

The National Intelligence Council (NIC) has made a prognosis for 2030. According to its findings, individual empowerment is the most potent global trend, making it unlikely that authoritarian regimes can survive indefinitely. At the same time, however, illiberal forces are increasingly empowered. Hence, the most likely direction of political evolution is toward "hybrid ideologies." We are also likely to see a mixing of modernity with aspects of tradition in fast-developing states—pulling politics in different directions.[5] In other words, underlying trends seem to point toward a future where non-Western democracy is a phenomenon of high significance.

Of course, not everyone agrees with these arguments. Some Western politicians and democracy promoters insist that if democracy is losing legitimacy, it is not because of a rejection of liberalism but rather because the focus on liberal democracy has not been resolute enough. Niall Ferguson argues that the rise of "the rest" lies not in their repudiation of the West but in their acceptance of basic Lockean concepts of liberalism and property rights.[6]

Such skeptics suggest there is less appeal in global alternatives to liberal democracy today than there was before 2008. Some see the talk of alternative models as a passing fad undermined by the Arab Spring and the increasingly apparent hollowness of Putinism. They see the real challenge as coming not from legitimate alternatives to liberalism but from tactically savvy "smart authoritarianism" that seeks to broaden its legitimacy and builds careful pressure valves to calm social tensions. They worry that today's smart autocrat has deployed the "differentiated democracy" discourse to dupe both domestic opposition and Western powers. What passes as non-Western democracy, doubters insist, is the familiar power grab and prickly nationalism merely dressed in the language of pluralism.

To many such critics, the only meaningful divide continues to be between democracies and nondemocracies—not between supposedly differentiated forms of democracy. Skeptics tend to insist that so-called hybrid regimes simply reflect the feckless pathologies of state capture (whereby vested interests effectively control public institutions and decisionmaking) and political polarization. Hybrid regimes are less of a model than a distortion of local demands. One writer deplores an "epistemological inflation": democracy is now meant to be everything to everyone—the solution to all political, social, and economic problems—and has lost its definitional sharpness.[7]

Such skepticism helps caution us against swinging too uncritically in favor of non-Western arguments. Yet, the case for variation in democratic forms is a powerful one. In this book, I maintain that it is a search that is legitimate and indeed necessary. While many power-grabbing autocrats undoubtedly deploy the notion of non-Western democracy disingenuously as a democratic veneer for their self-serving rule, such hijacking should not be allowed to discredit the effort to look beyond "standard" templates of minimal, liberal democracy. However, skeptical voices do raise some issues pertinent to my argument that the need for democratic variety is not best defined in the terms used by many advocates of non-Western democracy.

AN ACKNOWLEDGED IMPERATIVE

There is no clear starting point to the increased tempo of calls for non-Western democracy. But during the past decade, the frequency and intensity has risen. In 2007, the United Nations (UN) General Assembly stepped into the fray: "While democracies share common features, there is no single model of democracy."[8] The UN secretary-general's message for International Democracy Day in September 2011 repeated that "the UN does not seek to export or promote any particular national or regional model of democracy. It works on the understanding that the democratic ideal is rooted in philosophies and traditions from all parts of the world."[9] An initiative run by the International Institute for Democracy and Electoral Assistance (IDEA), a multilateral institution devoted to supporting democracy globally, concluded that the forms of democracy that exist in the West "are fundamentally alien to most countries and regions, notably in the global South. Viewed from this perspective . . . innovative institutional responses offer a . . . better understanding of the workings of local, as opposed to imported, democracy."[10]

The UN secretary-general's formal policy paper on democracy reinforces the point that "there is no one model ... Local norms and practices must be taken into consideration and [woven] into emerging democratic institutions and processes."[11]

Politicians and diplomats from different regions around the world have bought into the discourse on non-Western democracy. In December 2013, India's Minister of External Affairs, Salman Khurshid, said, "We are in favor of democratic pluralism and religious moderation but it is up to the people of the region to decide the pace and the means to achieve those goals, keeping in mind their traditions and history."[12] In Indonesia's 2014 election contest, one of the main contenders, Prabowo Subianto, made waves when he argued that Western-style democracy "doesn't suit" the country. Singaporean government representatives advocate what they present as an Asian view: "Democracy is a concept best understood in reality as elastic. The birth of nations does not come with a clean slate. Societies have history, traditions and different ethnic and religious mixes and endowments of natural resources. Democracies evolve."[13]

It is also a terminology, however, that has appealed to leaders who are not democrats. Kazakh President Nursultan Nazarbayev stated in April 2012, "There is not one model of democracy. People should themselves decide their futures in line with their cultures, traditions, and political systems." The West errs, he claimed, in equating democracy with "creating people who are pro-protest."[14] Egyptian President Abdel Fattah el-Sisi argues that while U.S. democracy prioritizes "life, liberty, and the pursuit of happiness," Islamic societies value the principles of "fairness, justice, equality, unity, and charity."[15] As a consequence, countries in the Middle East should establish democracies "based on Islamic beliefs" that demonstrate "respect to the religious nature of the culture."[16]

In July 2014, Hungarian Prime Minister Viktor Orban spoke about the failure of Western democracy and the need to create "a new illiberal state" in Hungary. He said:

> Understanding [political] systems that are not Western, not liberal, not liberal democracies and in some cases probably not even democracies, but are still making nations a success is a top issue these days. . . . The new state that we are building in Hungary today is not a liberal state. It doesn't deny liberalism's basic values such as freedom but doesn't make it its core element. It uses a particular, national approach."[17]

Prominent figures in the West have also spoken about the need for democratic variety and their openness to it. In 2005, then U.S. secretary of state Condoleezza Rice acknowledged that democratic values "will find expression in local circumstances and we believe fully that the forms of democracy will be very different across the world. The forms of democracy are different in Europe or in Asia or in Latin America. And the Middle Eastern people will find their voice and find the form of democracy that is best for them."[18] In 2012, U.S. Ambassador to Cameroon Robert Jackson, discussing democratic prospects in Africa, averred that "there are many models of democracy and each must incorporate a country's history and culture."[19] Former U.S. secretary of state Madeleine Albright is of the same view: "There is not one model of democracy ... What is universal, however, is people's desire to make decisions about their own lives ... There are different ways of doing [this]."[20]

President Barack Obama has expressed the same sentiment:

> The message I hope to deliver is that democracy, rule of law, freedom of speech, freedom of religion—those are not simply principles of the west to be foisted on these countries, but, rather what I believe to be universal principles that they can embrace and affirm as part of their national identity. The danger, I think, is when the United States, or any country, thinks that we can simply impose these values on another country with a different history and a different culture.[21]

In an important Middle East speech, he reiterated a similar position: "Not every country will follow our particular form of representative democracy. . . . But we can, and we will, speak out for a set of core principles."[22]

As secretary of state, Hillary Clinton said in 2011:

> [W]e recognize there are many paths to democracy, and we recognize that true and sustainable democracy is about far more than elections. Each society will work to realize its own democratic values and build its own democratic institutions in its own way, because we also recognize the uniqueness of culture and history and experience.[23]

In a *Foreign Policy* article on Asia, she developed the theme:

We cannot and do not aspire to impose our system on other countries, but we do believe that certain values are universal— that people in every nation in the world, including in Asia, cherish them—and that they are intrinsic to stable, peaceful, and prosperous countries. Ultimately, it is up to the people of Asia to pursue their own rights and aspirations, just as we have seen people do all over the world.[24]

Former deputy secretary of state William Burns echoed the sentiments on a trip to Cairo in 2013:

Only Egyptians can determine their future. I did not come with American solutions, nor did I come to lecture anyone. We know that Egyptians must forge their own path to democracy. We know that this will not mirror our own, and we will not try to impose our model on Egypt. What the United States will do is stand behind certain basic principles, not any particular personalities or parties.[25]

Michael McFaul, during his time as a senior White House official in the Obama administration, commented: "We don't support one individual or one political view and we most certainly don't support an American-style democracy. That's not our policy at all. There are lots of varieties of democracy around the world. There is no one truth, there is no one way to build democracy."[26]

The then European Union (EU) foreign policy high representative, Catherine Ashton, stated the same view: "While democracy is the cornerstone of the European Union, it is clear there is no single model for democratic government."[27] Asked in Cairo about specific details of the EU's reform aims, Ashton stated,

[W]e are here to help. We are not here to impose. The people of Egypt will determine their own future and those who have the privilege to be in leadership positions have the responsibility to ensure that that happens. We have some experience that might be of value and we can help by having conversations with everyone, to listen, and to be able to offer some thoughts. . . . The solutions are for the Egyptian people, the solutions must be found by those who are in the position to be able to lead from the different aspects of the political spectrum.[28]

The European Parliament's Office for the Promotion of Parliamentary Democracy states its position: "Promoting democracy does not entail exporting a single model."[29] A senior European External Action Service diplomat involved in the EU's Eastern neighborhood policy recognizes the need for reassessment: "I think we are increasingly seeing that Eastern Europe is not the same as the countries which joined in 2004 and the same sort of value systems are not self-evident . . . The underlying question should be what democracy is fundamentally about, and that's ownership of political processes and accountability of leadership."[30] The then Norwegian minister of foreign affairs, Espen Barth Eide, pointed out: "The relations between majority and minority must also change. Democracy is more than majority rule. There is not one model of democracy, but we must be aware of this fact. Minorities are particularly vulnerable in periods of transition."[31]

Many more illustrative statements of the same kind could be listed. They are now pretty much par for the course. But, such proclamations do not move on to explain what different models of democracy actually look like. It remains unclear whether these leaders and ministers have thought through what non-Western democracy really means—or how to avoid some regimes' using the same discourse to shore up what is in practice their distinctly nondemocratic rule.

A NEW BUT FUZZY CONSENSUS

The case for exploring non-Western political models has gained widespread support. With many Western democracies underperforming politically and economically, it is harder to maintain that their institutional model is naturally superior. This is compounded by the larger trend of power shifting from the West to "the rest." There is more intense interest in the idea that new democracies should not reflexively seek to imitate Western political forms but rather try to develop their own.

In short, a growing weight of opinion insists that the global zeitgeist is toward different, non-Western and nonliberal forms of democracy—and that the West must not only tolerate but actively support such alternative models. Yet fundamental questions remain. What do advocates of non-Western democracy want that is really different from Western democracy? Do we not risk mixing debates over the shortcomings of liberal democracy with those over its presumed universality? What examples can we identify of emerging and promising non-Western democracies? Are countries such as Brazil, India, and South Africa non-Western societies with basically Western-democratic systems, or are they truly non-Western democracies? What is legitimate variation in democratic forms?

One of the points commonly raised in any discussion of international democracy is a challenging one: Many developing country participants say they want democracy, but not Western-style democracy, or even more commonly, American-style democracy. These participants believe they should have their own authentic form of democracy (whether Arab, Asian, African, or other). When one asks the questioner to explain further what they mean, the responses are often uncertain.

Often people have in mind certain features of Western societies that they do not like and do not want to see brought to their country. These features may include social norms such as gay marriage, high divorce rates, or what they perceive as the prioritizing of individual values over those of the community. These features may also include economic aspects (such as inequality) and operational aspects of the political system (such as chronic conflict between political competitors or large amounts of money flowing into political campaigns). The issue of ownership is also paramount. Although the Universal Declaration of Human Rights spoke the language of universalism, it was signed without much input from non-Western states. As the latter's confidence has grown, they have increasingly felt justified in revisiting some of its precepts.

There is empirical uncertainty about what kinds of variation in democracy people seek. World Values Survey results indicate that 80 percent of citizens across the world support democracy as the preferred system of government.[32] Regional polls confirm the high levels of general support for democracy in Africa, Asia, and the Middle East.[33] But such polls do not probe what different populations around the world understand by democracy or aspire to in terms of the political characteristics of a democratic system.

Those wishing to see a non-Western style of democracy are usually not clear how their national or regional variants should differ from Western templates. Often what proponents want is something aspirational that has never been present in their country, such as true social justice or national political unity. The impression these advocates give is that there is a set of core non-Western values waiting to take root if only their country could be freed from Western impositions.

If given a list of Western democracy's basic elements, people in developing states will usually acknowledge that they want similar attributes, such as choosing their leaders, enjoying basic rights of free and fair expression, and benefiting from the rule of law. So, when pressed, it sometimes seems that they do approve of the core Western model, but with different attachments or accessories.

Of course, as has long been the case, some advocates of non-Western democracy use it as a cover for nondemocratic systems. Their intent is to abridge core democratic processes and values under the appealing rubric of local authenticity. The clearest recent example of this is Russia under the rule of Vladimir Putin.

But at least some of the push for non-Western democratic forms is genuinely democracy-oriented. For example, as some Middle Eastern countries struggle to move away from decades of authoritarianism, their citizens have a deep interest in building a democracy that is authentically, distinctively Arab. Of course a fierce debate exists in this region between those who prefer a more strictly Islamist conception of democracy and those who do not. Yet many in both of these camps insist that they do not want to simply imitate Western democracy. Similarly, in Burma, the stuttering drive for democracy takes place in a context where respect for certain Asian values is high.

As non-Western states find themselves in the midst of vertiginous change, analysts have come to focus on the *process* of political development. One of their key observations is that in Western countries, democracy came long after liberalism. Indeed, those defined as liberals in the West were for a long time paternalistic elites that only reluctantly reconciled themselves to democracy. In other places of the world, democracy has arrived without prior centuries of liberalism.[34] This seems to strengthen the case for non-Western, nonliberal forms of democracy.

The various calls for and debates over non-Western varieties of democracy exhibit a number of core elements and concerns. However, the main concern is the high importance placed on individualism in Western democracies. Western societies are seen as collections of autarkic individuals not working together to advance communal interests and values. Although there may be variation among Western societies, many critics paint with a broad brush. In short, for many (but not all) critical voices in emerging and developing countries, the problem with Western democracy is that it is *liberal* democracy.

There is also a prominent emphasis among those who espouse non-Western models of economic justice. The widespread desire is for democracy to deliver at least a basic standard of protection and material life. The critique of Western-style democracy is to some extent a critique of Western capitalism. Equally present is the dream of greater popular participation—a desire for inclusion and political involvement that involves much more than just voting.

These points raise two overarching questions. The first is whether we are talking about different political principles or different institutional forms. Many supporters of non-Western models commonly insist they are fully committed to democratic principles, but that these values can be expressed through different institutional forms. These proponents criticize the West for having long conflated its institutions with universal democratic values—for thinking that only its institutional forms can give expression to democratic norms. But the imprecision in calls for non-Western democracy leaves much doubt over whether it is only institutional forms that are being questioned. As we will see in what follows, in at least some cases, advocates of non-Western democracy seem to be pressing for a reinterpretation of the basic principles upon which democracy is built. The familiar values-forms distinction does not fully capture the nature of today's debates over democratic variation.

The closely related second question, which was noted in chapter 1, is whether non-Western democracy is the same thing as nonliberal democracy. This is a complex issue, as will become clearer as we explore the debates across different regions. Many exponents of non-Western models quite explicitly challenge the liberal elements of Western democracy, objecting to the "liberal" part of liberal democracy. They want a form of democracy that is not wrapped so tightly around the primacy of individual rights. But others are searching for locally distinctive processes or institutions that would seem to fit within the liberal democratic template. In these cases, non-Western democracy may not necessarily be a less liberal democracy. The question of whether the legitimate quest is for forms of democracy that are nonliberal or "liberal plus" is pivotal to the book's core arguments.

RESPONDING TO NON-WESTERN TRENDS

Calls for non-Western democracy can in part be explained by the way that politicians, diplomats, and thinkers have reacted to a number of other trends that push against political uniformity. Three of these trends are worth summarizing briefly. The first relates to the recent failures of high-profile conflict interventions; these failures have prompted much soul-searching about the possible advantages of less liberal forms of governance in fragile situations. The second is the increasing prevalence of transitions resulting in hybrid regimes that incorporate illiberal features. And a third trend is toward legal pluralism, which is built on calls for non-Western concepts of the rule of law.

NONLIBERAL POWER-SHARING

The failure of conflict resolution efforts has been a key driver of interest in non-Western democracy. Events in conflict states such as Iraq and Afghanistan have led many to argue for a "postliberal" model of peacebuilding.

Such a model would celebrate hybrid templates that are not purely liberal. Critics say international conflict interventions that include support for liberal democracy have been prejudicial for peace across Africa, as well as in Iraq and Afghanistan. This failure calls for "needs-based activities" and "contextual legitimacy" to be constructed around non-Western political models. So far, Western powers have failed to live up to their own rhetoric about building consensus and social justice. A standard criticism is that in conflict situations, the West has been too concerned with "institutional development" rather than using traditional bodies and forums for reconciliation.[35]

In Iraq and Afghanistan, the combination of military invasion followed by extensive institution-building programs has failed to produce either stability or well-rooted democracy. This, critics argue, is because the conflict resolution models too rigidly followed a template of liberal democracy. In particular, they relied heavily on elections in a context of deeply riven political rivalries.

Critics may not be entirely right that the United States and other powers blindly imposed liberal democratic templates in these cases. Many with experience on the ground in Afghanistan insist the problem was more complex: the United States engineered quite-limited electoral democracy and then flanked it with support for traditional structures, uncritically assuming they were what Afghans wanted—even as many Afghans told them they opposed this approach.[36] Yet, whether critics' readings are entirely correct or not, the role of liberal democracy as a tool for conflict resolution is certainly more widely questioned today than prior to the Afghanistan and Iraq experiences. In fact, these interventions have engendered fundamental rethinking on the role that different political models play in conflict and stabilization.

As a result, analysts have more widely advocated negotiated settlements between warring factions—what political scientists refer to as arrangements of consociational democracy. Some argue that "corporate consociationalism" fares better than liberal models. Corporate models accord rights to groups on the basis of their ethnicity or religion—and in accordance with the weight of each ethnic or religious group within the overall population. What is defined as "liberal consociationalism" shares power on the basis of how groups perform in elections. Although the liberal model is more fluid and less rigid, it has also failed in Iraq and Afghanistan. As a result, many groups have pushed back against it—saying it is a model imposed from outside and unsuited to local conditions. The trend is toward power-sharing on nonliberal or noncompetitive bases.[37]

TRANSITIONS AND HYBRID REGIMES

The non-Western debate also reflects a trend evident in so-called transition states. As noted, many incipient transitions are not conforming to the supposed transition paradigm. This paradigm has long held that modest political reform leads inexorably toward a state of liberal democracy. Instead, the evidence suggests that many such cases have become what political scientists now call hybrid regimes. According to the transition paradigm, a lack of liberalism was a temporary and anomalous hiccup in a country's slow move toward the telos of liberal democratic consolidation. In hybrid regimes, a lack of liberalism is often an intrinsic and permanent characteristic of a political regime, not a temporary shortcoming.

Regimes can remain in a state of hybridity for extended periods of time. Hybrid mixes of democracy and autocracy are not so much a staging post in an incremental march toward liberal democracy as a quasi-permanent form of regime type. Advocates of non-Western democracy often seem to be referring to what are in fact various types of hybridity. They believe that some elements of hybridity embody context-appropriate deviations from liberal democracy. They seem to be grasping for a distinction between benign and malign hybridity.

Hybridity should not be defined merely as something less than democracy but as a distinctive type of regime. Taking hybridity seriously effectively broadens the search for different institutional expressions of democracy that reflect cultural specificities. Some hybrid regimes rest on genuine forms of legitimacy and not only repression or the co-opting of opposition forces.[38] This includes some personalistic regimes that seem to have secured a traditional, Weberian from of legitimacy—an issue we will return to later in the book.[39]

LEGAL PLURALISM

As a more specific offshoot of the non-Western discourse, the demand for legal pluralism has become stronger. This has opened up a rich vein of debate on the complex relationship between the rule of law and different forms of democracy.

In many countries, the use of customary or traditional justice systems has become more widespread in recent years. In some states, these systems account for more than 80 percent of legal cases heard. National, formal judicial institutional structures left by colonial partners exist in parallel with the more traditional dispute-settlement mechanisms at a local level. Many analysts argue that such legal pluralism is likely to increase in the future and that it represents a concrete expression of societies' desire for their own models of social and political organization. Analysts suggest legal pluralism should be welcomed and encouraged.

A wide-ranging UN study found that increasing support for informal justice systems is based on their providing justice that is cheaper and quicker than formal legal institutions built on Western templates. Informal processes have delivered an increase in the overall level of justice, owing to the inadequacies and remoteness of formal legal systems. Local systems provide culturally rooted remedies—solutions based on trust, patient dialogue, mutual consent, mediation, and the reintegration of offenders back into the community. Citizens often compare such restorative solutions favorably to the imposition of antagonistic penalties through the formal system.[40]

Legal pluralism is underpinned by broader political justifications. The rule of law must be defined not only in terms of formal institutional patterns but also in a more ends-oriented fashion. Western rule of law attaches importance to a certain set of judicial institutions being embedded within a system of formal democratic control. Other cultures have a long history of thinking about how rulers should be constrained by laws, even if that thinking is not manifested in the same institutional ways that it is in Western rule of law.

Social justifications also play a role. The focus of many cultures is not so much on the liberal concept of law protecting individual rights and private space as on forms of dispute resolution that contribute to certain social ends. In such societies, the impersonal rule of law is sometimes seen as being too neutral in terms of substantive social outcomes. Trends in legal pluralism question the singular focus of the rule of law that underpins Western, liberal democracy.

CONCLUSION

The rising interest in the concept of non-Western democracy is striking. This chapter has pointed to the reasons why this must be taken seriously. A number of factors have come together in recent years to spur such debates. Some factors relate to the successes of non-Western societies. Others are the product of shortcomings in the Western model. And still others flow from the frustrations increasingly expressed by non-Western populations. The growing interest in non-Western democracy is seen among citizens, civil society groups, political thinkers, diplomats, officials, and politicians—outside the West but also within it.

Yet, the non-Western debate remains imprecise. Some of those calling for non-Western democracy are clearly talking about the need for fundamental revision of core democratic principles. Others seem to want more limited changes to democracy's institutional architecture. Some seem genuinely concerned with improving democratic quality; others seem to be implying that Western standards are simply too demanding for other societies. Clearly, the momentum behind the non-Western argument merits more detailed investigation. The following chapter unpacks the way in which such debates over non-Western democracy have unfolded in greater specificity within different regions.

CHAPTER 3

REGIONAL MODELS AND TRENDS

T
he most detailed debate on non-Western democracy is about specific regional models. Many politicians and writers argue that various regions warrant their own distinctive institutional templates. And indeed, it is in these regions where most of the substantive characteristics of non-Western democracies have been molded—and most ferociously debated.

The case for non-Western democracy revolves around the claim that regions house enough specificity and commonality to merit their own distinctive form of politics. This debate has been long present in projects for African, Asian, and Latin American democracy. Each of these supposed regional varieties of democracy has gained new disciples and some degree of practical implementation in recent years. And in the wake of the Arab Spring, there has been a re-energized pressure for a unique Middle Eastern form of democracy. This chapter outlines the current state of the debates in these regions. It looks at the claims made in the name of such regional varieties—as well as at the doubts raised about them.

THE MIDDLE EAST: ISLAM AND DEMOCRACY

Reflections on democracy in North Africa and the Middle East have often appeared to be an offshoot of a long-running and extensive debate about whether Islam is compatible with democracy. Although some insist that Islam is inherently undemocratic, a strong majority of writers argue that Islam has evolved in response to fluid political factors and that there is nothing that prevents it from accommodating democracy.[1] However, whether or not Islam is inherently antidemocratic is *not* our concern here. Rather, our focus is the more nuanced debate about whether Islam provides a framework for a distinctive *type* of democracy.

Muslim scholars have long explored religious approaches to politics, suggesting ways in which religious values underpin conceptions of legitimacy and rights that differ from liberal individualism.[2] In the aftermath of the Arab revolts that began in 2011 and revitalized political debates across the region, a widening current of opinion suggested that democracy in Muslim-majority societies should not follow the Western secular model. Rather, as Islamists rose in popularity and influence after 2011, they insisted that incipient processes of democratization should preserve a role for Islam in public life and build on traditional Islamic concepts. Many in North Africa and the Middle East aspire to a democracy that is defined differently than in the West, encompassing Islamic notions of community and solidarity.[3] The kinds of distinctive features often put forward include the following:

- A concern with social justice, which places a premium on institutions that provide for social cooperation and mutual assistance, mercy, and compassion in social interactions.[4]

- The principle of *shura* or consultation, which requires a process of decisionmaking based on open discussion with members of the community affected by a particular issue. *Shura* is seen as demanding popular participation in politics as well as accountable government and collective deliberation.[5]

- The principle of *ijma*, which refers to consensus or the collective judgment of a community.[6] Islamic *ijma* and *shura* together seem to chime with looser forms of deliberation.

- The principle of *ijtehad*, which refers to the power to decide a public issue through reasoning and informed judgment. Many Islamic jurists have argued that the authority of *itjehad* should lie with the legislature and judiciary. However, *itjehad* can also be used to argue that Muslims today should not be bound by one definition of sharia law but should use reasoning and judgment to interpret a public issue in light of social changes and new complexities.[7]

Muslim scholars broadly agree that these precepts are central to most interpretations of Islam. However, it is not clear whether these notions provide for a distinctively "Islamic democracy." Many Western political projects are also based on the search for social justice. Many Western political systems are built on multiple layers of "consultation" and seek consensus. Yet Muslim scholars sometimes seem to view Western political systems as completely lacking in consultation and an interest in justice.

However, the differences between these precepts and Western forms of democracy are not clear because Muslim scholars interpret them in different ways.[8] Disagreements exist regarding the nature of the shura process, for example. The Quran does not specify who should participate in a consultation, how decisions should be made if participants fail to reach a consensus, and whether the outcomes of an open discussion should be binding.[9] Shura might be taken as a call for the kind of collective deliberation and popular participation in civic discussions that many citizens in the West want as part of Western democracy.

Some analysts insist that Islam provides a framework for *limited* rather than distinctive democracy. Omar Ashour points out that while some Islamists embrace a liberal concept of protecting minority rights, many favor a more limited form of electoral or Schumpeterian democracy.[10]

Islamist scholars often advocate for boundaries on what is considered a permissible individual right, commonly rejecting what they see as the moral relativism of Western liberal democracy, in which everything "is subject to referendum and debate and . . . nothing has a solid and an a priori 'foundation.'"[11] The thinking is that a democratic system must be underpinned by certain moral principles that are based on religious values.[12] These should be nonnegotiable and outside the sphere of competitive politics. Religious boundaries should limit the openness of civil society and critical discourse, prohibiting criticism of religion and Islam, for example. The public arena should be governed according to certain religious principles; or at least there should be guarantees that laws do not contradict Islam.

Communitarian and Islamist thinkers reject the idea that individuals have a "public, political" identity and a "private, religious" identity. They consider these two identities to be inseparable and that religious convictions cannot simply be "bracketed" to the private sphere.[13] Some Islamist thinkers conceptualize society not as an association of individuals, but as an integrated group that strives to realize a supreme good—the aim to have the right relationship with God. Therefore, these scholars do not insist on individual autonomy to the same degree as Western thinkers. Islamists complain that the Western liberal state protects the rights of religious minorities only as long as they accept that religion is a private rather than a public matter.[14] Islamists "envision a political order that is founded on Islam's fundamental principles about community life and moral behavior." The resulting political system will inevitably blur the boundaries between the private and public person and entail some form of community control over individuals.[15]

How do these conceptual debates relate to real-life trends, especially in the wake of the Arab Spring? It is difficult to identify common trends across the Middle East. The Arab awakening has produced wide variation in reform processes among Middle Eastern states. The divergence between regime types has widened notably in recent years. In countries such as Bahrain, Egypt, Libya, Syria, and Tunisia, opposition forces tried to oust regimes and attempt wholesale democratization—with varying degrees of success. In countries such as Algeria, Jordan, and Morocco, many—even if not all—parts of the population seem content with cosmetic processes of reform toward a slightly more open form of authoritarianism. Table 3.1 shows the range of democracy scores across North Africa and the Middle East.

Regional convergence has been more limited here than in earlier waves of transition in Eastern Europe and Latin America. If there are traces of a common trend across the region it is that democratic Islamists are now on the defensive, squeezed between resurgent autocrats and new jihadist formations. Analytical debates may focus on the finer details of the relationship between Islam and democracy, but real-life politics and security concerns are of a more visceral and brutal nature in most Middle Eastern states today.

TABLE 3.1. **DEMOCRACY INDEX 2014: NORTH AFRICA AND THE MIDDLE EAST (0 TO 10 SCALE)**

REGIME TYPE	COUNTRY	RANK	OVERALL SCORE	ELECTORAL PROCESS AND PLURALISM	FUNCTIONING OF GOVERNMENT	POLITICAL PARTICIPATION	POLITICAL CULTURE	CIVIL LIBERTIES
FLAWED DEMOCRACIES	Israel	36	7.63	8.75	7.14	8.89	7.50	5.88
	Tunisia	70	6.31	7.00	6.07	7.22	6.25	5.00
HYBRID REGIMES	Turkey	=98	5.12	6.67	5.36	4.44	5.63	3.53
	Lebanon	=98	5.12	5.67	2.14	7.22	5.00	5.59
	Palestine	106	4.72	4.75	2.86	7.78	4.38	3.82
	Iraq	111	4.23	4.33	0.79	7.22	4.38	4.41
AUTHORITARIAN REGIMES	Morocco	116	4.00	3.50	4.29	2.78	5.00	4.41
	Algeria	117	3.83	3.00	2.21	3.89	5.63	4.41
	Libya	119	3.80	2.25	2.50	3.33	5.63	5.29
	Kuwait	120	3.78	3.17	3.93	3.89	4.38	3.53
	Jordan	=121	3.76	3.17	3.93	4.44	3.75	3.53
	Qatar	136	3.18	0.00	3.93	2.22	5.63	4.12
	Egypt	138	3.16	2.17	2.86	5.00	3.13	2.65
	Oman	139	3.15	0.00	3.93	3.33	4.38	4.12
	Bahrain	147	2.87	1.25	3.57	2.78	4.38	2.35
	Yemen	149	2.79	1.33	1.43	5.00	5.00	1.18
	UAE	152	2.64	0.00	3.57	1.67	5.00	2.94
	Iran	158	1.98	0.00	2.86	2.78	2.50	1.76
	Saudi Arabia	161	1.82	0.00	2.86	1.67	3.13	1.47
	Syria	163	1.74	0.00	0.36	3.33	5.00	0.00

Source: *Economist Intelligence Unit, Index of Democracy 2014*   = denotes a tie with another country

Even the social makeup of these states seems to have splintered in various directions.[16] There is little evidence today that the region is headed toward a singular, distinctive non-Western form of democracy. Election results and the re-imposition of military rule in Egypt make it clear that political Islam does not have the monopoly on political thinking in the region. Many secularists across the Middle East reject the claim that the region needs a distinctive, religiously cast form of politics.[17]

Perhaps the most increasingly evident aspect of commonality across the region it is the erosion of civic rights. A recent Bertelsmann report shows that behind the variation in regime types there is a common deterioration of civic rights in many Arab countries.[18] Notwithstanding the evident divergence in states' political trajectories, Shadi Hamid argues that support for illiberal democracy is growing across the region. Islamist parties have been pushed in this direction by conservative public opinion. Polls suggest that majorities in Middle Eastern states today want sharia enshrined as the main source of legislation, clerical oversight of new laws, and extensive powers to be given to religious judges. Majorities also want to see alcohol banned, strict Islamist punishments for those found guilty of certain crimes, and less tolerance toward homosexuality. Such values point toward ultramajoritarian democracy. Hamid insists that this illiberal form of democracy is rooted in social demands and values, whereas in other places in the world, illiberal democracy is an elite strategy for limiting opposition. In these other regions, regimes limit political competition, while Islamists focus more on limiting liberal rights.[19]

Alfred Stepan and the late Juan Linz argue that the Middle East may be heading toward a model of democracy in which religion plays more of a political role than it does under a strictly secular concept. This is likely to be based on the concept of mutual "toleration" between state and church, in which each refrains from seeking to restrict the other. Stepan and Linz point out that this would not be entirely different from the situation in most European states. This model could be defined as a "civil state" rather than a "secular state," the latter having more antireligious overtones. The substantive difference with Western states would be one of nuance. None of the existing Muslim-majority democracies have so far imposed sharia as the only source of law. Arguably, the area of most meaningful difference with the West is that in Arab countries, state bodies consult religious authorities to advise on areas of public policy.[20]

Others disagree with these readings. Many analysts insist that the Middle East's cultural specificity is evaporating.[21] Olivier Roy sees a sociological convergence with other regions of the world. Even as authoritarian regimes hang on, the region is undergoing a process of individualization. The hold of patriarchy is declining. Roy's analysis questions the view that there is some unique form of illiberal politics that fits the region's social and ideational peculiarities.[22] Professional middle classes have become far more critically engaged citizens, concerned with practical issues of combating cronyism and the delivery of services.

The distinctive political model of democratic Islamists remains elusive. Although Islamists may use theological references in their discourse, they have not designed fundamentally different institutional structures. Citizens in the region often say they want an Arab democracy and not a liberal democracy. But they do not necessarily have a different set of institutional preferences in mind. Rather, they conflate liberalism with secularism and, in turn, godlessness. People want sharia not so much for jurisprudential or ideological reasons, but because they see it as a path to social justice and greater fairness in public life. This thinking makes the call for sharia almost a social democratic agenda, but with more conservative notions of personal morals than such an agenda might include in the West.

Debates over the notion of citizenship suggest that it is difficult to predict how processes of change will unfold. Identities are still being formed across the Middle East. This fluidity is not fully incorporated into standard explanations of transitions. Many citizens are more religious than previously but demand stronger civic rights and personal liberties than has been their lot under autocracies. It is questionable that they aspire to a curtailed democracy. Many polls in the region show that substantial majorities strongly desire the core individual freedoms of speech, religion, and assembly and do not want religious leaders to be directly involved in day-to-day governing.[23]

As democratic breakthroughs have failed to materialize, Islamist parties are refocusing their efforts at the local-community level. This local focus is pursued though their social and charitable networks rather than a wholesale, existential challenge to a certain type of liberal democracy. Islamists' priority is, once again, how to survive and work in nondemocratic conditions. This is a long way from the hopes that the Arab Spring would open the door for Islamist parties to implement a new and distinctive type of democracy.

FACTORS BEYOND ISLAM

It is important to realize that Middle Eastern specificities are not only about Islam. Some argue that the military's role in the region is part of a distinctive democratic model. However, again, there is huge variation here. In some states, the army is large and relatively independent from particular political figures. It is thus able to stand as guarantor of the nation, and it enjoys considerable popular prestige. In other states, the army is either small and weak or widely hated because it serves sectarian or elite interests. And in still other places—Indonesia and Turkey are prominent examples—armed forces continue to receive privileges in return for accepting democratic rules.

It is also important to remember that not all of society in North Africa and the Middle East approaches the issue of democracy through an Islamist lens. Initially, the lead role in the Arab Spring was played not by Islamists, and not by organized civil society, but by "social nonmovements." These were loose forms of nonobedience that coalesced into mass protests.[24] Some analysts argue that these actors presented a different kind of Arab challenge to Western democracy—a challenge that had nothing to with Islam but rather with the emergence of new forms of civil society organization.

However, it is not clear today that all this mass mobilization entails a qualitatively new type of political process. And the role of information and communications technology (ICT) in steering political change in the region has complicated matters further. There is a huge divide between the region's wired and globalized coastal elites—the digital activists who challenge "tradition"—and those living in the conservative hinterlands. Although many talked of Tunisia's revolution as being the first driven by social media, only a small part of its society harnessed ICT's potential: only one in six Tunisian families have a computer; and only one in 33 in the poorer regions of the interior where the revolt actually started.

ICT activists want to change traditional power structures and tend not to think in terms of "an Arab model." The digital elite are much more globally linked. They press for more effective government responses to citizens' practical concerns. These reformers see citizens as consumers using cloud computing to participate in the design of "democratic products." Arab ICT leaders have launched many initiatives that use ICT, including cloud computing, to monitor parliaments and offer input in the drafting of legislation. This activism is concerned with effective accountability rather than imagining a distinctly Arab form of democracy.

New ICT is not the sole province of the Western-educated, secular elite. Some imams have millions of followers on Twitter. Yet, most Internet content in the Arab world is still not locally produced but comes from the West. In addition, some observers point out that links between digital leaders in various Arab states have not deepened significantly so as to promote regional innovation. Rather, debates are still structured along national lines. All these factors must raise doubts about whether the role of ICT really points in the direction of "Arab specificity" or rather tempers such regional claims.

It is instructive to see how these debates have played out in different country contexts.

EGYPT: A STATE ON HOLD

Many democracy advocates both inside and outside Egypt lambasted the Muslim Brotherhood's short reign from 2012 through 2013 for restricting the liberties of women and minorities in the constitution and in other legislation. Other democracy supporters insisted the Brotherhood was flexible on these points in the name of consensus. For erstwhile president Mohamed Morsi, some rights restrictions were clearly part of a power-preservation strategy.

Soon after being elected, the Brotherhood's power became an issue because it held public office while still being a social movement more than a traditional political party. The Brotherhood's identity as a social movement meant that its mission was one of changing Arab states' social fabric, morals, and mores; it was not simply concerned with offering alternatives in public policy. At the same time, there was growing popularity of the conservative Salafist movement. Morsi therefore shifted toward more illiberal views to defend the Brotherhood's political position against the Salafists. There was fierce debate on the precise wording with which sharia would be included in the constitution introduced by Morsi in 2012. Would the latter be guided by the loose "principles" or firmer "rules" of sharia? The document fudged this question in an effort to keep different factions on board. The Salafist Nour Party opposed the constitutional term "civil state," fearing that this term could undermine the prospects for a strict application of Islamic law.

After the July 2013 military coup that ousted Morsi and the Brotherhood from power, the relationship between democracy and liberalism became even more complicated. Most self-declared democrats in Egypt insisted the July coup was a popular expression of democratic will, given that huge numbers protested against Morsi. The Brotherhood's very majoritarian understanding of democracy had rebounded against it. As some liberals said: to defend liberalism, it was necessary to curtail democracy. Protesters called for the restoration of liberal personal rights. The military pushed through a new constitution that was more authoritarian but that offered more protection for personal rights (including those of Christians, Nubians, and women) than did the previous document drawn up by the Brotherhood administration. Some liberal secularists welcomed this; others feared it created a kind of sectarian-based authoritarianism.

Now, of course, Egypt has reverted to authoritarianism under the military-backed government led by General Abdel Fattah el-Sisi. Debates about different varieties of democracy hardly seem relevant at this juncture. The new constitution introduced by the military strengthened the army and weakened the parliament. It also banned religion-based political activity and, in effect, the Brotherhood. With hundreds of its members now detained, its younger cadres are drifting toward more violent and extremist positions. Hopes that the Brotherhood would move back toward a more liberal-democratic agenda have for the moment been dashed.

TUNISIA: THE SEEDS OF POTENTIAL

If a more liberal democracy appears possible anywhere in the region, it is in Tunisia. Rached al-Ghannouchi, the highly influential cleric-philosopher and notable figure in Tunisia's post-2011 transition, has expressed doubt that Islamist principles require a different kind of political system:

> If by democracy is meant the liberal model of government prevailing in the West, a system under which the people freely choose their representatives and leaders and in which there is an alternation of power, as well as all freedoms and human rights for the public, then the Muslim will find nothing in their religion to oppose democracy and it is not in their interests to do so.[25]

Back at the political front line in Tunis after years of exile, Ghannouchi talked of a "civil state" and insisted that the newly elected Ennahdha party build a coalition with secular parties, rather than head in the direction of an Islamic template for democracy. The model he supported is more one of consensual democracy—to placate the sectors of opinion that are still distrusting of Ennahdha.

In this vision, Islamic principles can serve "as a sort of 'bridge' between Islam and modern democracy," but do not by themselves justify an Islamic political structure.[26] It may be that distinctively Islamist precepts provide a different framing for or way of justifying democratic principles—but these precepts do so without implying a fundamentally different model of democracy. As Ghannouchi suggested, democracy in the region might be theoretically based on Islam—and framed in terms of "the Medina not the Agora"—even if in practice it works in ways similar to Western democracy.

With Tunisia having more of an embedded tradition of French secularity (or *laïcité*) than other Arab states, Ghannouchi has been nuanced in his interpretation of sharia. He sees sharia as a framework but with rights being shaped through democratic debate. So, Tunisia's (fairly liberal) personal status code can be defined as part of the general sharia framework. However, critics say Islamists in Tunisia have not squared the circle. Where conservative sharia collides with democratic preferences, they ultimately veer toward illiberalism. Many observers point to a discrepancy between Ghannouchi's statements (especially those in English or French) and the way that Ennahdha acted in power from 2011 through late 2014.

Indeed, during its period in government, the Ennahdha party in Tunisia was criticized by liberal opposition groups for colonizing state institutions and for being more concerned with strengthening its own networks of power than with extending necessary reforms. The Ennahdha administration tolerated hardline Salafists that many suspected to be guilty of major instances of political violence. The new constitution did not give unequivocal protection to minority rights—these were downplayed relative to a more Arab-nationalist spirit.

Still, many aspects of Tunisia's recent political development do not obviously point in the direction of illiberal democracy. Although Ennahdha did not live up to its relatively liberal rhetoric, it did not push the new constitution toward any fundamental repudiation of the tenets associated with Western democracy. In September 2013, Prime Minister Ali Larayedh stepped down. This was in part because Ennahdha was sobered by what was happening to the Brotherhood in Egypt and in part because of pressure from the opposition. This salvaged a National Dialogue within which all major political forces eventually agreed on a new constitution. There are still differences between Islamists and secularists regarding the balance between universal human rights and Islamist values—something on which the constitution is ambivalent. However, the consensual model of the constitutional assembly succeeded in setting a basically liberal democratic template for Tunisia's political-institutional structure.

Ennahdha was voted out of power in October 2014. The elections suggested that Tunisian citizens voted on the basis of Ennahdha's performance in government—and especially its inability to resolve the country's economic problems—rather than the precise role of religion in the constitution. The elections broke new ground insofar as Ennahdha accepted its loss of power without complaint.

The elections' less positive implication was the extremely polarizing stance of the victorious, secular Tunisia Calling party—an unwieldy coalition of different parties united only in their antipathy to Islamists. The party deployed harshly anti-Islamist rhetoric in its campaigning. Despite agreeing to a limited coalition, it is not clear whether the new government will maintain a fully inclusive political process. There are also concerns over the rise of radical Salafists in Tunisia—security imperatives may once again militate against democratization.

TURKEY: THE DEBATE DEEPENS

The debate over whether Islamists are drawn to a highly majoritarian form of democracy now has great resonance in Turkey. Excluded from power for so long and still mistrustful of other actors, the ruling Justice and Development Party (AKP) has articulated this form in positive terms as an alternative model of democracy. Under the government of Recep Tayyip Erdoğan, Turkey is widely seen to have moved toward an extreme form of majoritarianism, with only limited protection for opposition secularists and minorities. The AKP has built its ideological project on traditionalism and globalism at the same time, espousing a conservative internationalism.[27]

The result is a combustible mixture of a highly majoritarian shade of democracy and simmering social discontent. The country's political sociology stands at odds with its style of leadership and the party system, where a right-wing nationalist party is still the main available alternative to the AKP. Turkish protesters have mobilized against the regime's attempts to restrict personal freedoms by implementing dress codes and drinking laws. Many protesters have called for more liberal democracy, rejecting Erdoğan's idea of a Muslim democracy. The AKP's dramatic loss of support in Turkey's June 2015 elections suggested Erdoğan's political project might be on the defensive.

DEMOCRACY ELSEWHERE IN THE REGION

Yemen's recent political transition has exhibited democratic elements that many see as appropriate to a local variation. After President Ali Abdullah Saleh agreed to step down in late 2011, a national unity government was sworn in. Elections in February 2012 confirmed the consensus candidate, Abd Rabbu Mansour Hadi. A national conference then deliberated on detailed reform options, concluding in early 2014. The resulting governing model was even more oriented toward dialogue and consensus building than the one in Tunisia. This reflected the enormous challenges of dealing with several factors: the remaining vested interests of the Saleh family, the frustration among southern secessionists, the powerful tribes, and a northern Shia Houthi rebel campaign. The consensus building was a process based on striking delicate bargains among elites, leaving many citizens' demands unmet. Yemen returned to open conflict in early 2015, when Houthi rebels forced President Hadi to abandon office.

Many analysts argue that there is widespread support among Moroccans and Jordanians for curtailed forms of democracy overseen by popular monarchs with deep tradition-based wells of legitimacy. But both King Mohammed VI and King Abdullah have advanced only limited reforms since 2011. Many democrats in Morocco and Jordan now regularly take to the streets and argue the reforms are not far-reaching enough.

As the monarchies' supporters point out, both countries have retained a degree of stability that is absent in most places in the region today. Defenders of these monarchies also speak of their unique models: neither is authoritarian, but neither goes as far as the Western model of constitutional monarchies in subjugating the king to democratic checks and balances.

Many voices reject such benign views. As repression has increased in both states against journalists, civil society organizations, and some minorities, critics insist that Morocco and Jordan have simply entrenched authoritarian dynamics. The two regimes now round up political opponents in the name of counterterrorism—and do so while successfully promoting a false image that they combine the best elements of democracy, stability, and historically rooted legitimacy.

The Justice and Development Party–led government in Morocco has not struck out to forge a distinctive type of democracy. Rather, it has sought to find maneuverability within the existing system's nondemocratic boundaries. The party's caution has increased since the Brotherhood's ouster from power in Egypt. In Jordan, there is much talk of "tribal democracy"; but many civil-society organizations are critical of the influence exerted by tribal leaders in stymieing deeper liberal-democratic reforms.

It is commonly pointed out that Lebanon represents a distinctive model of democracy. The country enjoys relatively open political and civic debate, but it has a system of institutional representation divided among oligarchic confessional sects. The instability that has overflowed from the neighboring Syrian conflict has made Lebanon even more reliant on this fragile power-sharing arrangement. Sunni, Shia, and Christian factions all fear what would happen if the confessional system were replaced by a more liberal-majoritarian system. With Hezbollah enjoying de facto power and the process of government formation becoming increasingly complicated, however, many doubt that Lebanon is a sustainable, distinctive model of successful non-Western democracy. Overdue elections have been postponed several times. The current parliament has simply extended its own period in office, citing the security situation as the reason why elections cannot be held. Lebanese civil society groups protest that the country is increasingly sliding into a form of confessional autocracy and away from its famed power-sharing democracy.

Following Bahrain's November 2014 election, the parliament was filled almost entirely with pro-regime independents—helped by government gerrymandering. The country's distinctive political societies suffered. Sunni political societies won virtually no support, while Bahrain's main Shia party boycotted the polls. Disaffection prevailed on both sides of the Shia-Sunni divide. A locally legitimate model seems a distant prospect in Bahrain.

In Kuwait, by contrast, debate and accountability are channeled through a lively parliament that often challenges the government in an effective manner. It is the parliament that is the country's center of debate and accountability rather than any distinctively non-Western forums or gatherings. But Kuwait differs from other states in the Gulf Cooperation Council. Qatar, for example, has supported a religion-centric democratization similar to the one led by the Brotherhood in other parts of the region. The United Arab Emirates and Saudi Arabia, however, have sought to block such developments—these states do not concur that such a form of democracy would represent a welcome and distinctively Arab form of political change.

In Saudi Arabia specifically there is much talk of tribal democracy, but it is hard to see very far-reaching elements of democracy in this concept. Princes receive petitioners and grant favors to settle private grievances. Supporters claim that this has made the ruling Saud family more responsive and legitimate and that the process harnesses very traditional forms of tribal representation. Critics say it reduces citizens to supplicants of royal favor.

In sum, while there is much talk in the new Middle East of a non-Western form of democracy, current trends are too varied or insufficiently developed to conclude that such a model is in fact emerging. One of Orhan Pamuk's most famous revolutionary characters pondered that in the Muslim world it was impossible to further both European enlightenment values and democracy at the same time.[28] But it is debatable whether the post-2011 dynamics of Middle Eastern politics can be captured by quite such an absolute, binary trade-off.

LATIN AMERICA: POPULISM AND DEMOCRACY

The diversity of Latin American democratic models is also notable. It is difficult to identify a single Latin American model.[29] Table 3.2 shows Latin American states' varying levels of democracy. On the one hand, the two largest Latin American countries, Mexico and Brazil, currently seem to be heading toward a more standard liberal-democratic model. The continent

TABLE 3.2. **DEMOCRACY INDEX 2014: LATIN AMERICA (0 TO 10 SCALE)**

REGIME TYPE	COUNTRY	RANK	OVERALL SCORE	ELECTORAL PROCESS AND PLURALISM	FUNCTIONING OF GOVERNMENT	POLITICAL PARTICIPATION	POLITICAL CULTURE	CIVIL LIBERTIES
FULL DEMOCRACIES	Uruguay	=17	8.17	10.00	8.93	4.44	7.50	10.00
	Costa Rica	24	8.03	9.58	7.86	6.11	6.88	9.71
FLAWED DEMOCRACIES	Chile	32	7.80	9.58	8.93	3.89	6.88	9.71
	Brazil	44	7.38	9.58	7.50	4.44	6.25	9.12
	Panama	47	7.08	9.58	6.43	5.56	5.00	8.82
	Argentina	52	6.84	8.75	5.71	5.56	6.25	7.94
	Mexico	=57	6..68	8.33	6.07	6.67	5.00	7.35
	Dominican Republic	59	6.67	8.75	5.71	5.00	6.25	7.65
	Colombia	62	6.55	9.17	7.14	3.89	3.75	8.82
	Peru	63	6.54	9.17	5.00	5.00	5.00	8.53
	El Salvador	64	6.53	9.17	6.07	3.89	5.00	8.53
	Paraguay	71	6.26	8.33	5.36	5.00	4.38	8.24
HYBRID REGIMES	Ecuador	79	5.87	8.25	4.64	5.00	4.38	7.06
	Honduras	80	5.84	8.75	5.71	3.89	4.38	6.47
	Guatemala	82	5.81	7.92	6.07	3.33	4.38	7.35
	Bolivia	=83	5.79	7.00	5.00	5.56	3.75	7.65
	Nicaragua	94	5.32	6.17	3.29	4.44	5.63	7.06
	Venezuela	100	5.07	5.25	4.29	5.56	4.38	5.88
	Haiti	118	3.83	4.75	2.21	2.22	3.13	6.76
	Cuba	=127	3.52	1.75	4.64	3.89	4.38	2.94

Source: *Economist Intelligence Unit, Index of Democracy 2014*   = denotes a tie with another country

also includes what have become "showcase" liberal democracies such as Chile, Colombia, Costa Rica, Peru, and Uruguay—countries that have firmly embedded democratic institutions despite suffering from serious economic inequalities and challenges to traditional party politics.[30]

On the other hand, however, developments in countries such as Bolivia, Ecuador, El Salvador, Honduras, Nicaragua, Paraguay, and Venezuela suggest the emergence of a different political model. Many celebrate this as a democratic alternative that is based on greater participation and inclusion. Critics deride this model as illiberal, populist, and only weakly democratic. In Latin America, debates about alternatives to the liberal democratic model have mostly—although not only—been framed in terms of populism. The core debate is whether leftist populist regimes represent a different type of democracy or camouflage a form of quasi-authoritarianism.[31]

The analysis of democratic transitions that dominated in the 1990s and early 2000s has been replaced by debates about the kind of democratic model that best suits the specificities of Latin American societies. As electoral democracy and civilian rule have been consolidated, popular dissatisfaction with the lack of social justice has increased. Consequently, new attempts to establish a "deeper" democracy have emerged.[32]

One complaint is that legislatures only serve to distribute patronage through clientelistic networks. They do not faithfully represent citizens' interests and concerns.[33] Opinion polls in Latin America reveal declining trust in political institutions and a perceived lack of connection between civil society and the state. This is mainly due to the persistence of clientelism, corruption, and poor socioeconomic outcomes. Democratic accountability is ineffective, as politicians and parties are rarely held to their campaign platforms. This can be traced back to the absence of horizontal accountability: state agencies are not sufficiently empowered to control the executive.[34]

This general context is the key to explaining the appeal of populism and alternative models of representation—the theme that has come to serve as a reference point for the region's politics in the past decade. Democratization and democratic reform movements in Latin America are bound up with demands for the redistribution of resources and greater economic inclusion.

A separate, yet related, element of Latin American discussions is a focus on the relationship between democracy and a market economy. This preoccupation can be traced to high levels of income and wealth inequality, compared with other regions, and the concentration of property and land in the hands of a very small elite. Proponents of alternative political models in the region seek ways to limit the sanctity of property rights and prioritize social solidarity.[35] Inequality is so bad in the region that the rule of law is widely perceived to be a mechanism for protecting elite interests.

Many analysts insist that populist regimes in Latin America offer a more direct form of democratic accountability than does standard representative democracy. Populism can be defined both as a strategy of political mobilization, appealing to the people against the establishment, and as a way of organizing political engagement, centered on a charismatic leader who embodies the "will of the common people."[36]

Laurence Whitehead refers to Latin American populism as the "republican model." This is a response to the perception that democratic constitutional systems have been "hijacked by liberal individualism and the market privileges of an oligarchic minority." According to Whitehead, these systems need to be reclaimed by the population, and this needs to happen through direct democracy rather than traditional parliamentary representation. While the mainstream liberal ideal sees politics as driven by individual interests and preferences, the republican ideal suggests that politics should be accountable to a collective public sphere.[37] Other prominent characteristics of this model include mass mobilization and popular participation, a personalistic leadership style (the leader presented as having a direct connection with the masses), and the de-emphasis of private property rights.

Proponents of populist policies argue that populist leaders and governments give voice to citizens who were previously excluded from the political system. Such policies do this by institutionalizing a direct democracy that circumvents elitist, unresponsive, and oligarchic political institutions. The root of populism is the desire to fulfill democracy's "emancipatory promise"—that is, to make sure it delivers freedom in tangible and not merely formal ways.[38] To their cheerleaders, leftist populist regimes reestablish a truly democratic order that has been subverted by liberal democratic institutions that only serve the privileged few. The goal is to restore the power of the legitimate holders of sovereignty, namely the demos.

The tensions between populism and democracy in Latin America are a product of the region's democratic shortfalls. The primary support bases of Latin American populists are the urban informal sector and the rural poor, rather than organized labor, although followers tend to be recruited from all segments of society.[39] This new style of populism first emerged in Latin America in the 1980s, when traditional party systems and the means of elite control began to collapse and rural populations moved into urban areas.[40]

The pejorative judgment is that the new wave of populism masks a weakening of horizontal checks and balances. Political scientists have long referred to this as delegative democracy or *caesarismo democratico*. Left-wing populism explicitly aims to loosen the central pillars of liberal democracy; but many insist that populism also undermines several core principles of *any* reasonable understanding of democracy.

Another danger inherent in such populism is the forced homogenization of diverse social groups under the banner of "the people." It concentrates power in the hands of an unaccountable leader who claims to be representative of the country as a whole. The primary antidemocratic element of the populist model is the idea that "the people" are a coherent whole, rather than an amalgam of multiple competing interests and visions.[41] Populism disregards the fact that pluralism and difference form the core of democratic ideals.[42] The tendency of this model is to exalt the charismatic leader—and to see such a ruler as almost infallible and entitled to indefinite rule—which contrasts with the democratic idea of political leadership as an institution filled very temporarily by different individuals.[43]

In truth, the relationship between democracy and populism differs across Latin American states. In its practical record, populism has shown itself to have some democratizing potential, but it has had some antidemocratic results as well.[44] Opposition to populist leaders raises the specter of militaries once again intervening to eject leftist leaders and ostensibly "save democracy"—as happened in recent years in Honduras and Paraguay. That is, some of the region's authoritarian tendencies on the left risk reawakening militarist tendencies on the right.

The broader debate about participatory democracy has sometimes been lost from view in recent years by the focus on controversial leaders such as Hugo Chávez. This is because Chávez attracted so much personal attention—favorable and critical. A more promising "democratic participatory project" points to the accountability mechanisms that have been tested in different Latin American countries—mechanisms such as participatory budgeting in Brazil and self-management councils in Mexico. Brazil is investing heavily in the welfare state, rather than ploughing resources back into reinvestment as China does. The Bolsa Família is now one of the best-known and most developed welfare programs in the world.

These initiatives also aim to address the limits attributed to liberal representative democracy and achieve greater social equality. Accountability was conceived as the means for ensuring public social control and popular co-management rather than improving government performance and efficiency.[45] Several Latin American countries have implemented constitutional reforms that establish new mechanisms of direct democracy. These reforms have been driven by traditionally excluded political sectors.[46] Eight countries currently allow for citizen-initiated procedures, namely Bolivia, Colombia, Costa Rica, Ecuador, Nicaragua, Peru, Uruguay, and Venezuela.[47] Their impact is still uncertain.[48]

A correlation between new types of politics and economic improvement has so far not been convincingly demonstrated. Sixty million people have been lifted out of poverty in Latin America during the past decade, in both liberal democracies and populist regimes, yet there is little correlation between economic gains and regime type. Moreover, in countries such as Brazil, the "vulnerable" population is not monolithic in its political references, one part supporting centrist-liberal options, another drawn to more populist rhetoric.

So, recent trends in Latin America are mixed. It is not clear whether the region is moving toward a distinctive form of democracy. The more populist democracies have advanced the political inclusion of social groups that historically have been consigned to the margins of the region's politics. Bolivia has an indigenous president. A trade unionist was the president of Brazil. In Argentina, Brazil, Chile, and Costa Rica, women are presidents.

Hand in hand with this inclusiveness, however, the core institutional aspects of democracy are unraveling in several countries. Venezuela is becoming more straightforwardly authoritarian. The Maduro government's reaction to revolts in June 2014 and its imprisonment of political opponents demonstrated a willingness to use repression to safeguard the Chavista Revolution.

Protests shook Brazilian democracy through 2014. Although the Dilma Rousseff government committed to listening to protesters' demands for better public services, the revolts revealed limits to the inclusiveness of the democratic process. The basic tenets of liberal democracy appear firmly rooted in Brazil. But in the wake of a polarizing election in 2014, calls for measures of more direct democracy became more prominent.

Across Latin America strong presidents, weak parliaments, supine judiciaries, and dysfunctional party systems still dominate—all features that have been with the region for a long time. It is an open question as to whether these add up to a distinctive form of Latin American democracy or whether the persistent concentration of power is actually a malign distortion of ostensibly liberal democratic systems. Either way, it is a type of politics that seems to be paying off for its architects. Incumbent or former presidents, including populists, are winning elections in the region. Rafael Correa won a new term in 2013 in Ecuador. Michelle Bachelet is back in power in Chile, and Jose Manuel Santos won the 2014 election in Colombia. Evo Morales won his third election in Bolivia in October 2014.

AFRICA: RETURNING TO DEMOCRATIC ROOTS

African thinkers and political leaders have long suggested that the Western liberal-democratic model does not fit the social, historical, and political context of African societies. In support of this opinion, these thinkers and leaders highlight the traditional elements and characteristics of African societies, including the strong role of religious, ethnic, and communal ties that sit uneasily with the Western emphasis placed on individual rights.

The legacy of colonialism also weighs on political configurations. It has reinforced sectarian divisions and helped produce a sui generis set of political institutions. These institutions were structured to favor particular segments of the population and are today easily co-opted by self-serving networks. Given their provenance and frequent misuse, these institutions are often viscerally disliked by African populations.

Two claims are made in African debates. One is that organic forms of local democratic representation and accountability were overridden by colonialism and need to be reinstalled—these forms should no longer be gainsaid by implanted institutions. Another claim is that local democratic forms today function well even where African states may fail by the standard (Western) measurement of liberal democracy. The policy implication is that external powers should focus on the subnational level and informal types of political engagement rather than seeking to superimpose modern forms of nation-state norms and structures at the center.

Many experts insist that the strong African tradition of consensus building is at odds with the Western focus on political competition, the silent and secret ballot, and majority rule. The ethnic, religious, and linguistic pluralism of African societies raises the danger of sectarian conflict and chaos in a system where those who gain an electoral mandate play winner take all.[49] Advocates of adapting democracy to the local context argue that Western conceptions overlook the importance of traditional loyalties in African society.[50]

Reflecting the continent's diversity, potential African democratic variations are suggested. Theocratic models are seen as relevant for societies with a Muslim majority, such as Sudan and Somalia. The persistence of underdevelopment leads many to advocate popular democratic models based on direct forms of political participation, greater economic inclusion, and a focus on marginalized communities. The most prominent and distinctive focus, however, is on so-called nativist models or consensus-oriented and consultative forms of democracy. These are based around traditional political practices and institutions such as chieftaincy and village councils.

Today, the argument is rarely made that traditional characteristics render democratic rule in Africa impossible or that African societies need authoritarian, "strongman" leaders. Instead, it is suggested that democracy in the African context needs to be based on and adapted to long-standing local democratic practices and traditions. These are seen as enjoying greater legitimacy than Western-style institutions.

Analysts blame the imposition of alien structures and processes for the failure of democratic consolidation and the persistence of neopatrimonialism and kleptocracy in most African countries. According to Claude Ake, in African conditions, Western liberal democracy "is not in the least emancipatory . . . because it offers the people rights they cannot exercise, voting that never amounts to choosing, freedom that is patently spurious, and political equality which distinguishes highly unequal power relations."[51] Ake insists that the liberal democratic model is based on a definition of interests that is too "particularized" for Africa, where the notion of a common societal interest still holds sway.[52]

African political traditions are consistent with democratic values such as accountability and participation.[53] They include the ideas of dialogue and consultation, systems of checks and balances, and the idea that political power should be derived from the people.[54] Many African precolonial political systems are said to have fit the notion of communalist democracy.[55]

Many experts suggest that African identity is reflected in one's ethnicity, religion, and communal traditions. Hence, a democratic paradigm is required that guarantees a genuine representation of all ethnic and religious groups. In contrast to the West, political parties in Africa are often organized around ethnic and religious ties, not political ideology.[56]

Putting all this together, it can be said that the core features of an African governance model based on traditional political institutions should include the following:

- *Communalism*: Communal governance at the local level, for example, takes the form of village councils and assemblies. Some argue that models of governance in which ethnic groups and other communities are represented as collective entities work well in the African context, if they are designed to include informal institutions.[57] Considerable decentralization would be required to allow local ethnic and other communities to govern themselves more democratically.[58]

- *Nonpartyism*: Some scholars and policymakers argue that instead of implementing multiparty democracies, African political traditions are more aligned with "nonpartyism." This is "movement democracy," which is not based on party competition. Nonpartyism is fundamentally distinct from one-party rule because it is based on direct mass participation and consensus building, rather than on the repression of the political opposition, and is meant to avoid sectarianism.[59]

An example of such a model is Uganda under long-time president Yoweri Museveni. The main characteristics of his rule have been the suspension of party involvement in elections and the reliance on mass participatory democracy. Candidates compete as individuals, and every citizen votes as part of a supposedly all-inclusive national movement and participates in policymaking through local committees. The idea is to minimize sectarianism.[60] The general argument in favor of such a model is that multiparty systems do not fit the multiethnic context of African societies and would lead to power grabs by the dominant ethnic group, followed by conflict and state fragmentation.

- *Consensual democracy*: Prominent African scholars have argued for a consensus-oriented, decentralized form of political decisionmaking. Nigeria has a system of alternating presidential rule between a northern Muslim and southern Christian and sharing power to prevent the exclusion of key ethnic groups. Kwasi Wiredu suggests that in multiethnic countries such as Nigeria, this kind of consensual model of governance is needed to temper sectarianism and partisan party politics.[61]

- *Chieftaincy*: Traditionally, local chiefs have played a crucial role in African politics. They arbitrate many local disputes and represent citizens and clans in interactions with the government. Chieftains are still important political players in countries such as Mozambique and South Africa. Advocates of this practice insist local chiefs can be incorporated into democratic institutions.[62] In Botswana, for example, chieftains have played a crucial role in negotiating on behalf of clans in land disputes. In many African societies, the chieftaincy still carries more political weight than the institutions of a national or regional government that lacks deep roots in the community.[63]

There are problems with any concept of African democracy that incorporates these elements. One such problem is that it rests on apparently contradictory arguments. On the one hand, Africans are said to value consensus rather than adversarial competition over political ideas. On the other hand, it is said that African societies are riven by too many ethnic, religious, and linguistic divisions for unrestrained majoritarian democracy to work. In other words, it is said that Western democracy is inappropriate because African societies value consensus and also because they value difference.

Another issue is how conceptual debates relate to real-life developments in Africa. Political trends in the region are extremely diverse (as shown by table 3.3). Macrolevel political trends suggest that while traditional, village-level forms of decisionmaking are strong, they coexist with very different levels of overarching democracy at the national level. In 2014, Freedom House scored ten African countries as free, 20 as not free, and nineteen as partly free.

"Free" countries include Benin, Botswana, Ghana, Lesotho, Namibia, Senegal, and South Africa. These appear to meet the criteria for liberal democracy. For example, South Africa qualifies as an essentially liberal democracy, according to Freedom House and Polity Project scores—though it shows some shortcomings. The African National Congress's persistent dominance means the parliament is weak and that it is rather the judiciary that represents the strongest constraint on government. Some restrictions exist on minority rights. But South Africa does not exhibit enough difference from standard liberal democracy to make it a wholesale, distinctive type of democracy.

More generally in Africa, the largest number of countries are categorized as "not free," including Angola, Cameroon, Central African Republic, Chad, Congo-Brazzaville, Democratic Republic of Congo, Equatorial Guinea, Eritrea, Ethiopia, Rwanda, Somalia, South Sudan, Sudan, and Zimbabwe. In these states, most indicators suggest that authoritarianism is the abiding dynamic, as opposed to genuinely distinctive models of democracy. At best, it could be said that to define any of these regimes as constituting benign varieties of democracy would require an extremely expansive definition of the term.

TABLE 3.3. **DEMOCRACY INDEX 2014: SELECTED AFRICAN COUNTRIES (0 TO 10 SCALE)**

REGIME TYPE	COUNTRY	RANK	OVERALL SCORE	ELECTORAL PROCESS AND PLURALISM	FUNCTIONING OF GOVERNMENT	POLITICAL PARTICIPATION	POLITICAL CULTURE	CIVIL LIBERTIES
FULL DEMOCRACIES	Mauritius	=17	8.17	9.17	8.21	5.00	8.75	9.71
FLAWED DEMOCRACIES	Botswana	28	7.87	9.17	7.14	6.11	7.50	9.41
	South Africa	30	7.82	8.33	8.21	.78	6.25	8.53
	Cape Verde	31	7.81	9.17	7.86	6.67	6.25	9.12
	Lesotho	60	6.66	8.25	5.71	6.67	5.63	7.06
	Zambia	67	6.39	7.92	5.36	4.44	6.88	7.35
	Ghana	68	6.33	8.33	5.36	5.56	5.63	6.76
	Namibia	73	6.24	5.67	5.00	6.67	5.63	8.24
	Senegal	74	6.15	7.92	5.71	4.44	5.63	7.06
HYBRID REGIMES	Mali	=83	5.79	7.83	3.93	4.44	6.25	6.47
	Tanzania	86	5.77	7.42	4.64	5.56	5.63	5.59
	Malawi	89	5.66	6.58	4.29	5.00	6.25	6.18
	Benin	90	5.5	6.92	5.36	4.44	5.63	5.88
	Uganda	96	5.22	5.67	3.57	4.44	6.25	6.18
	Kenya	97	5.13	4.33	4.29	6.11	5.63	5.29
	Mozambique	107	4.66	4.42	3.57	5.56	5.63	4.12
	Sierra Leone	109	4.56	7.00	1.50	2.78	6.25	5.29
	Burkina Faso	114	4.09	4.83	2.86	3.33	5.00	4.71
	Niger	115	4.02	7.08	1.14	2.78	4.38	4.71

CONTINUES ON THE NEXT PAGE

TABLE 3.3. **DEMOCRACY INDEX 2014: SELECTED AFRICAN COUNTRIES (CONTINUED)**

REGIME TYPE	COUNTRY	RANK	OVERALL SCORE	ELECTORAL PROCESS AND PLURALISM	FUNCTIONING OF GOVERNMENT	POLITICAL PARTICIPATION	POLITICAL CULTURE	CIVIL LIBERTIES
AUTHORITARIAN REGIMES	Madagascar	110	4.42	4.25	2.50	5.00	5.63	4.71
	Mauritania	112	4.17	3.42	4.29	5.00	3.13	5.00
	Gabon	=121	3.76	3.00	2.21	4.44	5.00	4.12
	Nigeria	=121	3.76	5.67	2.86	3.33	3.13	3.82
	Ethiopia	124	3.72	0.00	3.57	5.56	5.63	3.82
	Cote d'Ivoire	126	3.53	0.00	3.21	5.00	5.63	8.82
	Comoros	=127	3.52	3.92	2.21	3.89	3.75	3.82
	Togo	129	3.45	4.00	0.79	3.33	5.00	4.12
	Cameroon	=130	3.41	0.75	3.57	3.89	5.00	3.82
	Angola	133	3.35	0.92	3.21	5.00	4.38	3.24
	Burundi	134	3.33	2.58	2.21	3.89	5.00	2.94
	Rwanda	135	3.25	0.83	5.00	2.22	4.38	3.82
	Swaziland	140	3.09	0.92	2.86	2.22	5.63	3.82
	Gambia	=141	3.05	1.75	3.93	2.22	5.00	2.35
	Guinea	143	3.01	3.50	0.43	4.44	3.75	2.94
	Djibouti	145	2.99	0.83	2.50	3.33	5.63	2.65
	Congo-Brazzaville	146	2.89	1.25	2.86	3.33	3.75	3.24
	Zimbabwe	150	2.78	0.50	1.29	3.89	5.00	3.24
	Sudan	153	2.54	0.00	1.79	4.44	5.00	1.47
	Eritrea	155	2.44	0.00	2.50	1.67	6.88	1.18
	Guinea-Bissau	159	1.93	1.67	0.00	2.78	3.13	2.06
	DRC	162	1.75	0.92	0.71	2.22	3.13	1.76
	Equatorial Guinea	164	1.66	0.00	0.79	1.67	4.38	1.47
	Chad	165	1.50	0.00	0.00	1.11	3.75	2.65
	CAR	166	1.49	0.92	0.00	1.67	2.50	2.35

Source: *Economist Intelligence Unit, Index of Democracy 2014*   = denotes a tie with another country

It is in the remaining states defined as "partly free" where there would seem to be the most advanced, genuine debate over forms of representation that might be democratic in spirit but depart from Western understandings. These countries include Burundi, Côte d'Ivoire, Guinea, Kenya, Mozambique, Niger, Nigeria, Sierra Leone, Tanzania, Togo, Uganda, and Zambia.

However, overall it is difficult to detect a strong trend toward a completely different model of democracy. Afrobarometer and other polls show not only that the demand for democracy is rising across Africa but also that ordinary citizens make the same judgments about what is and what is not "democratic" as elsewhere in the world.[64] Some fear that, in practice, leaders have emphasized the role of clans in order to freeze self-serving, anachronistic hierarchies. To many, Nigeria has been characterized more by ruling-party domination and fraudulent elections than by a healthy local variant of democracy. In the country's April 2015 presidential contest the system of pre-agreed quotas and alternation broke down; the change of government may signal the emergence of more competitive pluralism in Nigeria.

Similar to the "Asian values" debate, which is discussed next, the debate about local democratic traditions in Africa has been complicated by the fact that African leaders have embraced traditional political practices and ideas, such as consensus, to justify (their own) one-party rule.[65] Prominent political supporters of "African-style" democracy include Paul Kagame, Meles Zenawi, Isaias Afwerki, Yoweri Museveni, and Laurent Kabila—all of whom have taken their countries toward what most observers would define as more authoritarianism rather than more locally fashioned democracy. The abuse and resulting hollowing out of democratic concepts has been a problem for African democracy in recent years. Jacques Nzouankeu writes that democracy in Africa "appears to have become a hackneyed term applicable to any situation, to the extent that notorious dictatorships would take advantage of this ambiguity to pass themselves off as democracies."[66]

ASIA: THE INFLUENCE OF VALUES

The advocacy of "Asian values" can be traced back to the 1970s.[67] The "Asian model" of democracy first attracted international attention in part because of the economic success of East Asian societies.[68] The 1993 Bangkok declaration—signed by countries such as China, Indonesia, Malaysia, and Singapore—staked out a "distinctive Asian point of view" on human rights and democracy.[69]

Since the 1990s, the most assertive stance in the promotion of Asian values has been taken by the political leaders of Southeast Asia, and in particular the late Lee Kuan Yew.[70] The long-serving prime minister of Singapore is widely recognized as the leading advocate for an East Asian alternative to Western liberal democracy. The Asian values discourse reflected the emergence of a cultural nationalism. Initially, postcolonial Asian governments gradually asserted their local political and societal traditions against Western norms. Later, they reacted against Western triumphalism after the end of the Cold War. Persistently rapid economic growth bred self-confidence among Asian elites.[71] Although the 1997 financial crisis temporarily put the advocates of the Asian model on the defensive, the region's economic recovery seemed to add further weight to its claims to superior economic adaptability.[72]

The claim that there is a distinctive Asian approach to politics rests on three core domains: values; institutional frameworks; and an emphasis on economic performance. The region's distinctive values reflect a shared set of moral, cultural, and religious practices, traditions, and beliefs. These values are said to include "respect for authority, strong families, reverence for education, hard work, frugality, teamwork, and a balance between the individual's interests and those of society."[73] These values are based on Confucianism, which emphasizes duty, social harmony, authority, strong commitments to social cohesion, and family ties.[74] It is often argued that owing to the strong influence of Confucianism in the region, Asian societies are less focused on individualism and the concept of individual rights than the citizens of Western liberal democracies. Western ideals of active citizenship are seen to weaken communal commitments, such as family ties.

In terms of institutional frameworks, Asian values are said to result in a prioritization of social order and political stability. Because of the importance placed on respect for hierarchy and authority both within the family and in society as a whole, the political system is based on consensus and trust in political leadership. There is less focus on contestation and adversarial debate. There is stronger demand for standards of good governance than for competitive political debate. Patron-client relations are considered natural and essential to the functioning of the state. Leaders and citizens are tied together in a complex of web of interdependence and reciprocity: leaders provide goods and services, and citizens provide loyalty and support. A strong state is considered benign rather than threatening.[75]

Countries following this model have personalistic regimes, dominant political parties, limited pluralism, a strong corporatist state capable of intervening in and directing the economy, and lean bureaucracies with significant political authority and high levels of national prestige.[76] Political parties tend to be catch-all and consensus-oriented rather than conflict-oriented.[77] The prevalence of legalism is also noteworthy in East Asia. It reinforces the idea that a strong state and rule-based governance are necessary to address political and economic needs.[78]

It is widely claimed that in the Asian model, economic success brings greater levels of trust in political authority, social discipline, and a greater willingness to sacrifice individual rights and consumption for collective welfare goals. This is the inverse of modernization theory, which argues that economic development ushers in liberal democracy.[79] In the Asian model, the government is considered responsible for creating the conditions necessary for economic growth. Economic governance is based on both sound macroeconomic management and a strong state capacity to intervene in the economy.[80] Singapore is sometimes portrayed as a "trustee model of democracy"—overseen by a government that is not led by short-term economic and populist preferences, but by longer-term judgments. Some argue that Singapore has been better at advancing meritocracy in recent years than have Western liberal democracies, where the quality of electorally selected politicians has declined.[81]

Asian values are about adapting governance institutions to local cultural and social contexts, rather than searching for a universally applicable replacement for liberal democracy.[82] The pragmatic argument for Asian-style democracy suggests that Western style governance is ill-suited to promoting rapid economic growth and social stability in the Asian context. Supporters believe that a system of governance should not be judged according to abstract principles but assessed on its capacity to deliver certain concrete outcomes for its citizens.[83]

Notwithstanding its undoubted merits, the Asian values concept is often applied to justify authoritarian regimes rather than used to serve as a genuinely democratic alternative to Western models.[84] The proponents of Asian values have focused more on defending semiauthoritarianism rather than putting forth an alternative model of democracy. Many elements of what is described as the Asian model look very similar to those of standard semiauthoritarian regimes—present in Asia as well as many other regions. Malaysian politics, for example, are predicated on racial quotas, but in a context of semiauthoritarianism rather than as a model of democracy. The concept of Asian-style democracy has been most vigorously embraced by Asian political leaders who have a clear interest in maintaining a system that limits opposition and emphasizes respect for authority and order.[85]

To say that Asians are willing to sacrifice civil or political rights for economic development begs the question of who decides that. How do we know this is true if Asian citizens do not have a free voice to express their choices? There are strong proliberal, prodemocratic voices within Asian society who sharply rebuke the likes of Lee Kwan Yew for peddling self-serving notions of perpetual elite power.[86] If there are such strong consensual values that all Asians agree with, it might be asked, why is it necessary to enforce these by stifling political debate and imposing illiberal restrictions on rights? There are laws in several Asian countries that oblige children to care for parents; if this is such an embedded cultural value, why does it need to be imposed through legal obligation?

Moreover, as with the other regions discussed above, the political variation that exists within Asia today casts doubt on the notion that there is one single culturally appropriate form for the region. The whole gamut of governance models and varying degrees of political freedom, repression, and economic development now exist in Asia.[87] A full range of divergent trends exists, from moves toward relatively liberal democracy to the persistence of largely illiberalized autocracy. Table 3.4 gives a flavor of this diversity.

Indonesia has undergone a sustained transition in an effort to manage the diversity of the country's huge population—a transition that has succeeded through decentralization. Indonesian politicians involved in the country's transition placed a distinctive focus on consensus. They combined this with asymmetric autonomy arrangements for Aceh and Pap-

TABLE 3.4. **SELECTED ASIAN COUNTRIES (0 TO 10 SCALE)**

REGIME TYPE	COUNTRY	RANK	OVERALL SCORE	ELECTORAL PROCESS AND PLURALISM	FUNCTIONING OF GOVERNMENT	POLITICAL PARTICIPATION	POLITICAL CULTURE	CIVIL LIBERTIES
FULL DEMOCRACIES	Japan	20	8.08	9.17	8.21	6.11	7.50	9.41
	South Korea	21	8.06	9.17	7.86	7.22	7.50	8.53
FLAWED DEMOCRACIES	India	27	7.92	9.58	7.14	7.22	6.25	9.41
	Taiwan	35	7.65	9.58	7.50	6.11	5.63	9.41
	Timor-Leste	46	7.24	8.67	7.14	5.56	6.88	7.94
	Indonesia	49	6.95	7.33	7.14	6.67	6.25	7.35
	Mongolia	61	6.62	9.17	5.71	5.00	5.00	8.24
HYBRID REGIMES	Malaysia	65	6.49	6.92	7.86	5.56	6.25	5.88
	Singapore	=75	6.03	4.33	7.50	5.00	6.25	7.06
	Philippines	=53	6.77	8.33	5.36	6.67	4.38	9.12
	Bangladesh	85	5.78	7.42	5.07	5.00	4.38	7.06
	Sri Lanka	87	5.69	6.17	5.36	4.44	6.88	5.59
	Fiji	91	5.61	4.17	5.71	6.67	5.63	5.88
	Thailand	93	5.39	5.33	4.29	5.56	5.00	6.76
	Bhutan	102	4.87	8.33	5.36	2.78	4.38	3.53
	Cambodia	=103	4.78	4.42	6.43	3.33	5.63	4.12
	Nepal	105	4.77	3.92	4.29	4.44	5.63	5.59
	Pakistan	108	4.64	6.00	5.36	2.78	3.75	5.29
AUTHORITARIAN REGIMES	Vietnam	61	6.62	9.17	5.71	5.00	5.00	8.24
	Myanmar	80	5.84	8.75	5.71	3.89	4.38	6.47
	China	82	5.81	7.92	6.07	3.33	4.38	7.35
	Laos	=83	5.79	7.00	5.00	5.56	3.75	7.65

Source: *Economist Intelligence Unit, Index of Democracy 2014*   = denotes a tie with another country

ua—the only way to manage the diversity. The Philippines seems to have pulled though its recent crises well, with strong and reasonably liberal democratic processes.

Thailand's 2014 military coup revealed a confusing array of opinions about democracy. The country's urban middle class protested, as it wanted to stop further elections from being run under the control of a nominally democratic but de facto highly oligarchic government—a populist regime that had gained a solid majority among the rural poor. The battle for democracy in Thailand is being driven by changing class alliances rather than a desire for an Asian democracy. It has been difficult to determine who are the "good democrats" in Thailand, as social configurations are so different from those in the West. A corrupt elite has opportunistically used poor-quality democratic mechanisms to protect itself from being challenged. If this is presented as a type of regime specific to Asia, it is perhaps not an especially healthy one.

While Burma has taken some steps toward a more open political system, little reform has been seen in Vietnam or Cambodia. Malaysia has sought to retain a distinctive hybrid mix of autocracy and democracy, eschewing fully competitive politics. Some say that the Singapore model is now subject to more criticism within the region. Singapore and Malaysia are often described as "limited liberal democracies." In these two countries, constitutional rights coexist with controlled political competition—although in Singapore, competition is not primarily about alternative political choices; it is rather about merit-based selection for posts within the administrative system. This combination also marks the contours of Asian democracy in Indonesia, Japan, South Korea, Sri Lanka, and Taiwan.[88]

The AsiaBarometer reveals regionwide support for social traditionalism, but there are varied opinions about political models. Surveys conducted in the region find that good, clean, and competent government performance wins more popular legitimacy than democracy. Support for traditional values is strongest in Indonesia, Vietnam, and Cambodia, and so is not specific to regime type.[89] Moreover, there are non-Confucian cultures in the region, such as in Malaysia, Thailand, and Vietnam, and these also follow very different political models.

Reality sometimes sits uneasily with the common view that Asian countries seek more protective democracy. Some research finds that Asian societies are in fact characterized by low levels of trust beyond immediate family circles.[90] South Korea—perhaps the most successful case of Asian democratization in recent years—still spends only 8 percent of GDP on social welfare protection, compared with the European Union average of about 30 percent. Polls show South Koreans place even greater stress on egalitarianism and state benevolence than do Singaporeans, yet quite happily pursue these values through what are largely liberal democratic institutions. More than one-third of South Koreans say that economic equality is the most important feature of a democratic system.[91] South Korea and Taiwan are the Asian economies that have maintained strong growth for the longest period of time—not the region's autocracies.

Asian governments have certainly introduced interesting institutional variations. Thailand has constructed a fourth branch of government dealing with oversight. Several Southeast Asian parliaments have developed nonpartisan parliamentary chambers. Indonesia has what it classifies as a three-chamber parliament: the two standard chambers that sit together and a separate third chamber with unique powers. Fiji has introduced a House of Chiefs.[92]

Yet the main structural question mark remains over the relationship between social norms and political institutions. The different elements of Confucianism can be separated from each other; those concerning political governance are distinct from those concerning personal morality.[93] The Asian values concept is most obviously about social values, such as respect for the elderly and care for the family and the collective in preference to egocentric individualism. Asian values are against drug abuse, high crime rates, homosexuality, social malaise, and alienation.[94] It is not clear why generally desirable values such as respecting elders require restrictions on political parties, the media, and civil society.

The Asian values concept draws a dichotomy between liberal democracy and communitarian principles that is perhaps too absolute. It is not clear that liberal democracy necessarily implies the end of communal values or family ties. The political leaders that have embraced Asian values have failed to specify the concrete institutional makeup that would make Asian-style governance a better quality of democracy. Instead they emphasize vague concepts of societal and collective values. They have generally failed to clarify which Western political institutions would specifically undermine or contradict Asia-specific values. One of Confucius's central points was that rulers must earn the devotion of their subjects and never do anything to them they would not want done to themselves—a precept that is similar to Kant's (liberal) categorical imperative. Some Asian experts argue that the Confucian values of family and meritocracy are compatible with a form of democracy that need not involve abridged notions of liberal freedoms or pluralism.[95]

Furthermore, Asian cultures have not been static, but subject to change. It is therefore specious, critics say, to maintain that a certain culture does not "fit" with liberal democracy—the same could have been said about many Western societies at a previous point in time.[96] Cultural change can also be encouraged and accelerated by political elites. Culturalist arguments about Asian values quickly blend into Orientalist stereotypes about the "Asian mentality."[97]

Others have suggested that rather than a singular divide between Asian values and Western culture, there is a much broader philosophical debate about the role of political authority. According to this line of thinking, the Asian critique of Western liberalism corresponds to the conservative political-philosophical challenge to liberal democracy. Seen through this lens, Asian values correspond to a form of illiberal, ultra-conservatism that has been on the rise in the West itself.[98]

Authoritarian China has stood somewhat aside from these debates. However, today in China, many political options are vigorously debated, including democracy of a distinct type. The general feeling is that fundamental change is now required in China, owing to growing protests, corruption, inequalities, and the lack of welfare provision. A small number of village elections are now allowed once again. The system is more responsive and open and permits more genuine debate. The question is whether this is a coherent model of accountability without elections. Many insist it is. Social media sites are constrained in China, but the Communist Party uses them to rouse opinion against corrupt local officials who it wants to expel. The use of Weibo opens up the prospect of direct outside links to Chinese citizens—links that are not mediated through the Communist Party. Official debates have moved from talk of administrative reform to political reform. Noted experts predict that China will contribute to new and distinctive forms of accountability and not be a monolithically closed political system that is simply good at creating growth.[99] It remains to be seen whether such trends will extend into a fully convincing alternative approach to accountability.

A final, highly pertinent area of debate relates to developments in a very different part of Asia: Afghanistan. Some assessments stress that the Afghan government and the international community have supported hybrid institutional forms. The country's High Peace Council is essentially a form of *loya jirga*, a traditional communal gathering. This has helped incorporate a wider range of communities than was the case before 2002. There has been a mix of old and new, formal and informal institutions. Legal pluralism has given people a choice of traditional, sharia, or modern courts. Although the Taliban was the one actor that stayed outside this plural framework, local traditional forms have even been useful more recently in bringing some Taliban into the tent, too. The "bad" side is where the government tends to use hybrid forms in an instrumental way to back its own positions; it has done this on several occasions to mobilize *loya jirga* opinion against the United States, for example. Certainly, when the Karzai government, in power until 2014, was at odds with traditional bodies, it favored more standard institution-building templates.

MODELS OF DEMOCRATIC VARIETY

There is a more specific subcategory of debate about Asian democracy. Japan and India hold a curious position in debates about democratic variety. They have both been firmly democratic for many decades and do not challenge the core concepts of democratic pluralism. Yet these countries' respective political systems clearly harbor many intricate and sophisticated elements of originality. Although neither country follows a model that is fundamentally different from or at odds with Western, liberal democracy, both exhibit elements of notable specificity. Japan and India are non-Western societies that fit within a broadly liberal democratic template, but whose politics have important specificities.

JAPAN: CONSOLIDATED BUT UNIQUE

Although few would contest Japan's place among the world's consolidated democracies, its political system is characterized by several distinguishing features that are tied to the country's historical, religious, and cultural context. Perhaps the most unusual aspect of Japanese democracy has been the dominance of a single political party, the Liberal Democratic Party (LDP), in the postwar period. With the exception of two brief periods from 1993 through 1994 and from 2009 through 2012, the LDP's ruling-party status has remained uncontested since 1955—despite a series of political scandals, internal divisions, and decreasing popular support.

This one-party dominance has been attributed to a variety of factors, including the Japanese electoral system, political campaign regulations, and the weakness of the political opposition. Opposition parties have generally failed to mobilize grassroots support and present themselves as a credible alternative in a centralized and clientelist political environment. Some scholars have questioned the extent to which Japan can be characterized as a democracy, given that it has a single dominant political party and that party relies on state resources to co-opt the country's most powerful interest groups, such as big business and agriculture.[100] Others argue that the current system is not as exclusive or uncontested as suggested and that regular free and reasonably fair elections are enough to ensure its democratic legitimacy.[101]

A further unique feature of Japan's political system is the power of the administrative bureaucracy, particularly the power of the Ministry of Finance and the Ministry of International Trade and Industry. The bureaucracy's dominance can be traced back to the prewar period and the belief that a strong, centralized leadership was needed to facilitate Japan's economic modernization. Scholars disagree on whether the dominance of nonelected bureaucrats and institutions represents authoritarian tendencies or whether the bureaucracy's power is in fact sufficiently constrained by elected officials.[102]

Lastly, Japan's political system is closely tied to its economic model, which has been described as state-regulated capitalism with elements of corporatism or "redistributive regulated party rule." The dominant party allocates the country's economic resources among various sectors of society, thereby bringing a wide variety of political and societal factions into the ruling structure and preventing political conflict and instability.[103] Long celebrated for facilitating Japan's remarkable economic growth in the postwar period, this system has come under criticism in recent years for being too rigid and preventing much needed reforms.[104]

INDIA: SUCCESSFUL DESPITE CHALLENGES

India is routinely lauded as the world's biggest democracy. With more than 1.2 billion inhabitants, countless ethnic, regional, linguistic, and caste divisions, and widespread poverty and illiteracy, the country's democratic track record remains a puzzle for political scientists.[105] The uniqueness of India's democracy lies less in its institutional model than in its ability to function despite immense political and economic challenges, including persistent underdevelopment, mass poverty and exclusion, corruption, and ethnic and regional tensions. Democracy was interrupted only briefly by a state of emergency from 1975 to 1977.

In order to understand Indian democracy, most scholars point to its origins in the pro-Independence movement that set the foundations for the country's political development. Although India inherited a relatively centralized state and a well-established civil service from the British colonial system, nationalist elites played a crucial role in institutionalizing secularism, universal adult suffrage, and a federal system.[106] Contrary to what political scientists would predict in a highly heterogeneous society, India is not a consociational but a liberal and adversarial democracy based on the majoritarian Westminster model.[107] It did incorporate some features of a power-sharing model. The grand governing coalition that was the Congress Party successfully aggregated a wide variety of regional, caste, and ethnic interests.[108] Yet this political arrangement has been challenged in recent decades by higher levels of political mobilization and participation, resurgent sectarianism, the decline of the Congress Party and the rise of the Bharatiya Janata Party (BJP), as well as numerous ethnic and regional parties. As a result, Indian democracy since the 1990s has become significantly more fragmented—a trend that has deepened appreciably under the current Modi government.[109]

India's relative success at managing societal cleavages rests on a complex political balance between centralization and decentralization.[110] India remains a comparatively centralized federal state, even though considerable power has been devolved to state and local governments as a result of regional pressure. New Delhi retains the right to suspend representative government at the state level and impose emergency rule from the center, a law that is meant for emergency situations but has in the past been abused for political purposes.[111] Although center-state conflicts have at times led to violent breakdowns of relations and separatist movements, political conflicts in India tend to remain confined to individual regions. They have not undercut democracy as a whole.[112]

In contrast to other postcolonial states, traditional governance institutions were to a large extent rejected or abolished in the postindependence period owing to their association with colonial rule. They have played a relatively insignificant role in the overall functioning of Indian democracy. However, customary village councils continue to play a role in certain regions of the country, and tend to operate in harmony with formal local institutions and elected officials.[113]

On the national level, two institutions have played a particularly important role in sustaining democracy. One is the independent Electoral Commission, which oversees elections at all levels of government. The other is the country's judiciary and, in particular, the Supreme Court.[114] At the core of India's democratic system are regular elections characterized by mass participation of India's poorest and most disadvantaged citizens. India's lower classes and castes constitute the country's most important voting bloc.[115] However, the increase in political inclusiveness and its "reservation" (or affirmative action) policies have not significantly improved the plight of the country's poor.[116] The state has failed to provide citizens with basic goods and services, reduce socioeconomic inequality, or fight endemic corruption. Analysts criticize India's democratic system for its incapacity to deliver more substantive democratic outcomes.[117]

In some senses, debates about Indian democracy remain very much unresolved. Some analysts point to India's measured use of power-sharing to include the country's myriad groups and religions. Others, however, doubt whether India stands as a good and distinctive model. Corruption and de facto discrimination remain rife in India. Politics works on the basis of the "in group," hindering equality. India's super rich have pulled away from the rest of the population, earning more of their money from outside the country. Tensions increasingly flare between the regions. And Naxalite unrest in recent years is testament to the limits of inclusion.

CONCLUSION

The regional debates summarized in this chapter have existed for decades but have gained a new lease on life in recent years. These discussions constitute powerful lenses through which the issue of non-Western democracy is viewed. For many, regional specificity provides a legitimizing force that universalism does not. The desire for some form of ownership of political ideals—even if only vaguely formulated—means that many would feel more enthusiastic about democracy if it could be presented as developing in a way that is "Arab" or "African" or "Asian." Some elements of regional specificity are now at the forefront of political developments.

And some of these elements are about fairly core values, not minor institutional tweaks to democracy as it exists in the West. The frequently made claim that democratic variation is about different institutional expressions of universally shared values does not fully capture the nature of regional debates. These debates are also not simply about pitting an illiberal non-Western democracy against a Western liberal democracy. Some features of widely advocated regional models are indeed illiberal, but others are not. The form-versus-values and liberal-versus-illiberal dichotomies are useful to a point, but they are insufficient to fully appreciate the concerns specific to different regions.

The very longevity of these regional debates suggests they cannot be entirely without foundation. Francis Fukuyama has recently pointed out that regional variations are so enduring because they have long roots in different historical processes and sequences of political development. In Latin America, the prevalence of oligarchic structures before and after independence militated against a strongly redistributive state; the pursuit of liberal equality has for many centuries had an antisystem tone in this region. In Africa, tribal structures were utilized by colonial powers and then retained influence in the absence of strong state-building projects. In Asia, a strong and relatively impartial state developed early on, embedding support for a notion of societal goals being fairly pursued above particularistic gain.[118] With such strong roots, the focus on regional variation is certain to continue.

However, the chapter also uncovers serious limitations to all these regional debates. Overall, the empirical evidence suggests that uniform regional clusters of particular types of democracy do not exist. Rather, there is a high degree of variation that exists within regions.

In comparing different components of democracy across a large number of countries, one project finds that there is no Western-versus-non-Western divide. Older democracies tend to be more liberal than younger democracies, including younger Western democracies. The use of referenda, as a proxy for direct democracy, tends to be a function of how new a democracy is, not whether it is Western or not. Several Eastern European states are closer to Latin American states than to Western European democracies. Some non-Western democracies are majoritarian (such as Turkey); others are highly consensual (such as South Africa). Degrees of centralization do not split along Western-versus-non-Western lines; neither do degrees of judicial review.[119] Some Asian political institutions are based on smaller government and leaner state bureaucracies than in the West.[120]

This finding can be widened into a more general observation. Democracies make choices: a republic or constitutional monarchy; a unitary or federal government; a unicameral or bicameral legislature; common law or civil law; monism or dualism with respect to international law; an inspirational or technical constitution; and a majoritarian or proportional representation electoral system. The choices governments make do not split along regional lines.

Analytically, most of the supposedly specific regional variations remain well short of being mapped out in firm and comprehensive detail. They all define as aspects of "democracy" at least some features that seem, in practice, to merge into authoritarian dynamics. Critics of each regional model have become as outspoken as their supporters in recent years. All the models struggle to explain how modernizing social trends fit into tradition-based templates. They tend to paint a rather static concept of regional identities, ignoring that these are in fact changing fast. Some of what they profess to be radically different from Western democracy in fact mirrors current concerns in Europe and North America. In sum, these regional debates reveal why the question of non-Western democracy has become not only so potent but also so frustratingly difficult to address.

CHAPTER 4

PROBLEMS WITH THE NOTION OF NON-WESTERN DEMOCRACY

The calls for non-Western democracy are increasingly ubiquitous, but they lack clarity. The principles and institutions that such a concept might entail in practice are nebulous and ambiguous. When talking about non-Western democratic alternatives, politicians and analysts make any number of claims. Some argue that liberal democracy per se is flawed and that fundamentally different models are required; these critics assume that other such models exist in sharp contradistinction to a single Western model.

In contrast, some point out that liberal democracy may be suited to the West, but it is not a governance model others want. More subtly, some suggest that while liberal democracy may be a legitimate universal aim, conditions outside the West make it impracticable. Yet others maintain that liberal democracy's focus on individual rights needs to be complemented with more effective means of holding powerful political and economic elites accountable and that this applies both in and beyond the West.

This chapter unpacks the deficiencies of many of the claims made in the name of non-Western democracy. These include

- the questionable link between social norms and political processes;

- the thinking that economic justice requires an alternative democratic model;

- the tendency toward overly static cultural essentialism; and

- the way the non-Western narrative is used to cloak authoritarianism.

SEPARATING SOCIAL NORMS FROM POLITICAL PROCESSES

Delve beneath the surface of many calls for non-Western democracy and very often the concern is more about certain Western social norms rather than about specific types of democratic political processes. In some debates, there appears to be a conflation of liberal social values and democratic practices and institutions.

Concerns over Western democracy often come down to the question of whether liberal political institutions necessarily lead to liberal social norms, such as tolerance for divorce and homosexuality, the embrace of secular morality, more relaxed attitudes toward drug use, a loss of hierarchical deference, and an insistence on the full panoply of women's rights. Many critics of Western democracy believe that liberal democracy results in liberal values and that this is a malign feature of these political systems. Several of the most prominent challenges to liberal social values come from authoritarian leaders, such as Russia's President Vladimir Putin. But governments of countries that are at least partially democratic also attack Western democracies as epicenters of social decay. Examples can be seen in many African states and recently in Turkey.

But does this argument really stand up? Are certain Western social choices influenced by a particular political system? Although there is undoubtedly some linkage between political arrangements and social outcomes, the claim that liberal democratic politics necessarily entails excessive social liberalism is highly questionable. Permissive social norms may flow from the nature of Western society, but they do not inexorably derive from any specific mechanisms of democracy.

Indeed, a number of liberal democracies clearly embody persistently conservative values. Chile, Poland, and South Korea are examples. Compared with many European populations, a high proportion of U.S. citizens have conservative religious values. Western democracies separate church and state, but they do not intrinsically obliterate religious values or completely exclude them from public life. Figure 1 shows that there is no neat correlation between types of political regime and prevailing social values. The figure gives examples of countries placed on a spectrum of social values, as measured by the World Values Survey. On one end of the spectrum are societies adhering to "traditional" values; on the other end are those preferring "secular-rational" values. Matching this spectrum against the Economist Intelligence Unit's categorization of regime types, we can see that within each category of social values, there are political regimes of different types—autocracies, hybrid regimes, flawed democracies, and fully democratic systems. A particular form of social values does not correspond to any one type of political system.

Moreover, doubts must surely be raised about those who purport to determine outside a democratic system that particular societies want illiberal social values. If it is the case, for example, that a commanding majority of Asians want a less liberal society than Westerners do, how do restrictions on democratic competition serve that orientation? Even some proponents of Asian distinctiveness speak of a "great convergence," as some kinds of political values are spreading across cultures. Asia and other regions of the

FIGURE 1. **REGIME TYPE BY SCALE OF SOCIAL VALUES**

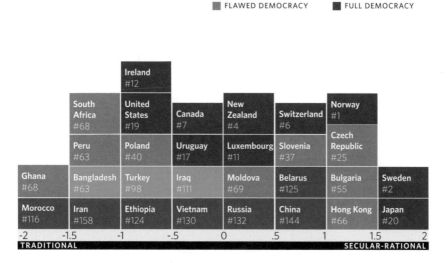

Source: *Economist Intelligence Report, 2014,* and *World Values Survey, 2008*

world are increasingly adhering to the norms of reason, law, and accountability as a result of economic progress advancing so spectacularly, even though their social values may still differ from those of the West.[1]

In this sphere, communitarian thinkers have struggled to design full alternatives to the Western liberal model. These critics disparage Western liberalism for its flawed assumptions of universal validity, arguing that liberalism devalues the importance of community and overemphasizes the rights of the individual in society. Yet they have not developed comprehensive institutional alternatives.[2]

Social illiberalism currently appears to be one of the world's most notable trends. It lies behind many of the most forceful calls for non-Western democracy. This is ironic given that in the West, advocacy of non-Western democracy is often associated with a leftist progressive agenda that at home champions social liberalism. Indeed, the various groups that espouse the cause of non-Western democracy make for uneasy bedfellows. In many developing countries, those leading the charge for non-Western democracy see it as a means of pushing back against precisely the kind of socially liberal values for which Western progressives have campaigned so hard.

SEPARATING NEOLIBERAL ECONOMICS FROM LIBERAL DEMOCRACY

Many proponents of non-Western democracy most ardently seek different economic policies—and equate this aspiration with the need for a different system of political governance. In particular, calls for non-Western democracy are often a search for an alternative to neoliberal economic policies, which they believe generate poverty, inequality, and other socioeconomic ills. Supporters of non-Western democracy seek an alternative that would produce greater social justice. It is important to clarify whether the hostility is toward Western-style democracy or market capitalism.

In fact, the desire for social justice and a fairer arbitration of markets does not necessarily entail a rejection of liberal politics. In the years immediately following the Cold War, many proponents of liberal democracy saw it as inextricably bound up with neoliberal economic reform. In dealing with today's pushback against Western-style democracy, we now reap the problematic harvest of that conflation.

The complex relationship between economic and political liberalism has lain at the center of writings on democracy for many centuries. These writings tell us that there is not an absolute dichotomy between liberal politics and social justice. Indeed, the later work of John Stuart Mill famously pointed to the mutually reinforcing links between liberal political rights and social democratic ends.[3]

A common line of reasoning is that economic justice needs strong state capacity. So a key question is whether there is a trade-off between state capacity and liberal rights. This is the core claim underlying at least some calls for alternative democratic models. Yet the examples of Western democracies with strong states, such as Sweden and other Nordic countries, invalidate such a blanket assumption. Defenders of Western democracy insist there is no crisis specifically related to liberal democracy's economic performance. Rather, we see variation in performance across different regime types—including liberal democracies, autocracies, and other types of democracy. The variables that most clearly explain economic performance and social outcomes do not seem to include those relating to regime type. So, for example, the Gini coefficient, a measure of income inequality, is improving in several developing regions but not in a way that is correlated to any particular political model. In many countries outside the West, the democratization process went hand in hand with a strengthening of state capacities; in many others, it undermined the central state. There was no single pattern of political development, and as a result, there is no uniform correlation between effective state capacity and a particular form of democracy.[4]

Of course, radical critics of liberal democracy insist there is an intrinsic link. They argue that liberal democracy feeds neoliberal economics and that the latter negates de facto liberal rights. This means that a properly social democratic model can be seen as requiring more than fair policy outcomes; it should also involve a distinctive political process. In this line of thinking, the priority is for greater democratic control over economic processes and the aim is to democratize socioeconomic power relations, which are considered sites of political power.[5] The argument here is that leftist populist varieties of democracy *require* a repression of some individual rights in order to implement heterodox economic policies.

It is one thing to call for flanking measures of workplace "economic democracy" (mechanisms giving workers influence over decisions within companies), but it is another to support a more generalized assault on liberal democracy in the name of economic justice. The record suggests that, in practice, the chain of causality often runs the other way: regimes use the popularity they win by challenging neoliberal economics to consolidate their power in illiberal fashion—and in areas and in ways that are quite unconnected from the implementation of more equitable economic policies. The pursuit of fairer economic policies does not necessarily require illiberal politics as much as it tactically enables them. Today's Robin Hood leader easily becomes tomorrow's despot. Venezuela during the past decade stands as an example of this danger.

There is a need to better link procedural with substantive democracy. But this does not necessarily mean that any non-Western alternative to liberal democracy will be superior on this score. Critics of Western democracy make this argument often without firmly demonstrating exactly how a qualitatively different form of democracy would deliver on economic justice. Too much focus on substantive output sometimes leads to a neglect of vital procedural principles—a danger lurking in some alternative forms of democracy that are often proposed.

CULTURAL ESSENTIALISM

So, advocates of non-Western democracy are making some questionable claims about the relationship between liberal democracy and liberal social and economic policies. But the problems go beyond such confusions. The deficiencies also flow from some highly questionable assumptions that are made about the fundamental nature of non-Western societies.

The non-Western argument often crosses the line into essentialism—the assumption that certain values are intrinsic to given cultures and not likely to evolve. Liberal democracy's universality is often disputed with the claim that some cultures are not compatible with the core tenets of liberal democracy and that such cultural identities must be preserved and respected. However, such cultural claims are disputable. One reason is that it is unclear who decides which norms and traditions belong to a certain culture and which aspects should be protected politically. The prevailing "culture" is invariably contested and changeable.[6]

Historians of political development have charted how changes to politics and changes in cultural values interact. They often point out that norms of representation are a product not of different cultures, but of different structures of production: agrarian societies fit with more oligarchic forms of representation; more industrial societies need interest aggregation through modern political parties.[7] The implication is this: illiberal values may exist because change is still under way, not because a society uniformly supports these values as eternal truths.

In this vein, we must distinguish illiberal democracies from nonconsolidated ones. The former are stable illiberal states; the latter are nations with a form of illiberal politics that rests on still-evolving social structures. Transitions have always taken time. Yet, in the wake of the Arab Spring revolutions in Egypt and the Maidan Revolution in Ukraine, many writers seem to have forgotten the decades of violence and effort that have usually been midwife to modern Western democracy. The "normal" problems associated with such an arduous transformation are often mistaken for an existential crisis of liberal democracy per se.

Similarly, the call for wholesale nonliberal democracy must be distinguished from advocacy for a "role for some traditional institutions." Traditional institutions may indeed have some traction today, but that does not necessarily mean that cultural values require a wholesale alternative to liberal democracy.

A society's core values quite patently change over time; to suggest otherwise buys into the notion of static cultural relativism. The non-Western discourse has gained political correctness, but in its more extreme forms it elides into something akin to a contemporary form of Orientalism. As a result, when Western analysts talk of different "indigenized" forms of democracy in developing regions, it can annoy many self-consciously and acutely modern democratic activists in these localities.[8] In essence, a sequencing problem is that traditional forms of family and village solidarity have broken down in developing countries, but the modern form of (state) solidarity common in advanced Western democracies has not been built up to take their place. Moreover, many pro-democratic voices in developing states complain that "traditional" structures are actually a hangover from colonial efforts to find ways of backing friendly allies. And they see ethnicity-based mechanisms as transmission belts for the clientelism that keeps the same elites in power year after year. Experts point out that in many rising economies, the problem is that social change is happening so fast that it is outstripping existing institutional structures.[9]

Indeed, some aspects of change happening outside the West might be more oriented toward modernity and forward-looking than some aspects occurring within the West. The middle class is growing in developing states but shrinking in the West. Hence, the notion that liberalism is tied to middle-class interests and perspectives has an interesting twist in this sense: inherited belief systems may be evaporating in developing countries just as Western citizens are increasingly searching for the protection of traditions.

The non-Western argument tends to assume that nonliberal preferences are firmly rooted in complex internal processes of identity formation. Some celebrate these choices as resistance to liberal hegemony. Others decry them and insist that democracy promotion strategies need to be more invasive to change these "mistaken" choices. But both views neglect the social and economic factors that shape such views—the crucial point being that these factors fluctuate in their impact over time.[10]

Difficult questions follow from this. Do developing societies really want to lock in forms of representation that are based on traditional cultural practices? Do such societies really want their politics to be based on noncompetitive and hierarchical structures—and do they believe these structures are really best suited to guaranteeing peace and harmony between otherwise clashing ethnic or religious communities? Critics say that, far from being benignly suited to non-Western societies, power-sharing deals that amount to elite bargains are often rejected by local parties that seek to maximize their own gains. In practice, competitive jockeying for position destabilizes many such settlements that are reached. Indeed, Western actors have often pressed for consensual settlements *against* reluctant local actors.[11]

In many countries, people say Western democracy seems too conflictual and adversarial. They seek more collegial forms of resolving differences. Yet these communal institutional forms have their own power dynamics, their own vested interests, and their own forms of manipulation. Liberal democracy is viewed critically for allowing the powerful to prevail, whatever the formal narrative of equal rights. However, traditional forms are themselves hardly bereft of such dynamics, even if the latter function without the harshly and visibly competitive aspects of liberal democracy.

Moreover, the style of Western politics should not be attributed to liberal democracy per se. Contemporary politics in the West may be abrasive and adversarial—and many non-Western democrats may genuinely recoil from the unedifying tone of debate that now prevails. But this is a choice of political style—not something that follows unavoidably from the political structure of liberal democracy. Non-Western countries can easily have a set of fully open democratic institutions and liberal guarantees as well as a less aggressive style of political debate.

JUSTIFYING AUTHORITARIAN DYNAMICS

Although knee-jerk rejections of the alternative-models discourse should be avoided, it is nevertheless important to be alert to instances where covert support for authoritarianism lurks behind calls for non-Western democracy. The search for political variety is valuable and should not be dismissed as disingenuous. But it is crucial to be attentive to arguments that are really only justification for authoritarian dynamics. Calls for "different democracy" are sometimes made with the intent of "less democracy."

For example, the notion that consensus is more important than competition between ideas—a favorite claim of some advocates of non-Western democracy—is easily manipulated. As already suggested, if consensus is indeed so natural to non-Western societies, they should not *need* to have more restrictions placed on their political freedom. There should be less of a need to, say, restrict political party activity if local communities are naturally drawn to consensus-building deliberative processes. Hannah Arendt's comments on communitarianism take on new relevance today. One of her themes was that ancient, participative liberty should not justify an infringement of modern, private liberty.

As noted in the previous chapter, conceptual debate has for several years centered on boosting participative and deliberative dynamics as a corrective to liberal democracy's shortcomings. Yet many non-Western governments talk of their local cultures requiring more *restrained* civic debate. Politicians are critical of participative and deliberative theories—complaining that these have developed almost uniquely on the basis of Western writings and are as insular as concepts of liberal democracy.

As already highlighted, the rise of populism—especially in the Latin American countries discussed in the previous chapter—is closely related to calls for non-Western democracy. This is despite the fact that populism is not in itself non-Western and has been on the rise in many Western countries as well. Moreover, populist appeals are clearly sometimes used to legitimize authoritarian control. Although scholars differ over the question of whether populism is a healthy corrective of or a threat to democracy, in at least some cases it has clearly become the latter.

Although populism increases inclusiveness, it seems to undermine the dynamic of competitive and open contestation. The positive interpretation of this equates populism with a democracy that is legitimately direct, while shorn of liberal checks and balances.[12] Many see populism as a de facto and legitimate form of democracy on the basis that it widens inclusiveness.

But, does populism boost inclusiveness on a democratic basis? This governance model admirably seeks the betterment of excluded segments of society. But does populism give them a free voice and a role in holding decisionmakers accountable, or does the model broaden inclusiveness on the basis of paternalism? If the latter, is it not stretching to define populism as a distinctive, nonliberal model of democratic enhancement—however welcome any improvement in the well-being of marginalized communities may be?

Populist regimes should be judged, case by case, on their own terms: do they in practice guarantee a form of democracy that is more responsive to what formerly excluded citizens themselves define as their interests? And does this responsiveness suffice to protect such groups if and when the populist leader "turns bad"? Regimes differ. Evo Morales is a more positive example than Hugo Chávez and his enduring legacy, for instance. When the answers are negative, however, doubts must arise over whether a populist regime practices a deeper and fairer form of democracy than liberal democracy.

There is a striking irony in non-Western leaders' support for concepts such as managed democracy and soft authoritarianism. These concepts echo Dahl's classic concept of democracy's "guardian institutions" operating beyond the scope of competitive politics. Many claim that the need for wise, nation-guiding guardians is an essential pillar of non-Western politics. The irony, of course, is that the originator of this idea, Plato, was as Western as Locke. When non-Western illiberal soft authoritarians base their actions on a discourse of "authenticity," they are actually drawing on ideas that have as much Western pedigree as does liberal democracy. It was Plato who first developed the idea that there is objective right and thus states should be ruled by reason and laws to restrain individual interests, rather than by democracy. It was Aristotle who extended the idea of states needing an enlightened oligarchy, chosen by the people but capable of autonomous, rational planning for the population. And it was Alexander who spread such aspects of Hellenism outward.

CONCLUSION

Many conceptual weaknesses and doubts persist when the calls for non-Western democracy are interrogated more closely. A lack of clarity—at the policy and analytical levels—is evident on a number of crucial questions. These include: the relationship between social illiberalism and liberal democracy; the link between economic justice and forms of democracy; and the point at which alternative forms of democracy elide into something that cannot convincingly be defined as democratic. This chapter cautions against an uncritical acceptance of the non-Western argument. We need to draw very selectively and carefully from the calls for non-Western democracy. The key is to situate these calls within a broader debate over democratic regeneration—to which we now turn.

CHAPTER 5

THE DEBATE ON DEMOCRATIC VARIATION

G iven the problems with the non-Western argument, how can we best explore the need for democratic variation? In recent years, broader debates have gathered steam that urge a rethinking of democracy. These debates are not framed in terms of non-Western democracy per se, but they are concerned with finding new innovations in accountability and representation.

This chapter summarizes some of the scholarly thinking behind these debates. The chapter does not delve deeply into abstract democratic theory; rather, the purpose of this chapter is to explain some important analytical issues in a way that points us toward policy-relevant conclusions. Recent conceptual thinking helps us establish a bridge between the non-Western debate and a broader, more useful means of exploring democratic variation.

The chapter covers several areas of the broader debates over democratic variation:

- the conceptual questioning of Western democracy;

- the impact of global power shifts and the current economic crisis;

- the focus on participative democracy and new social movements;

- what liberalism is and isn't; and

- new ways to measure democracy.

This chapter is a conceptual interlude. So far, I have argued that we need to take seriously the calls to look beyond the standard model of Western democracy, but we must also avoid fully buying into the notion of non-Western democracy. Consequently, we need to step back and think about the kind of analytical foundations that might be capable of framing a search for democratic variation. Examining the wider debates that are taking place about democratic regeneration helps lay the groundwork for the policy suggestions that are set out in the following chapters. The scholarly debates are presented here in a separate chapter so that those not engaged at such an analytical level can proceed directly to the next chapter.

REEXAMINING WESTERN DEMOCRACY

Democracy requires some redefinition not only outside but also within the West. Concerns about the parlous state of Western democracy have prompted much soul-searching in recent years. Today's debate is not simply about making non-Western adaptations to a fixed and unquestioned set of Western democratic institutions. Many of the calls for non-Western democracy are best understood as reflecting the challenge of reimagining democracy in a general sense. Democracies and would-be democracies everywhere struggle with similar challenges, as disaffection grows with politicians because of inequality, corruption, and a lack of meaningful policy alternatives.

Concerns outside the West are not entirely different from those that have gathered pace within the West. This is categorically *not* to say that Western democracy is ahead of the game or that it is on top of all the criticisms thrown at it by non-Western critics. Quite the opposite: Western democracies are floundering; they need to improve democratic quality in many of the same ways as non-Western countries.

Michael Saward points out that the very meaning of democracy has been extensively debated within the West over the past twenty years. Indeed, democracy's very essence has become "the contest over its meaning." Efforts focus on thinking beyond the minimal Schumpeterian definition that democracy is elites competing in market-like fashion for citizen support. It is now clear that it's a "definitional fallacy" to define democracy in terms of the U.S. model simply because it is assumed to be the exemplar of a democratic regime.[1]

Western debates have shifted significantly since the seminal 1973 Tri-lateral Commission worried that liberal democracies were becoming un-governable because of almost unmanageable and clashing constituencies.[2] Today, citizens say they feel disenfranchised due to governments' failure to respond to their demands or protect their basic interests. An increas-ingly prevalent view is that traditional mechanisms of representation in the West are being sidelined by other forums—and at the same time be-ing deformed by power interests. Consequently, there is a need to think anew.[3]

Prominent historians note that the juncture resembles previous mo-ments when liberal democracy suffered deep conceptual challenge.[4] Then as now, many prominent books were scathingly critical of democracy's liberal variant and called for alternative ideas for revitalizing democracy.[5] A recent account argues that the historical development of Western lib-eral democracy was based on a series of balances and alliances between different social groups; however, the unrestrained dominance of today's "merchant class" has undermined these configurations, requiring a deep political reinvention to keep democracy afloat.[6] Debates over models such as republican, deliberative, and associative democracy have gained new life. And analysts have added contemplation of other models, such as feminist, green, virtual, and religion-rooted democracy.[7]

The author of the most extensive history of democracy, John Keane, insists that we need a "more capacious, globally sensitive understanding of freedom, citizenship and democracy." He detects the emergence in the developing world of a "monitory democracy," conceived as a "continuous public scrutiny, chastening and control of power." This is seen taking root in places such as India in the form of local consultation schemes, tradi-tional dispute resolution, and quota-based representation to spread civic capacity. He sees these forms coming to supplant the traditional institu-tional parameters of Western, liberal democracy.[8]

Liberal democracy now squirms uncomfortably under a harsh spotlight of critical scrutiny. Moises Naím argues that the problems facing West-ern democracy have become so bad that it almost seems like an excess of liberalism and pluralism has sapped governments of the power they need to solve basic needs or even retain order. He suggests that the dispersal of power has almost gone too far.[9]

Mark Chou believes that recent trends show liberal democracy to be inherently unstable, as its "rampant liberalism" inevitably clashes with and undermines core democratic principles.[10] Indeed, there is concern that in many countries Western liberal democracy is breeding exclusionary illiberalism. Indeed, many worry that liberal individualism has come to contradict itself: liberal Western systems now constrict genuine individual autonomy and influence over government choices. Liberalism has been appropriated by a select, dominant part of society. A standard refrain of political theory inveighs against the "liberal irony": liberalism has become its own inverse. That is, liberal political systems have facilitated the dominance of increasingly less tolerant, less equitable, and less liberal views.

A widespread feeling is that, against the backdrop of so many predetermined power constraints, liberal democracy today reduces a noble ideal to merely formal procedural rules. Critical voices see the international agenda of spreading liberal democracy as being inherently linked to Western power interests, and that this is what has prevented Western governments from genuinely exploring alternative models.[11]

This reminds us that the challenge to liberalism is far from being entirely of non-Western origin. Many of the most vociferous critics of Western democracy and advocates of non-Western or non-liberal democracy are Westerners. In July 2014, Hungarian Prime Minister Viktor Orban announced explicitly that he sought to abandon liberal democracy in favor of an "illiberal state." Within the West as elsewhere, strong currents of thinking have pulled opinion back to pre-Enlightenment, Aristotelian visions of society's interests having primacy over the individual's rights.

There is no singular Western malaise. The problems with democracy in the United States are almost the opposite of those in Europe. U.S. democracy is designed with so many checks and balances that gridlock has become endemic. In Europe, the issue is more about populations having little effective sway over the decisions elites make with apparently little regard for shifts in public opinion. U.S. democracy is predicated on restraint of the majority, European democracy on elite autonomy. In the United States, the crisis of democracy is one of polarization; in Europe, it is one of frustration with elite consensus providing citizens with no real alternatives. There is no uniform Western democratic disease; the United States suffers from the problem of a weak executive, while Europe's distress is the prominence of extrademocratic technical agencies.

Indeed, as problems deepen, it becomes more evident that there is no single Western template. Many variations of democracy persist even within a basically liberal model, and particularly around a division between "protective" and "developmental" democracies.

The extensive reach of the worried debates about effective politics reveals a broader point. There is disaffection today with all mainstream political elites—not with only one particular model. It is an age of higher expectations and more impatient populations—again, both within and beyond the West. All political systems are struggling to respond. Protest is not directed uniquely at one particular type of regime. Nor is disaffection the preserve of one culture or one region. A creeping "privatization of politics" blights all regime types.

These trends have helped revive a classical idea: republicanism. Many democratic theorists advocate returning to republican liberty and moving away from liberal varieties of political organization. A common argument is that the "ancient republican liberty" of engaged and duty-bound citizens is needed to underpin the "modern liberty" of rights-claiming individuals.[12] Mark Mazower argues that liberal democracy has shown itself incapable of redressing the fundamental tensions and societal polarization that have arisen in recent years. This, he insists, points the way toward a necessary return to republican elitism to render decisionmaking manageable.[13]

Indeed, it is striking how many recent calls for democratic variation revolve around the republican ethos of classic democracy. Republicanism evokes the concept of civic virtue and of accountability to the collective as opposed to the liberal notion of the primacy of the individual. Both Athens and Rome expected public involvement of their citizens. Of course, Rome (and later, the Italian city states) did this in a more oligarchic, less democratic fashion than Greece; the republican spirit can have democratic and nondemocratic manifestations—the difference between Rousseau's and Machiavelli's republicanism. Yet, something of its potentially democratic spirit pervades current analysis of liberal democracy's apparent woes.

Finally, real-world developments have influenced political philosophers who increasingly talk in terms of "differentiated universalism" and "thinner" forms of cosmopolitanism.[14] Under these terms, they focus more on the political philosophy of flexibility and the tolerance of variation. John Rawls's theory of justice has been the cornerstone of the liberal case. But political philosophers increasingly take issue with some elements of this theory.

Communitarian philosophers have gained a higher profile by arguing that standards of justice must be based on a particular society's traditions and ways of thinking that vary from place to place. This contrasts with Rawls, whom communitarian philosophers berate for proceeding from an individualistic conception of the self and for neglecting that the individual is always defined by communal ties and identities. Thus, politics should be not only about autonomous choice and freedom but also about sustaining social attachments.[15] Communitarians would argue that when conflicts of interest arise, individual rights should not outweigh collective concerns. The question of toleration as a matter of rights is what today most sharply divides liberal and nonliberal beliefs.[16]

GLOBALISM, ECONOMIC CRISIS, AND DEMOCRATIC VARIATION

Globalization and ongoing economic crisis lie behind the need to rethink democracy. The increasingly evident tension between democratic vitality and economic globalism is perhaps the most notable factor that drives these debates. The assumption that international liberal economics represents an integral pillar of liberal democracy is more widely questioned today than it was ten years ago. Analysts argue that "market sovereignty" today undercuts democracy's core spirit. Social democrats are more insistent today than ever before that the economic and political spheres cannot be separated: economic injustices compromise the de facto quality of democratic rights and menace a more communitarian version of rights.[17]

Social democracy fits under a developmental—rather than liberal—variety of democracy. The developmental model is said to provide more and "thicker" democracy than does protective liberal democracy. This is because developmental democracy encourages more active participation among citizens and creates a state that is more active in defending democratic values.[18]

Prominent leftist intellectuals argue that the economic crisis, which began in 2008, has brought class back as the prime shaper of global politics. These thinkers insist that this change negates the notion of universal, cosmopolitan, and liberal norms. A legacy of the economic crisis is that analysts use it to validate fundamentally different political and economic models.[19] Radicals insist the crisis behooves us to look beyond liberal democracy: the financial debacle shows that neither capitalism nor individual rights-based liberal democracy is up to the job.[20] Some commentators insist that the global turmoil of 2014 strengthens the case for local models that are alternatives to a Western political-economic package of "predatory modernization," which is now more clearly questioned.[21]

Other experts insist that the West's ongoing economic crisis has pushed opinion back toward the not-so-liberal notion that democratic politics should be conceived as a means to particular, state-decreed ends.[22] A powerful and convincing interpretation comes from critical thinkers who argue that citizens in the West have been bought off by the easy provision of debt, which was used to mask the narrowness of their democratic political choices.[23] Influential leftist thinkers insist that the crisis obliges Europe to return to the Hegelian notion of a strong state and move away from support for liberal individual empowerment.[24] The crisis and the rise of populism reinforce the growing tension between liberalism and democracy—a tension that existed for most of history when liberalism and democracy were rival notions and not bedfellows. Curiously, many European populations today agitate to preserve the leftist vision of the welfare state even while they shift to the right on identity politics.

In parallel to globalism and the financial crisis, power balances are shifting within the international community. It is widely felt that the shift of global power has ensured a genuine opening for competition among fundamentally different ideas of how democracy and legitimacy are best secured.[25]

Internationalization alters the very core parameters of democratic accountability and representation. Jan Aart Scholte foresees a future of "postmodern global democracies" in which all levels of political action and identity have equal worth, from the local to the global; all varieties of values are taken equally seriously as non-Western actors gain power. This thinking is entirely different from current cosmopolitan projects to democratize the international order—projects that merely seek to scale up standard liberal democracy.[26]

Critical scholars maintain that Western power interests have always underlain the liberal order and that the demise of American hegemony opens the way to a benign rethink. This must involve reconsidering the assumption that particular rights-based concepts of politics necessarily form the core of a liberal order.[27] There are growing tensions between established and new democracies. Competition over various models of democracy is one element of this tension. An impending "clash of democratizations" can be expected. The extension of democracy, some analysts aver, brings with it not a more liberal world order but greater rivalry and zero-sum competition.[28]

Some feel that the global power shift has gone so far that Western democracies must look seriously at how legitimate forms of accountability and representation can be developed in systems that have traditionally been described as entirely nondemocratic. Here, China represents the main conceptual challenge. China's supporters say it has learned responsiveness and self-correction better than Western democracies. These supporters insist that China involves its citizens in consultative forums more than Western democracies do, is more meritocratic than the West, has succeeded in generating deeper wells of public legitimacy, and has widened private freedoms to the point that only those dedicated to overturning the system per se are meaningfully restricted. From the Chinese perspective, in historical terms, political parties are a very recent addition to the definition of democracy, making them a contingent—not an essential—aspect of the model. Chinese leaders laud rationalism as more democratic than liberalism. They argue that strong state action helps overcome the collective action problem of small groups and thus provides for a more democratic outcome than does a mere protection of individual rights.[29] Of course, such claims may not be entirely convincing, but they are perhaps not quite as disingenuous as they seemed even quite recently.

PARTICIPATIVE DEMOCRACY
AND NEW SOCIAL MOVEMENTS

A call of clearly global reach is for more participative forms of democracy that ensure effective accountability. Critiques from the Global South have for some time suggested that greater participatory democracy is particularly apposite outside the West. This is because in many developing countries the gap between political representatives and the public is so large that thicker participatory mechanisms are needed. As a result, a constrained, Madisonian liberal democracy is less likely to work well.[30] However, although non-Western democracy is often judged to require more bottom-up participative dynamics, recent tends within the West have revolved precisely around this same concern.

New social movements have erupted onto the scene in Western and non-Western countries. Donatella Della Porta suggests that these movements have fundamentally redrawn what citizens understand by democratic legitimization. Political identities are today constructed through more deliberative and participative processes than was previously the case.[31]

New social movements in Brazil, Egypt, Greece, Spain, Thailand, Turkey, Ukraine, and many other places work to develop forms of leaderless democracy in their own decisionmaking. These movements set themselves the challenge of resolving how to function without leaders, without formal voting, without programmatic policy platforms, and without group representatives.[32] New civic action is more fragmented, but it is also oriented toward local communitarian ideals rather than big, international causes and solidarity. It is more collectivist but not in the way of old-style, mass organized labor.[33]

The EU's economic crisis in particular has brought forth a raft of social movements across Europe motivated by concepts of nonhierarchical participation and "horizontality."[34] The economic crisis has left a legacy of extensive debate in Europe over the need for more participatory forms of democracy. In the United States, too, the Occupy movement and other groups were organized to instill consensual deliberation. Critical thinking on the notion of "liquid democracy" has provided a reference point for a wave of active, participative initiatives, such as the *Indignados* movement.[35]

These kinds of new movements and organizations are widely celebrated as having representational legitimacy. The recent trajectory of this civic activity has been about "guaranteeing heterogeneity" and a taming of formal institutional structures.[36] Many urge a return to what was the essential spirit of the "Greek ethos," namely the conviction that discord and contestation are integral to the good society—an open challenge to the notion of small cabals of elites handing down solutions to a passive citizenry. This echoes the very rage and wrath that drove the Iliad.

In recent years, global civil society activity has shifted from professional nongovernmental organizations to broader citizen activism. This activity has rebalanced from international-level social forums to more locally rooted concerns. And it has begun to question democratic effectiveness at a more fundamental level.[37] This has happened not only in the developing and emerging worlds but also in the West. The notion of civic watchdogs more effectively monitoring public policy resonates with many initiatives at the local level in Western states. What is specifically non-Western or illiberal about such a notion is unclear.

These shifts have been picked up and explored in many key scholarly works. Pierre Rosanvallon labels protest politics as a whole new "counter democracy."[38] Charles Tilly has argued that both within and beyond the West, democracy hinges upon the better "integration of interpersonal trust networks into public politics."[39] Pippa Norris has uncovered a new form of "critical citizenship."[40] David Held has used the concept of "autonomy," which entails democracy not only protecting individual rights but also according citizens the capacity and effective independence to exert influence and hold decisionmaking accountable.[41] There is a broad consensus among theorists that moves to relegitimize democracy must be built around loose forms of deliberation and localism, even cutting across the traditional container of the nation-state, around smaller units better able to defend against centralized institutionalization.[42]

These trends are closely related to the scholarly focus in recent years on the concept of deliberative democracy, which points to the importance of active debate among citizens as a means to mold preferences into common understandings. Deliberative democracy contrasts with the notion of citizens being merely egotistical voters with preconceived selfish interests, as assumed by many theorists of liberal democracy. Deliberative democracy insists that legitimacy and accountability must come from decisions being justified collectively. Democracy must be more than the aggregation of preexisting and self-regarding interests. This is often assumed to fit with non-Western societies' focus on mutuality over individualism. Many analysts see calls for more dynamic participative and deliberative dynamics as a fundamental challenge to liberal democracy's assumption that citizens are passive and that they simply cede policymaking autonomy to oligarchic elites between elections.[43]

Some writers are less upbeat. Skeptics worry that protests now occur in a form that cuts across democracy's representative institutions. Popularity is today garnered by individuals with followers on Twitter, Facebook, and in the blogosphere. This is instantaneous punditry and commentary, not political engagement. Single-issue social movements are not able to generate collective action.[44]

Skeptics say that protests around the world are now about atomized and disgruntled individuals; they reflect individual demands, not coherently thought-through group interests. Today's protesters oppose and seek to undermine governmental power; but they have no ideology and no comprehensive governing manifestos of their own. These individuals propose no solutions and oppose certain austerity policies but have no systemic alternative worked out. Indeed, various factions of protesters advocate a whole array of totally incompatible options, from more state to more market, from more internationalism to nationalist parochialism. Ivan Krastev defines them as hyperlibertarian rather than democratic. Disruption has become an end in itself. Participation in politics today stands at odds with political representation.

Critics charge new civic movements with being anti-institutional; they do not seek actively to strengthen the institutional checks and balances of liberal democracy but rather seek direct action as a means of circumventing the channels of representative democracy. They see elections as increasingly meaningless, because governments change time and again with no significant change in policies. The strength of new social movements—the critics say—is more of a threat to than a regeneration of liberal democracy. These organizations no longer provide a transmission belt between the individual citizen and the political sphere (parties and government), but reflect a spirit of pure "rejectionism."[45]

In short, new ideas on participation abound, but they remain contested and relatively undefined. The issue with deliberative democracy is not whether it is Western or non-Western but that it still struggles to define itself with sufficient precision, in terms of the exact form and site of deliberation. Most work on direct democracy now sees it as a complement to representative bodies, not a substitute. There has been extensive effort to measure the quality of deliberative discourse in recent years; some of the best known experts carrying out such exercises acknowledge that the advances of deliberative democracy have gone the furthest within standard Western representational institutions—further than alternative civic forums.[46]

In the future, debates about democratic variation may divide along generational lines rather than cultural ones. A younger generation of civic protesters appears less oriented toward culturally traditional forms than its elders. A debate in both Western and non-Western societies centers around a younger generation seeking more direct models of democracy using digital technology and crowdsourcing and what this approach means for existing concepts of both representational and direct democracy. Arguably, the most significant differences over democracy are among generations in all societies—Western and non-Western alike—rather than between Western and non-Western cultures. Similarly, the rural-urban divide within national polities is a more prominent cleavage in the democracy debate than the Western-versus-non-Western divide.

WHAT IS "LIBERAL"?

To the extent that many calls are for alternatives to *liberal* democracy, it is important to understand what liberalism is and is not. Some recent ideas on this topic are helpful to touch upon, as they provide some nuance that should be considered in the debates about democratic variation. This is also important because it lays the groundwork for an argument I make in chapters six and seven in favor of a "liberalism plus" concept.

Liberalism has had a rich history. Although developed in the West, liberalism has shown itself a capacious creed. At many points in its intellectual unfolding, liberalism has been acutely concerned with the very things it is ritually attacked for ignoring. Since originating in the eighteenth century, liberalism has frequently been declared "in crisis" and yet has adapted itself to changing contexts. Its roots were about tackling privilege and power, not only establishing formal rights. Liberalism's association with laissez-faire economics played a very small and relatively brief part in its historical journey.

In France, liberalism developed under the banner of "republicanism." There and elsewhere, the concept was centrally about civic engagement. Liberalism's early concerns were as much about creating a strong, modern state capable of impartial oversight of the economic realm as they were about gaining personal civil rights. For many liberal thinkers, the focus lay with justice and economic mutualism. The liberal concept of the general will prefigured notions of communitarianism. Liberal thought has long gone beyond Isaiah Berlin's "negative liberty," which was a very time-specific rebuttal of totalitarian ideology. At particular moments in history, liberalism has been concerned primarily with correcting intolerance and with preventing citizens' dissent from morphing into political disengagement. Many theorists from within the liberal tradition have also been concerned with liberalism's cohabitation with religion, custom, and community.[47]

The "liberal" component of liberal democracy is more nuanced than is often portrayed. A whole strand of liberal thinking rejects the supposed tension between liberalism and communitarianism, noting the branch of explicitly communitarian liberalism. From this perspective, liberalism is more than simply not interfering with others, but rather facilitating the strong community needed to protect individual rights: many liberals reject the supposed choice between the individual and the community as a false dichotomy. Analysts point out that Western societies often have strong communal, religious, and social bonds that exert pressure on the individual and induce conformity and, therefore, the dichotomy between individualistic and communitarian societies is routinely drawn too starkly.[48] Prominent political thinkers point out that the contemporary liberal notion of negative liberty has in practice still left of lot of room for state curtailment of individual freedoms—that is, within Western democracies themselves.[49]

Since the publication of John Rawls's *Theory of Justice*, liberalism has sought to work through a stress on social justice and community that is based on liberal principles. Rawls's argument is liberal because it supposes that it is individual choice that leads toward social justice: it is what individuals choose behind the "veil of ignorance," what they would prefer if they were unaware of their own social position. Social justice is not the utilitarian adding and subtracting of overall wealth levels that treats citizens as means, not ends in themselves; rather it is the product of a rational exercise of individual freedom.

Where classic liberalism seeks constricted and rules-constrained government, the competing notion of "welfare liberalism" foresees limited but active government. Mill's seminal *On Liberty* observed that social welfare was needed to give real meaning to the liberal celebration of individual choice. Modern liberals also insist they are not hostile to traditional forms of institutional organization; rather, they think informed individual choice should undergird these forms and not a repressive and ingrained hierarchy.

Liberalism is equally not inconsistent with new forms of association. Indeed, its very core is that of individual innovation and questioning. And as said, nor is liberalism so resolutely counter to religion: for Locke, individual rights were inviolable precisely because he understood man to be the work of God.[50] Many would question critics' charge that Western liberal democracy leaves no room for religion, considering the role played by the Catholic Church in promoting liberal democracy in the post-Soviet states of Central and Eastern Europe.

In original enlightenment thought, liberalism was about individuals' virtue residing in a concern for society's general welfare beyond base and selfish desires; its aim was to bring man center stage in creating a communal ethics. This was indeed the whole Nietzschean and postmodern critique of liberalism; namely, that it retained *too much* of an appeal to the kind of common ethical values inherited from religion. Nietzsche's will to power was about individuals breaking through this and discovering their own notions of right and wrong. Heidegger, in turn, charged globalized capitalism with undermining the original political sense of liberal ideals— liberalism not as indifferent amorality but as a sense of civic moral ethics driving engagement in politics.[51]

Robert Dahl's emblematically liberal works also gradually pushed toward a more active concept of citizenship. In fact, campaigns for more active citizenship have been at the heart of democratic struggles in the West for some time. Classical writers' "protective" view of democracy has been supplanted by more active notions of citizenship. Madison and Locke, with their limited, elitist, and republican notions of democracy, hardly stand today as uncontested reference points. Indeed, the protective, Lockean understanding of rights can be seen as one but only one necessary part of the liberal essence of democracy.

Debates in the West over the need for more participatory democracy go back to the 1960s and 1970s. In turn, these debates also draw on their own classical, Western reference points in Rousseau and Mill. Many citizens' monitoring bodies were introduced within state bodies and companies beginning in the 1970s, a reflection of this trend in thinking. Beginning in the 1980s in the West—as much as outside the West—there was abundant talk of postparliamentary democracy and much attention paid to alternative channels of representation. Associative democracy added a different focus in turn, seeing the role of localism to be key in bringing the management of services back closer to citizens and outside the central state. Many liberals today posit a kind of group-based pluralism as important to context-specific democratic and vital citizenship.

Many liberals have also shifted the focus onto the need for more consensus-building processes within Western liberal democracies. In fact, the consensus model of democracy was itself of Western origins and aimed at, among other things, resolving problems within some European states.[52] Many Western states have moved toward some form of coalition or consensus-based government in an effort to mitigate polarization. There is debate about how best to avoid division and about stricter checks on majority power and guarantees for minority groups. Western democracies strike various trade-offs between representation (proportional systems) and accountability (majoritarian systems). Lijphart was the vanguard advocate of consensus over majoritarian democracy, using Belgium and Switzerland as his emblematic cases. This notion was based on interest group corporatism, a system whereby civic groups are linked in a structured "insider" relationship to corresponding parts of the state to avoid colliding in a free-for-all civic marketplace of ideas and interests.

If liberal democracy is seen to be precisely what limits majoritarianism, then there is a huge variety *within* the West in terms of how constraining states choose to make their constitutionalized rules. Some states have strong and rigid formal rules to guarantee liberal rights, while others (such as the UK) see pluralist debate as the best guarantor of liberal rights.[53] Debates have intensified over which approaches should be prioritized now to strengthen consensus and inclusiveness.

There is also much deliberation within Western democracies over developing better "state guidance"; non-Western critics are wrong to argue that liberal democracy completely neglects this question. Tony Judt observed that welfare states were the culmination of "reformist liberalism" and not a challenge to liberalism.[54] Recent debates challenge the view that Western democracy is built on an untrammeled liberalism that lacks any concern for state-managed public policy. In the past decade, much concern within the West has focused on the weighing of individual freedoms and state-guided protection of national interests and the shift toward the latter.[55] Many continental European polities have drifted toward the model of Madisonian, constrained democracy, as a widening slew of policy areas have been placed beyond parliamentary interference.[56] A whole strand of democratic theory in the West argues in favor of an even more "depoliticized" form of democracy that overrides sectional interests by extracting a wider range of policy choices from the public realm.[57]

NEW WAYS TO MEASURE DEMOCRACY

New approaches to measuring democracy have taken shape—approaches that reflect these various debates. Much analytical work has concerned itself with classifying democracy on grounds other than liberal tenets. Debates over how best to measure democracy feed into wider uncertainties about the universal validity of the way in which Western indicators define democratic quality.

An influential Varieties of Democracy project captures this new spirit. It starts from the premise that the worldview of democracy is based on indices and measurements that are insensitive to democracy's various forms or components. Given that countries emphasize different varieties of democracy, comparisons must be disaggregated. The project sees existing rankings, specifically those of Freedom House, as instrumental to the United States' interest in spreading a particular, uniform template of democratic reform. It dismisses these rankings as too subjective, insofar as they rely on the judgments of a small number of local experts.

The project proceeds from the argument that current indices measure a very roughhewn impression of freedom along a singular axis. Therefore, these indices are simply not set up to compare the respective quality of various forms of democracy. Even where they are disaggregated into subcategory measurements, the subcategories are highly correlated with each other. The indices are, in effect, measuring the same kind of dynamics rather than qualitatively distinct axes of pluralism. Additionally, the numerous indices all have highly similar results at the extremes—the scores that reflect whether a government is a mature democracy or a closed autocracy. The indices exhibit discrepancies, and thus uncertainty, in the gray zone of hybrid regimes. This is precisely where the debates over alternative forms of democratic legitimation are most vibrant and pertinent and thus where more broadly cast means of assessment are most necessary.[58]

The Varieties of Democracy project proposes to measure governments in accordance with some established varieties of democracy: electoral, liberal (which is based on the rule of law and protection of minority rights), majoritarian (which gives extensive power to a democratically elected majority), consensual (which supports power-sharing among groups), participatory, deliberative (which moves toward positions defined in terms of the common good), and egalitarian (a form that sees the provision of basic needs as a precondition to the effective exercise of political rights). The logic is that states will score well on some of these and less well on others. So, the project's data have "the modular quality of a lego set."[59] Influential scores such as those from Freedom House and Polity IV elicit differing interpretations. When analysts delve into the scores' respective disaggregated data, they draw contrasting conclusions on several questions regarding middle-range scores: Must they simply fall on one side or the other of a democracy-autocracy dichotomy? Do they denote a direction of change backward or forward? Or do they indicate some kind of stable and distinctive hybrid model?

The essential point is that current conceptual lenses, as embodied in the scoring systems that are traditionally used, do not help resolve these questions.[60] Hence, there has been a call to move away from single, comparative measures of states' "democraticness" and a perceived need for varied definitions of what defines democracy.[61] Along similar lines, other initiatives have sought to rank democracies in accordance with their success in fostering a form of "human empowerment" that challenges existing measurements on the basis of passive, liberal rights.[62]

CONCLUSION

Many of the debates about non-Western democracy duplicate those that today are flourishing within Western societies about Western democracy. Many worries about the general state of democracy are global. Western liberalism is itself more varied and complex than its non-Western critics realize or acknowledge. This chapter has given a flavor of debates that show it is unduly simplistic to posit a rigid and narrow Western concept of democracy in contradistinction to a fluid and innovative non-Western debate. Advocacy of non-Western democracy is replete with confusion about which features are intrinsic to Western democracy and which are optional.

This certainly does not invalidate the exploration of democratic variety. But it does enjoin us to be more precise in what it does—and does not—rightly entail. Understanding how this more subtle approach to variation is now rooted in new conceptual thinking helps us move toward more policy-oriented ideas. It raises very practical questions for the future of global democracy. Should we seek democratic innovation within or beyond the liberal tradition? Does democracy really require divergent forms in non-Western societies or in fact similar types of improvement everywhere? Having laid some firmer conceptual foundations, I now proffer more action-oriented guidelines.

CHAPTER 6

A FRAMEWORK FOR DEMOCRATIC VARIATION

N ow that we understand better what is at stake in the debates over non-Western democracy, this chapter outlines a framework for determining the necessary elements of democratic variation. This framework not only takes into consideration the motives behind the calls for non-Western democracy but also the doubts that have been raised about such a concept. I believe that the appropriate metric is one of variation that is *bounded within the parameters of core liberal principles*. Such an approach can help ensure an energizing and legitimizing plurality in democracy, while also guarding against the malign features of illiberalism.

There can and should be much legitimate variation that is genuinely different from the general principles that have to date informed democracy in the West. Non-Western societies will make democratic choices that are different from those of Western countries. These different choices will not only be about institutional forms but will also be influenced by values. And the paths taken by non-Western states can play a valuable role in defining democracy's future. The space for non-Western deviations should not be foreclosed.

At the same time, it is important not to overstate the Western-versus-non-Western division. Many of the core concerns with how to find a more accountable and equitable politics are shared across all regions; these concerns are often described in terms of different models largely because they are framed in relation to different reference points and through different terminology.

The future requires more effective and flexible democracy, but not a blanket non-Western or nonliberal democracy. With an eye toward striking a balance, this chapter proposes five axes along which democratic variation might best be developed, whether in Western societies or non-Western ones. These axes relate to different notions of rights, the means of pursuing economic justice, communitarian provisions, the role of new civic actors, and legal pluralism. Exploring democratic variation on these issues helps us to better understand the prospects for selective political divergence in various regions and countries.

THE SPIRIT OF DEMOCRACIES

The search for variation in democracy is genuine, legitimate, and desirable. The fact that African, Asian, Latin American, and Slavic autocrats have disingenuously used the discourse of democratic variation as a cover for patently undemocratic behavior does not mean that such variation is undesirable. Today, the developing world is much more democratic than it was in earlier periods when the initial calls for non-Western democracy were made. There is much more knowledge of democratic norms and much more respect for them. There are many more genuine efforts to look for alternative political forms than there were before. And it is clearer that democracy's value is different for different people. Calls for non-Western democracy do not emanate only from disingenuous autocrats.

The search for democratic variation is also not confined to non-Western states. The West is less certain of itself today. It is more open to doubt about its own systems and asking itself about alternative paths for its own politics. Although fully mutual and reciprocal learning among Western and non-Western states does not exist, there is a much greater sharing of political ideas across borders than there has been previously. Much rethinking springs from the recent financial crisis and its associated uncertainty. Yet this rethinking contains positive potential. After all, pluralism is at the core of democracy's appeal and legitimacy. Hegel's classic concept of "concrete universality" remains useful: the search should be for aspirations that are shared and expressed in concretely distinctive varieties. The world should be stirred not only by the "spirit of democracy"[1] but also by "the spirit of democracies."

Although the search for variation and plurality is a legitimate endeavor, it is a quest driven by contrasting motives. Different proponents have different agendas, and these agendas need unpacking. In contrast to those who claim that Western liberal democracy is fundamentally flawed as a concept, it is most constructive to consider how the principles can be better implemented—in particular, so that the rich and powerful do not influence decisions quite so overwhelmingly. And although many claim that there are distinctive non-Western formats, it is most appropriate to think of healthy democratic innovation leading to any number of institutional permutations that cut across regional divisions.

There is a distinction to be made between variation that posits a less liberal type of democracy and variation that involves fundamentally different forms of representation. The former seems to imply mainly a reduction in protection of Western-style individual liberal rights. The latter promises a potentially more far-reaching addition to established mechanisms of representation and legitimation and, therefore, seems most welcome.

These kinds of nuanced positions are how best to conceive the need for democratic variety. They help direct our analytical gaze toward legitimate areas of difference. There are no wholly non-Western models, but there is scope for legitimate innovation.[2]

Western liberal democracy is today beset by a malaise of sufficient proportions to merit ambitious rethinking on political accountability and representation. In turn, global challenges are too far-reaching simply to require more effort to extend the "Western political package" to other societies, as some are still willing to argue. Of course, to hold the core essence of Western liberalism culpable for today's problems would be unduly simplistic. The overdue pursuit of social equality and economic justice would not necessarily be served by a uniform non-Western political system. And respect for cultural tradition and conservative social mores doesn't require a wholesale non-Western politics. Yet states and societies around the world are certainly set to create their own democratic combinations, adopting some parts of Western systems and taking other parts from what appears to have worked in non-Western contexts. Variation beyond Western practices is possible and necessary—for developing states and rising powers.

Of course, the variety among societies outside the West is vast and widening. If there ever was a neat dichotomy between "traditional" and "Westernizing" societies, it surely does not stand today. As we saw in the previous chapter, a variety of paths toward modernity—combining economic development, traditional social values, and political demands in various permutations—is evident across the world.

Critics of "the Western order" have added to international relations debates in enormously valuable ways. But these voices have a problematic tendency to extend their arguments into a defense of a non-Western template of political order that is rather unsubstantiated. Recourse to "customary" forms of dialogue and communal decisionmaking can be controversial in non-Western societies that are rapidly modernizing. It is entirely legitimate to consider how states' paths to modernity may express themselves in areas of institutional innovation and novelty. But this variety must be carefully thought through in the context of each country and matched to the requirements of its particular circumstances. Simply dismissing the relevance of Western democracy for other societies is not helpful to identifying such nuances.

Liberal democracy's varieties can be understood as particular forms of institutionalized self-rule. In the West, these forms were socially constructed and historically specific. Although liberal democracy has become widely seen as part of the West's hegemony, this does not invalidate the model's core ethos of self-rule. Modern democracy's mainly Western development reflects much that was historically contingent. This reminds us that the way the concept develops today will be shaped by new patterns of power, interaction, and shared learning among Western and non-Western states. Democracy never was an entirely fixed entity.

In some regards, recent trends *within* Western politics, societies, and economies challenge the liberal components of democracy more than these are menaced or questioned *outside* the West. Looking at the current rise in chauvinistic populism, institutional gridlock, and rights infringements within many parts of the West, it is not inconceivable that future debates will flip or invert in a confusing fashion: parts of the non-Western world may have the confidence and optimism to take on the liberal mantle of tolerance and nondiscriminatory freedom, while parts of an anxious and defensive West may become associated with illiberalism. How will we then frame or understand the debate between Western and non-Western democracy?

In an era of shifting global balances, there is likely to be a multidirectional mix of influences among states. A smorgasbord of institutional options is available today for reformers both within and outside the West. And the scope for difference extends well beyond familiar reform options—such as the choice between parliamentary and presidential systems—that have normally been raised when various models are debated. This will challenge the supposed distinction between Western and non-Western models and demands even further. As today's international influences flow in all directions, overlap, and loop back on each other, it will become more difficult to say with certainty what is properly Western and what is non-Western.

LIBERALISM PLUS

So what are the crucial vectors of variation? Democratic variation can and should be pursued in a way that builds upon liberal democracy, rather than subtracts from it. I propose an umbrella principle of "liberalism plus" that covers more specific tenets of legitimate variety.

This notion redresses the confusions the previous chapters identified in calls for non-Western democracy. Many criticisms of the performance of Western democracy are sound. But that must not give legitimacy to attempted cures that turn out to be worse than the illness. Non-Western governments and societies may well seek outcomes that many Western countries have neglected. And these non-Westerners may well be entirely justified in arguing that different political arrangements can help achieve those aims. Yet it should not be assumed that these arrangements entail less liberal forms of democracy and should not justify direct antagonism toward the core tenets of democracy in the West. The most desirable democratic variation is liberalism plus, not "liberalism minus."

Liberalism plus categorically does *not* mean simply more of what is Western. Rather, this principle calls for variation and experimentation to find local ways to give greater vitality to the core ideas of tolerance, participation, and holding the powerful to account. It does *not* mean simply more Western liberalism, without compromise to others' values. Rather, it calls for others' ideas to be taken seriously on how the core spirit of political liberalism can be better respected.

Variety is better posited in terms of additions to existing democratic templates than in terms of non-Western or less liberal democracy. Some aspects of the calls for non-Western democracy resemble more of a dilution of liberalism. This kind of option is more pernicious than the current shortcomings of existing democracies. It would be most promising to tease out how "alternative models" can complement, "re-radicalize," and deepen liberal democracy rather than supersede it.[3] The notion of a "floating but anchored" democracy is useful in this regard.[4]

As outlined in the previous chapter, liberalism is an elastic concept: it can mean absolute individual rights and limited state functions, or (as in Mill) tolerance and respect for a broader set of rights for all. My contention is that it is the latter ethos that needs to be rediscovered. Marshall's classic concept of "social citizenship" can be reinvigorated as a useful guide to revitalizing democratic quality.[5] Improvements do not require a less liberal spirit. More effective participation in decisions about rights or stronger accountability for finances are not a matter of constricting political liberalism—yet they are among the most pressing of today's problems.

In this sense, critical accounts contain much that is perceptive, but they also have misleading implications: they often advocate for social democracy hand in hand with deliberative and global democracy as a direct challenge to liberal democracy. But such reform options are best formulated as being "within and beyond"—not "against"—liberalism's basic core, if we understand liberalism properly as tolerance, effective participation, and protection against injustice and repression.

Limits on core freedoms should not be justified as a "locally credible" model for achieving economic growth and social justice. Experts are right to caution against stretching definitions too far and passing any illiberal practice off as a locally legitimate form of non-Western democracy. It is important to avoid "definitional gerrymandering"—introducing a new definition every time a case doesn't quite fit the common model.[6] Hybrid regimes may legitimately claim some divergence from liberal democracy that Western political science has tended to simply damn as shortfalls from full democratic quality. But the malign aspects of hybrid models should also be more firmly spelled out.

The protection of basic individual rights and the guarantee of free elections are the core pillars of liberal democracy that can and should be defended as universal principles that underpin a multiplicity of democratic models. For all the validity in calls for democratic variety, it is not convincing to argue that various models need to be built on a denial of rights protection or free electoral choice. Kate Nash argues that the classically liberal human-rights architecture has already developed in a relatively expansive fashion, beyond its presumed minimalist dimensions: "If human rights are liberal, they are a version of liberalism that is more collectivist than individualist . . . more 'New Liberal' than classical liberalism or neo-liberalism."[7] The idea of reversing this advancement within the liberal framework should not be advocated as progressively non-Western.

This discussion should not be taken as a defense of those aspects of market capitalism that have clearly undermined individual potential and negated citizens' practical capabilities to exercise their rights. The liberalism-plus notion categorically does *not* entail an automatic assumption that market reforms and economic deregulation should be unconditionally extended. It does *not* denote a conviction that extending market freedoms necessarily strengthens the foundations upon which political freedom stands. Various models of economic change may well be justified. Indeed, they may be necessary as a means of freeing the full potential of the empowered and "self-responsible" individual envisioned by the early liberal political theorists. As detailed later, democratic variation should include active participation in decisions about economic and social rights.

But this need for economic variation does not mean that political illiberalism is a means of resolving the social injustices brought about by market capitalism. This is an important point to clarify, because some critics think advocating an extension of political liberalism is almost the same thing as tolerating the injustices of economic liberalism. This association should be broken; developing a nuanced but genuine agenda of democratic variation can help do this.

Left-wing populist regimes have established themselves in many parts of the world. Although many democrats viscerally oppose these regimes, their complex root causes must be appreciated and their social achievements not entirely dismissed. But it must be doubted that such regimes constitute the basis for a coherent and sustainable political model for democracy—and this is because they are rarely fully consistent on their own terms. Illiberal populism is condescending to the poor: it paternalistically offers them social benefits instead of real ownership or empowerment over political decisions.

The relationship between political and economic freedom is nuanced. Critical theorists are right to point out that liberal perspectives too often hold the political and economic spheres to be entirely separate. And these critics are right to stress that social injustice is a blight on democracy's very essence and not a mere unrelated detail. These points are an important contribution to the debates over democratic quality. But critical theorists tend to go too far the other way and minimize the intrinsic value of political freedom to social development.

Although there is overlap between the political and economic spheres, they should not be conflated: if free market liberalism is not working, this does not necessarily invalidate political liberalism. A deeper social democracy must broaden the role of the state in facilitating necessary social and economic change—it cannot be delivered simply by providing "compensatory alleviation" that militates against modernization and reform.[8] The trend in many parts of the world is now toward unfettered capitalist accumulation that is married to carefully managed political control. To some extent, this equation needs to be inverted.

Marc Plattner reminds us that democracy needs a degree of liberalism to the extent that free elections require individuals' freedom of speech, association, and assembly to be protected.[9] The key should be to build outward from a base of pluralist institutions. More conservative social mores are not a threat or alternative to liberal politics.

In sum, although framing democratic variation in such experimental terms may not fit a non-Western agenda, this approach does move the debate toward areas where non-Western states can have more input into reflections about democracy's future than has so far been the case. It fact, this method opens a more fruitful path for non-Western variation to be taken seriously and for its proponents to be part of a global conversation about improving the performance of democracy.

The debate need not be couched solely or primarily in terms of non-Western democracies rejecting what is supposedly the "full menu of democracy" on offer in the West. Indeed, framing the challenge in terms of mutually beneficial learning stresses the potential for Western democracies themselves to learn and adopt ideas from other parts of the world—and to

MEASURING DIFFERENT MODELS OF DEMOCRACY

The Varieties of Democracy initiative sheds light on how various "types" of democracy relate to each other—which are alternatives and which can comfortably go hand in hand with each other. Some measurements of democracy can be strengthened together; the indicators of liberal democracy, for example, can be deepened in parallel with indicators of other strands of democracy. Only some collide with each other—for example, majoritarian and consensual measurements—and thus stand rather as mutually exclusive alternatives. These may seem like relatively unimportant design details for different democratic systems, but they are crucial to this book's argument.

In categorizing democracy, often analysts are referring to various weightings rather than to mutually exclusive variants of democracy. The project's March 2014 code book that guides detailed surveying of institutional variation around the world contains a subtle but important innovation that could help move debates in the direction suggested in this book: it distinguishes measures of liberal, egalitarian, participative, and deliberative components, on the one hand, from measures of liberal, egalitarian, participative, and deliberative *democracy*, on the other hand—the latter being measured by indices that take into account a country's degree of electoral democracy as well.[10] These may seem like rather arcane methodological nuances, but it is at this level that positive, non-Western variations are likely to be identified. That is, these nuances help direct our gaze toward variations that are not a cloak for authoritarianism or illiberalism, and which are not framed in terms of different regional models standing in wholesale antagonism to each other.

Indeed, the Varieties of Democracy project does not point us toward distinctive non-Western forms. It distinguishes the components of democracy that are already well established conceptually: liberal, egalitarian, participative, deliberative, and electoral. Variety is then seen to result from various combinations of these components. The approach does not specify particular permutations of combining the components—the various forms of rights to protect from the majority, the various understandings of achieving equality, the various forms of participation or deliberation, and the various forms of electing representatives. The project finds a close correlation in practice among the components, with the partial exception of the egalitarian element, which is also found generally to have increased in recent decades.[11]

do so without necessarily becoming less liberal or less pluralistic.

Such a framing clarifies that variation can be pursued without turning the core tenets of liberal democracy upside down. Western democracies currently grapple with many of the same dilemmas as other societies—in some senses their political and economic crises appear to be deeper today than those that beset developing states. However, the point is that if non-Western countries make choices that are "within and beyond liberalism," these nations should be supported—even if Western states do not opt for such choices. Whether this is labeled as an increment or alternative to liberal democracy is secondary.

FIVE AXES FOR DEVELOPING VARIATION

On the basis of this broad principle of liberalism plus, there are five areas where more variation in democratic forms merits encouragement:

FLEXIBLE AND EMPOWERING RIGHTS

Liberal rights must be recast to include elements that speak to the empowerment of community ideals and not only the protection of individuals. Although it remains unclear how or to what extent this can be done, it is undoubtedly one of the most pressing challenges facing democracy today.

A commonly made argument is that core human rights have universal appeal but that there are regional differences over political institutional models. In some places, this situation seems to have been inverted. Many emerging democracies have been happy to accept the same kind of institutional configurations that established democracies have, and do so without a great deal of controversial debate; but fierce and polarizing debate takes place over personal rights.

Non-Western societies are more likely to think that rights are about individuals' ability to assist communal goals than about individuals being protected from the state.[12] The so-called New Confucian understanding of democracy largely accepts liberal institutions and processes, but the notion rejects the idea that government should remain neutral among conflicting conceptions of what is a good life. Instead, the state should ensure a certain minimal morality.

Rights are not only protection from interference but also about empowerment.[13] In many developing regions, belief systems did not play the role
that Christianity played in the West in embedding the concept of inalien-
able individual rights. The notion that individual rights were secondary or
derived from communal rights thus persisted in non-Western societies—
and was not challenged as forcefully as it was within Western processes of
political development.

The challenge is to take seriously and advance the concept of "rights
as empowerment" without trampling on the liberal concept of "rights as
protection." There is strong demand for community-based deliberation
around this notion of empowerment. Such initiatives can help rebut criticisms that liberal democracy is based on atomized citizens merely claiming
individualistic rights from the state. Doubts about unfettered individual
rights may often derive from genuine and noble concerns about social cohesion and morality. The West should not condemn them a priori as being
driven by undemocratic intent.

This should not be taken as a green light for illiberal democracy, however. The need is not for illiberalism on rights questions but for liberalism
to be recast. The prioritization of individual rights has become seen in many
parts of the world as synonymous with amorality, excessive individualism,
and intolerance for religion. Liberalism has become code for an attack on
conservative tradition, restraint, and the community. It needs to dissociate
itself from this particular agenda and defend a notion of liberal procedure—
that is, fair and open political processes. The substantive agenda with which
it has become confused is not what the origins of political liberalism were
about. Liberalism was properly envisaged as a philosophy of toleration.

Political developments make the question of rights one of the thorniest of today's debates over global democracy. Many states now combine
competitive democratic politics with highly bounded individual rights.
Governments and some opposition movements in many countries espouse
the virtues of free elections, multiparty politics, and institutional checks
and balances, while seeking an often far-reaching curtailment of individual
rights. These politicians and activists routinely make the claim that this
constitutes a context-legitimate democracy.

This contrast is a difficult equation for Western governments to accept. They are more willing to tolerate greater flexibility in the institutional

forms of democracy than in core rights believed to be universal; indeed, this has become the standard, almost politically correct Western line. But many citizens outside the West seem to see the situation in precisely the opposite way: they apparently have different concepts of constitutionalized liberal rights even where there is little evidence that they want some major deviation from the basic institutions of Western democracy. This returns us to one of the core threads that runs through the book: the complexity of the norms-versus-values distinction.

Specifically in Muslim-majority countries, a battle is taking place between two types of ascendant illiberalism over rights. On one side of this battle stand Islamist parties that seek to impose religiously sanctioned restrictions on the scope of individual rights. On the other side of the battle are secular-autocratic forces that use the discourse of liberalism to constrain such religious concepts, but then restrict rights in the name of defending democracy against religion-based politics. Curiously, in today's visceral, existential conflicts between secularists and Islamists, both sides pursue a form of non-Western democracy rooted in restrictions on liberal, individual rights—and both sides insist that such restrictions will make democracy more likely to prosper in the Middle East.

So, what is the solution? Are there circumstances where limits to individual rights are justified and indeed necessary to safeguard other aspects of liberal democracy? Variation is justified in non-Western countries through definitions of rights that are about empowerment and community goals; these definitions are not focused on the primacy of individual entitlements. The search for more collective identity rights reflects deep social adjustment. Analysts relate declining levels of religious freedom in the past decade to globalism. This induces fears about the loss of identity and the sense of a disintegrating community and "leads to a retreat into the religious or cultural group of origin, accompanied by a tendency to become more protective of the group's values."[14] The contingent roots of preferences over liberal rights have to be understood.

The challenge is to help further such concepts and, at the same time, avoid serious infringements on individual freedoms. Templates for liberal rights need to strike a balance between the freedom from and freedom for religion. Proper liberalism requires both sides of the equation to demonstrate more respect for the other.[15] Religious rights have to be protected as part of a broader protection of all human rights, not through provisions that enable the latter, broader rights to be infringed.

The imbalance in some Islamist concepts of rights is this: they frame a democracy where society as a whole follows Islamist tenets and precepts. Liberals would say that liberal democracy defends Islamists' freedom to adhere to their beliefs and simply obliges them to accept that others may have a different point of view and a different set of moral values. In the Middle East and North Africa, many Islamists don't seem to accept this. They argue that laws that protect liberal rights would effectively impose a non-Islamist agenda on individual Muslims. This divergence of understanding is why pessimists feel there is no middle ground for compromise between Islamists and liberals. But there must be grounds to challenge this: the notion of liberal rights promoted and framed not as a threat to religious belief but a means to defend and enhance it, for those that desire such an identity.

There are incipient efforts to strike these kinds of balances. In Egypt, the large number of parties across Islamist, nationalist, and secular-leftist currents all talk of the country's religious identity and, at the same time, of the principles of democratic citizenship, equality before the law, and basic freedoms—reflecting a broad concern with trying to fashion a kind of synthesis.[16] Tunisia may be the most promising model: its 2014 democratic constitution gives the state competence in both protecting individual freedoms and in ensuring guidance for communal norms. This is an incredibly difficult balance to strike. Some will say it is a circle that is impossible to square. But democratic constitutions can at least try to define rights in a way that takes into account a community's broad moral compass and the fact that the state must often be mobilized to make formal rights a reality. If constitutions do so, the defense of individual rights will not so easily be held as synonymous with "Western individualism."

Such an approach may not provide complete solutions or entirely remove the tensions that beset many countries—not only in the Middle East and North Africa but also in a Europe—hit by violent attacks, intolerance, and tensions over free speech. But efforts in the direction suggested here would at least frame the balance between societal and individual levels in a way more conducive to tempering current levels of polarization. Some in Europe have begun to take this on board. After the killings of *Charlie*

Hebdo journalists in Paris in January 2015, some prominent progressive-liberal thinkers, such as Jürgen Habermas, shifted ground: they acknowledged that European liberal democracy needed to rebalance and offset the secular-rights narrative with the better integration of spiritual ideas on community solidarity.[17]

In sum, variety is merited not in the form of illiberal concepts of rights, but in liberalism being seen to allow for different normative orientations. Individual rights should not be diluted. But democratic variation could involve rules and procedural means aimed at moral agendas different from those that are most widely supported in the West. It might be said that we should be comfortable with the existence of *varieties of liberalism*, not only varieties of democracy.

LIBERALISM AS ECONOMIC JUSTICE

Greater variation is clearly legitimate and indeed positively needed in the types of economic models that are paired with democracy. As this book has made clear, many calls for non-Western democracy emerge from the conviction, in all regions of the world, that Western, liberal democracy has become too closely associated with neoliberal economic policies and obscene levels of wealth disparity.

In the eyes of many governments, officials, and citizens around the world, the idealism of liberal democracy stands discredited primarily because Western countries have in the past two decades suffered such a patent deepening of economic inequality. The principle of equality in political rights coexists today with an ever-more undeniable inequality in the exercise of economic and social rights.

Potential varieties of democracy that aim at fairer socioeconomic outcomes should be embraced, explored, and nurtured. Democracy of any form will suffer a rough ride in future years if it is judged to be the inseparable handmaiden of increasingly cruel economic injustice. Liberal democracy's failure to temper the de facto power of economic elites is one of the most powerful reasons for rethinking what effective accountability and representation today require.

The gravity of the situation is reflected in the impact of Thomas Piketty's book arguing that the West has returned to a model that existed for long periods during its history of growth strategies being predicated on widening inequality.[18] The quest for democratic variation can gain much from examining how best to break the association between political pluralism and neoliberal economics. This conflation emerged from an unfortunate temporal coincidence. The promotion of Western democracy gathered steam in the late 1990s, just as the free market economic doctrine of the Washington Consensus reached its peak of influence. The twin reform agendas of political liberalization and structural market reform were thrown together as part of a single package. Today, it is widely recognized that the (at least partial) failure of liberal market reforms has tainted the appeal of liberal democracy by association.

Emerging and industrializing countries generally suffer worse inequality than do advanced, Western economies; the governments of these developing nations habitually say that redressing such disparities has to be the absolute priority. Their doubts about liberal democracy are understandable, given that in their eyes, Western governments have not only failed to reduce inequalities but allowed them to deepen. In many developing countries, there is so much inequality that progressive liberalism is equated with the need for a more effective mobilization of the state to reduce inequities. In such circumstances, it is difficult to argue that democratic rules should be neutral about economic outcomes—that democracy should be one thing and economic policy should be another entirely.

The desire for more just socioeconomic outcomes is well established. The point of this book is not simply to echo the opprobrium directed at free market capitalism; such criticism is made in an endless number of books, articles, and opinion pieces. Rather, the issue for discussion here is whether such concerns over economic policy require a *different type of democracy* in order for them to be effectively addressed.

This is a more complicated and nuanced question, and it warrants a balanced line. The depth of economic challenges is serious enough that institutional variety and change should be explored. The need is not only for certain modifications to economic decisions but also for changes to the political process that arbitrates economic interests.

At the same time, this socioeconomic perspective must not be overstated. Many critics are overzealous in criticizing liberal-democratic institutional structures as a corollary of their plea for different types of economic policy. The entirely justified and indeed overdue call for "economic democracy" is increasingly used as an argument for diminished "political democracy."

The socioeconomic argument is now so strong that many analysts are tempted to embrace the opposite extreme that was prevalent in the 1990s and the early part of this century. They argue that any pressure for economic reform or freer trade is inimical to democracy. This is because the majority of the voters is likely to oppose more open markets and trade. Critics accuse Western states of simply using the mantra of liberalism to pursue their own economic interests around the world when the economic strand of liberalism stands fundamentally and by definition at odds with its political strand.[19]

This critique risks being as equally one-sided as the economic neoliberalism it excoriates. The concern with economic injustice should not morph into a blind antipathy to markets. In the right conditions, political liberty can still be assisted by an extension in economic liberty. It has often been simplistically presumed that neoliberal economics is the other side of the coin to democratic politics; it would be equally simplistic to replace this with an argument that deepening democracy axiomatically requires a restriction of free markets.

A line must be drawn between a legitimate effort to democratize economic policies and a more dubious restriction of political space in the name of "economic democracy." One of democracy's keystones is objective rules-based decisionmaking. Nonliberals say this is a convenient and false fetish that merely loads the dice in favor of powerful interests. But if a state lacks such basic equality of status in democracy's ground rules, then it's not possible to talk about democracy in any meaningful sense. As one writer avers, "A certain degree of neutrality between participants in a democracy is a fundamental prerequisite, not a cultural bias."[20] Economic justice is desperately needed to restore democracy's legitimacy, and democracy cannot be completely neutral or indifferent about substantive outcomes. But it also cannot sanction neglect of this core principle of institutional impartiality.

In short, a sense of balance should be sought. Variety in democracy is surely legitimate when countries seek to temper the disproportionate influence of economically powerful groups. Governments may legitimately wish to limit the extent of the free market. If they do so, this should not in itself lead to their being defined as less democratic. (Some indices confusingly still include a measure of market freedoms in their democracy scores.) Conversely, though, governments limiting free markets in the name of egalitarianism cannot claim that this agenda requires the limiting of political liberties.

Economic justice and political freedom must be understood as more interrelated than in the past, but the control of free markets must not pass as justification for the control of free politics. Indeed, liberal economics and liberal politics must be seen as more linked *and* more separate than hitherto. They should be seen as linked in the sense of economic justice being recognized as necessary for the effective exercise of liberal rights. They should be conceived as separate in the sense of liberal democracy's not being so integrally tied to neoliberal economics.

Two goals are then desirable. The first is to view good quality democracy as compatible with a wider variety of economic policies. The second is to adopt decisionmaking processes that widen participative input into decisions on economic reforms.

The question then is what kinds of institutional forums and variations can help meet the latter goal. Social forums capable of offsetting the more elitist pathologies of liberal democracy merit support. The challenge is to give a wider range of social actors access to decisionmaking processes without replaying the more problematic, hierarchical rigidities of corporatist forms of democracy. Broad social movements may have a role in non-Western societies, where they have gained representative legitimacy through their social functions within local communities. Crowdsourcing input into economic policies may have a greater role in future. The key principle in assessing such possibilities is that the state and civil society must be seen as mutually constitutive rather than zero-sum rivals.

Debates will continue to rage over the right mix of state and markets in the creation and distribution of wealth. Opinions will continue to differ on this question, and evidence will doubtless provide ammunition for both sides of the debate. The point here is not to argue that an optimal form of democracy requires a particular type of economic policy. Rather, it is to suggest that a more generally open and participative spirit is warranted: one where economic choices are subject to full democratic debate, ownership, and legitimation.

In the past two decades, in many countries around the world, economic institutions have been taken out of the realm of political debate, precisely to depoliticize the structural adjustment of free market policies. This trend must now be reexamined. Policies to develop markets and control government expenditure might often be a practical necessity. But these policies should be formed from a domestic political debate on various alternatives, rather than embedded in the political system as an unavoidable imposition.

The most important factor is not to stipulate that a certain level or degree of market reforms is most conducive to effective democracy. Rather, it is to reassess the *processes* through which economic choices are adopted. Although voters may be willing to bear tough market reforms if a convincing case is made for them, they recoil where privatization processes simply distribute new market benefits to members of a corrupt and nepotistic elite—which has been the norm in developing states in recent years.

Of course, there is a long history of debates over social democracy within the West, and there have been many years of experimentation with more or less corporatist institutional arrangements. Many Western governments reject the charge that they are blind to the potential tension between structural economic reform and democracy. After such deep crisis within the West, they may indeed be ready to look favorably at new ways to understand the complex relationship between economic and political democracy—and acknowledge that non-Western states might be innovating in helpful ways. The point here is not to suggest that there is a single replacement model that has the ready-made answer to socioeconomic imperatives. Rather, it is to argue that more participative processes are necessary to getting this economic-political rebalancing right.

POWER QUOTAS AS COMMUNITARIANISM

Power quotas—shares of political representation allotted to ethnic, religious, or regional groups—may play a positive role in many societies. In the right form, these quotas represent a healthy form of democratic variation. For this to be so, they should be accompanied by efforts to galvanize those aspects of identity that might be shared in common among groups. Quota systems can be seen as a concrete manifestation of communitarianism and inclusivity. Analysts have long pointed to the problem of majoritarianism being insensitive to minority interests. In some societies, such a drawback justifies some representation stipulated on ethnic grounds, rather than territorial divisions of power as are common in the West.

Liberal and communitarian identities do not have to contradict each other. Individual rights and political participation can sit alongside the values of consensus and social harmony. Daniel Bell argues that communitarian and liberal views of the self are not necessarily at odds: individuals have a strong interest in leading communal lives and having these sustained by political arrangements as well as in having the state protect their right to pursue individual ambitions.

The appropriate forms of community vary across societies. Cultural references affect how rights are legitimized. This does not imply a wholesale rejection of the liberal model; it does mean that political rules and practices should be based on what fits a given society, rather than on abstract and unhistorical concepts.[21] Confucianism, for example, is not antithetical to democracy, but the precepts point in the direction of more consensual forms of democracy. This variation is not entirely alien to the West, where many countries have favored consensual over majoritarian democratic procedures. But in many non-Western contexts, formalized inclusion may legitimately warrant a much greater priority.

At the same time, the downsides of power quotas must be tackled. Quotas can give a helping hand to the search for consensus and ensure that a broader range of groups is consulted. But quotas should not extend so far that they menace core liberal principles of rights and equality. The less benign face of quotas is a tendency to calcify politics into sectarian or factional ghettoization and commonly empower local oligarchies.

Often, the benefits of quotas flow to elites from each communitarian bloc. These elites preserve their own power interests when conducting well-practiced negotiations and when making trade-offs with each other. Much less advantage falls to the citizens that make up these blocs. Many such arrangements have clearly constricted citizens' ability to influence communal identities or to express changing sets of local demands and grievances. There is a thin line between the benign quest for intergroup consensus and elitist manipulation.

Quotas designed to ensure political voice for besieged minorities go with the grain of democracy's liberal ethos—when the aim is to safeguard basic rights against onslaught from the majority. Quotas are more subversive of liberalism's spirit where they ossify chauvinistic hierarchies. Many groups exhibit little democratic accountability internally. Each religious, ethnic, or linguistic "community" might be apportioned a guaranteed slice of power, but its own procedures can remain strikingly undemocratic. Democracy is then reduced to a predetermined balance among various power blocs, each somewhat authoritarian in its own internal decision-making processes. This is democracy as façade stability, not as protector of individuals' ability to express minority, communitarian identities. It is communitarianism sold disingenuously as the only recipe for maintaining stability—a stability that, in practice, it rarely guarantees.

Recent trends in institutionalized communitarianism have varied. Ukraine's conflict is related to debates over the protection of minority (Russian) linguistic and ethnic rights. The Kiev-based elite insists these rights are now fully respected in the country's putative democratic transition. Yet, the degree of tension and concern in many southern and eastern parts of Ukraine would seem to require more formal kinds of representation for these groups. Russia's plea for federal structures may be a disingenuous ploy for increasing Moscow's influence. Notwithstanding this, a more far-reaching degree of devolution and ways of combining the country's very different sets of identities would seem appropriate. The template agreed upon in the Minsk peace accord fleshed out in February 2015 moves in the direction of communitarian democratization—albeit with many details still to be agreed upon between the government in Kiev and Russian-backed separatists.

In Iraq and Lebanon, denominational power sharing has had a questionable benefit for democratic quality. Such arrangements increasingly feed into regional conflict and instability across the Middle East and breed frustration among disempowered citizens from all groups. In such cases, communitarian logics go hand in hand with politics that are increasingly undemocratic. Power sharing has not facilitated a benign and healthy local form of democracy that is finely tuned to local circumstances and welcomed by all citizens.

In Iraq, the fiercely sectarian Shia Prime Minister Nouri al-Maliki used an internationally sponsored power-sharing democracy as a platform for tightening his own authoritarian power. Communitarian harmony was shattered not only among the country's Sunnis, Shia, and Kurds but also within each community bloc. Maliki allowed little room for Shia organizations other than his own, provoking bitter intra-Shia rivalry and tension. The actions of the Sunni jihadist Islamic State alienated Sunni tribes and community leaders as it took control of large swatches of the country in 2014. By mid-2014, a badly fractured and poorly governed Iraq enjoyed little communitarian legitimacy at any level, local or national. A new government took power in September 2014 and agreed to a new power-sharing arrangement. This has produced a more balanced spirit of inclusion, even if the government still contains many familiar faces from the country's discredited elite.

In short, certain forms of communitarianism can add productively to democratic variation. Bottom-up rather than top-down forms offer more potential to add genuine democratic quality and vitality. The right debate is not simply more or less communitarianism. Rather, it is what *type* of communitarianism best chimes with citizens' democratic aspirations. Tolerance among community blocs is needed. But this should not merely be a negative, minimal tolerance—one that allows space for minorities as long as they acquiesce to institutional structures that almost predetermine their identities.

Quotas might be most appropriate within local governance arrangements. At this level, power-sharing can encourage various groups to work together on practical, local issues. These are the kinds of issues on which bridges can be built between factions. Such bridges can be harder to build when rigid shares of ethnicity or religion become the main structuring feature of high-level national politics—because this pushes debates toward the most sensitive and divisive issues of identity.

Trends point toward communitarian dynamics becoming stronger. The uncertainties of globalization push people to cling to communities that give them a sense of belonging. Deeper communitarianism is the flipside of deeper globalization. Communitarian identities must be given room for greater expression through varied forms of democratic institutional setups. Western democracies often form governing coalitions to widen inclusion; in non-Western countries, inclusion and consensus will often need to extend much further than this, as they are imperatives that are more socially rooted. Democratic institutions need to reflect group identities, while making sure that these identities do not take over the political debate. Institutional arrangements will need to respond to the growing demand for communitarian identity without making it harder for democracies to adapt to changes in social identities.

ALTERNATIVE FORMS OF ACTIVISM AND REPRESENTATION

There is a long-running debate over alternative forms of interest aggregation to political parties and over alternative consultative fora to the Western-style parliament. With repeated surveys showing that parties and parliaments are today among the least trusted political institutions, these are areas where democratic innovation is clearly warranted. Of course, beefing up a few symbolic civic initiatives does not go far enough in challenging underlying power structures. Instead, context-specific democracy should draw on distinct forms of representation.

A common view is that variation in democratic models will come mainly from the use of information and communications technology (ICT). New forms of mobilization and citizen groupings should be supported, but not to the detriment of more tried and tested vehicles of interest representation and aggregation. Some insist that mobilization based on ICT will increase accountability without implying democratization, as it has in China, for example. And they say that such accountability is where we may see more variation than in the past. Although such a possibility indeed holds potential, it would not amount to an entirely progressive form of the alternative democratic model.

Deliberative democracy should be pursued as a complement to formal aspects of democracy rather than as a non-Western alternative to free elections and formal rights protection. This model should not be seen as a means of circumventing the core tenets of polyarchy or core democratic norms. Deliberative democracy might entail a role for workers' councils or tribal mechanisms to articulate interests. The important challenge would be to ensure these mechanisms feed into existing ones far better than they do today and not weaken them.

Nonelectoral forms of representation have a role to play. However, systems that do not allow elections to run freely and without manipulation should not be indulged as part of a credible alternative to liberal democracy. The fact that democracy cannot be reduced to elections does not mean that better democracy results from the absence of free and fair elections. However, where supplementary, nonelectoral means of selection are proposed for certain functions, these should not be dismissed out of hand. The key is to ensure that if local forms of selection are widely seen to confer significant legitimacy, then these forms are implemented so that they feed into open election-based competition further up the chain of representative office.

In the future, representation is likely to be based on the performance of representatives and the dynamic interaction between them and the represented. Standard and rather static electoral representation does not need to provide the only bedrock of representative accountability. Thinkers insist that new avenues of performance-based representation offer the prospect of blending representative and direct-participative democracy. This is because the combination would offer the represented a greater degree of policy involvement and include a wider range of participants.[22]

Today's "social nonmovements" are looser networks of activists that are less hierarchically structured than professional advocacy groups. The members of these nonmovements often explicitly reject formalized patterns of nongovernmental organizations (NGOs) or party activity. In closed political environments, nonmovements focus on the "politics of presence"—innovative and creative ways of capturing public attention and setting thematic agendas. This is quite clearly not the kind of subversive activity that the more conservative of non-Western elites have in mind when they talk about locally "authentic" representation.[23] But such nonmovements have gained importance in many non-Western contexts that are not propitious to more familiar forms of associative or political party development. Such movements need to be encouraged to contribute toward wider political participation. Their skepticism of traditional politics should not extend to indifference toward democracy per se.

Expanding initiatives such as participatory budgeting could be useful. Participatory budgeting offers a much-lauded means of reinvigorating local democracy and is a good example of universal principles with local variation. This practice has spread during the past fifteen years most extensively across Latin America and into Europe; more recently, it has spread into Asia. In Latin America, participatory budgeting has been associated with the empowerment of local communities and has oriented public services toward poorer communities in a context of limited welfare states. In Europe, participatory budgeting has been used in a slightly more top-down manner and has not led to significant local redistribution; indeed, local authorities increasingly see it as a means of sharing responsibilities for cutbacks in public services. In Asia, there has been no single model: South Korea has pioneered Brazilian-style local empowerment, while in China, budgeting has been participatory in the sense of involving more layers of state bodies, not citizens. There is not one model of the practice specific to each region. Rather, a disparate set of national processes has taken shape reflecting the different rationale lying behind the impressive uptake of participatory budgeting.[24]

Of course, not all is rosy in the sphere of new civic activism. As explained in the previous chapter, critics argue that the explosion of protests led by new actors is far from being positive for democracy. These critics insist that the eruption of more conflictive civil-society activity around the world in recent years denotes a misfiring of the long-supposed connection between civil society and democratic quality. These skeptics base their case on the argument that today's new civil-society actors embody the very antithesis of democracy-enhancing qualities.

Some criticisms do need to be taken seriously. They reinforce the need to ensure more effective deliberation, so that civic actors do not simply replay their instinctive prejudices but look to other-regarding and constructive solutions—the essence of good quality deliberative democracy. In many countries, new civic actors clearly do not fit the dysfunctional picture that skeptics paint. Protesters in nondemocratic states have taken to the streets demanding the basic, core institutional features of liberal democracy, even as protesters in Western democracies complain these features have lost their meaning. Yet new social movements do need to be channeled toward more concrete forms of effective accountability. Their spirit of contestation needs to be harnessed and channeled in a direction that serves better-quality, stable democratic decisionmaking.

NON-WESTERN JUSTICE

Chapter two noted the recent trends in legal pluralism. An aspect of these debates relates to how variation in legal systems can contribute positively to locally rooted forms of democratic legitimacy.

This is another finely balanced question. Some traditional-justice systems sit more easily with democratic principles than others. Conversely, sometimes customary justice is carried out in a way that is problematic in terms of democratic principles. Locally rooted justice is intrinsically neither inimical nor beneficial to democracy. It is necessary to look very carefully at the specific conditions under which legal pluralism is able to "translate" the principle of democratic justice into local settings.

In some countries, the tribal, clan, or village chiefs responsible for customary dispute resolution pay little regard to human rights norms. In others, they are effectively pressed to adhere to basic liberal-rights norms. Some have proven more adaptable than others on the issues of women's and children's rights—areas where traditional systems have given most cause for concern. Some traditional systems are based on tribal or clan structures, some are based on religion, and some are organized around inclusive mediation forums. These variations can have very different effects on the formal democratic system. Some systems are at least partially incorporated into formal rules. Others are more antagonistic toward the formal unitary legal order.

Variation in legal systems should be seen as a legitimate avenue for exploring democratic innovation. Customary justice mechanisms can be developed in a way that feeds into and nourishes national-level democracy. At the same time, such justice should not be axiomatically extolled as virtuous simply because it is "traditional." Customary justice should not be held to a set of criteria that is likely to infringe on core democratic values.

The key question is the relationship between the structure of national-level judicial systems and local-level dispute-resolution mechanisms. In liberal democracies, one function of the rule of law is to constrain the way in which leaders rule; another is to deliver justice in a way that is predictable, efficient, guarantees equality before the law, and safeguards individual rights. These two functions must work in harmony. It is one thing to look for different and more effective ways of delivering justice; it is another to have basic rules governing justice that diverge fundamentally from democratic principles.

Several African constitutions try to enshrine universal principles of equality while also recognizing the role of customary law in delimited domains. In the best cases, citizens—and in particular women—draw on both customary and common law as a seamless whole. The balance is, of course, extremely difficult to strike: although there are growing demands for informal justice, parts of local communities—often those that are becoming less deferential toward traditional hierarchies—complain that such systems are discriminatory.[25] In some countries, traditional systems are reasserting themselves; in others, they are being challenged by universal legal principles. In still others, there is a struggle between different types of traditional justice systems—for example, between tribal and religious forms.

The United Nations argues that democratic reformers within developing states and the international community still tend to underplay rather than overplay the potential for informal justice systems to add healthy variety and legitimacy to democratic models. For all the difficulties, the aim must be to strike a mutually enhancing balance between formal and informal justice. On the one hand, the democracy community would be wrong simply to dismiss informal justice systems as failing to meet Western human-rights criteria. On the other hand, it would be wrong to support such systems on a purely expedient basis—because they deliver justice in a quick and cheap fashion—and not reflect on the broader rules that govern their operations. They cannot be a substitute for the strengthening of the unitary legal order.

Although both of these dangers are present in current debates, in general the greater risk has been the former—that of an overly dismissive attitude toward customary systems. These systems can and should be embraced, under the right conditions. Such conditions are those where traditional systems' human-rights standards, transparency, and appeals procedures can be improved.

The challenge is to improve coordination and learning between the formal and informal legal systems and to make the former more attentive to the reasons why traditional mechanisms retain appeal. If this is not done, tensions will continue to grow between formal and informal justice systems. This source of conflict and instability will be prejudicial to democracy at all levels.[26] Maintaining two entirely separate legal systems is not sustainable. The key is to develop a successful and more accessible state legal practice, and then allow traditional justice with appeals to the state courts. This combination would have the formal and informal dimensions functioning as a single, democratically accountable rule-of-law system.

CONCLUSION

This chapter has disaggregated the principles in accordance with which democratic variation can usefully be debated and encouraged. It has expressly not attempted to map out any kind of detailed alternative democratic model, as that would contradict the spirit of variation that this book advocates. Rather, it has proffered a set of principles to guide the deliberation about legitimate forms of democratic variation. The chapter identifies five such guiding arenas of possible variation, under a common principle of liberal democracy being enriched rather than diluted. In this way, the chapter has offered a way of framing the right kinds of debate about democratic alternatives. Of course, the question of how much variation is needed to constitute a completely different "model" is not easy to answer with precise objectivity. But the general spirit of the arguments made here is that variation is best seen as supplementing, correcting, and enriching the current practices of liberal democracy—not as an antagonistic substitute.

In all regions, the most evocative and audible rallying cry is for "inclusion." In all regions, there is a broad if often nebulous feeling that political systems have failed to reduce "exclusion." Exclusion—expressed as economic, social, ethnic, religious, rural, and gender imbalances—has worsened. The desire for a "more inclusive" form of democracy does not provide a clear, detailed, or universally accepted set of solutions. The call for inclusiveness is essentially the way that the debate over future democratic renewal is framed. That debate takes place in terms of which kind of political system can best augment "inclusion."

Liberal democracies have not performed significantly worse than any other regime type on inclusion, but neither have they excelled on this score nor incontestably proved themselves less exclusionary than other countries. Hence, a means must be found to confront debates on this terrain. This can be done by supplementing the core nucleus of liberal democracy with measures that improve the breadth and depth of inclusiveness. It is this spirit of inclusiveness that forms the common thread that ties together the types of variation proposed in this chapter—namely, variation in the areas of rights, economic equality, minority quotas, civic participation, and customary forums of justice.

The chapter has sought to draw attention to the balance between positive potential and boundaries. On the one hand, it has suggested the areas in which benign potential for democratic variation exists. On the other hand, it has drawn some lines that should limit what counts as genuine democratic variation. And, crucially, the chapter relates these conceptual considerations to real-world trends, taking a step from academic to international policy-relevant debates. The next chapter develops these policy implications in greater detail.

CHAPTER 7

THE IMPLICATIONS FOR INTERNATIONAL DEMOCRACY SUPPORT

The debates over non-Western democracy specifically and democratic variation more generally have practical implications for the design of Western foreign policies and for governments and organizations involved in democracy support. Although democracy supporters have mostly bought into the discourse of being open to "authentic democracy" and not hewing narrowly to a set Western model, they admit to being unsure how this outlook should be operationalized.

This chapter discusses international democracy-support policies. It assesses how far these policies have encouraged democratic variation and offers a number of guidelines to help inject genuine substance into the declared goal of nourishing democratic variety. These guidelines are matched to the suggested five-point framework for variation outlined in the previous chapter. There is much untapped potential for non-Western democracies to support different models through their foreign policies, and this chapter suggests drawing on that support in ways that could help reinvigorate and relegitimize the promotion of democracy.

HOW MUCH VARIATION DOES THE WEST CURRENTLY SUPPORT?

A common criticism of the West's democracy-support efforts is that they are inflexibly wedded to their own national models of liberal democracy.

Critics insist that the international community has failed to support or even to think very much about alternative or nonliberal models of democracy.[1] This has become part of the conventional wisdom about problems that beset the emerging world order. The standard picture that critics paint is of reductionist or narrow-minded Western powers unable to move beyond ethnocentric presumptions of their own superior models. Many writers lament that Western governments have been unwilling to move with the times and embrace political variation among newly successful non-Western powers.

Critics dismiss Western governments' claims that they seek to encourage democratic variation. Although donors may talk of supporting variation and funding programs designed by local stakeholders, skeptics see this as cosmetic and willfully disingenuous. They insist that donors still stick rigidly to a liberal model not only because of familiarity or a lack of original thinking but also because of their own power interests. Critics' familiar and standard line is that for proper non-Western variation to exist, Western donors should "keep away" and desist in the whole notion of supporting democracy. This is because their policies inevitably steer political trends away from locally legitimate institutions.

The most often repeated charge is that the promotion of Western democracy overemphasizes elections, which both narrows the understanding of democracy and precludes the consideration of alternative forms of representation. Although donors insist they are no longer guilty of "reducing democracy to elections," critics think that it is still done in practice.

Critics also admonish Western donors for the way they fund civil society. The standard criticism is that donors have been responsible for creating artificial spheres of civil society—civic organizations that fit a Western model and are unsuited to local contexts. Most evaluations conclude that donors err in taking "civil society" to be synonymous with professional, overtly political, advocacy nongovernmental organizations (NGOs). These groups have squeezed out the organic growth of looser, grassroots organizations. Critics charge democracy promoters with fostering an "engineered civil society" that has few local or organic roots but which fits donors' neoliberal conceptions of democracy and economic policy. This approach, critics insist, has displaced more legitimate local forms of organization. For example, in former Soviet states, democracy promotion policies sought to excise all traces of Soviet rule and, in doing so, overrode useful, traditional, pre-Communist forms of civic organization.[2]

Analysts increasingly focus on the distinction between civil society organizations and social movements. Western governments fund the former, analysts argue, but these donors seek to contain and tame those social movements that push for variations of democracy or more far-reaching policy changes—by keeping them at arm's length from decisionmaking and often restricting their ability to organize. These movements are about creating spaces for debate and consensus building. Their participants see social movements as an alternative to the rigid hierarchies of representative democracy. The new movements are about contestation, not about polite civility and the acceptance of status quo boundaries. This is why Western governments' external-funding initiatives withhold support.[3]

A different critique is that Western donors and democracy promoters subscribe to the highly liberal notion that civil society is a counterforce against the state—a concept that precludes initiatives that aim toward more cooperative problem solving between the state and civil society. Donors exclude from their work a concept that civil society is complementary rather than adversarial to the state. They do little to build up networks of trust and, instead, support individual groups that aim to restrict the state. Donors fail to focus on community development, because they see the civic sphere as being about the bold, antigovernment assertion of individual rights. Critics berate donors for being too drawn to high-profile opposition change agents—the outspoken liberal activists present in nearly all states, even if in small numbers—who are openly hostile to incumbent regimes. Donors do not prioritize the generic accumulation of social capital, though—something that is necessary to underpin effective prodemocracy activism as the opportunities for political breakthroughs present themselves. In this way, the argument runs, donors' liberal-democratic concepts draw the focus away from much needed coordination between civil society and state insiders.[4]

Although some of these criticisms are valid, they are overstated. Critical theorists generally make little effort to examine the kinds of democracy programs that are being run on the ground. Those thinking in theoretical terms about democratic models tend not to engage in detailed assessments of democracy support strategies.[5] Conversely, those involved in democracy support tend to eschew conceptual thinking about democratic models. Hence, there is a yawning mismatch between theory and practice.

The nitty-gritty detail of international democracy support in fact reveals a mixed picture. Some support policies reflect the narrowest parameters of liberal democracy. And there is certainly a tendency for some donors to fuse together pressure for neoliberal economic reforms and support for democratic reform. Critics' damning indictments of Western democracy support are not entirely without foundation.

However, many aspects of international funding show a genuine attempt to explore different concepts of democracy. Western governments, NGOs, and political foundations are not starting with a blank canvas when it comes to democratic variation. In recent years, donors insist they have taken steps to embrace variation in democratic forms and have become more open to new pathways to reform. Several see the promise of "alternative forms" almost as a panacea for relegitimizing the spirit of democracy support.

The standard critique that Western governments press elections on unwilling populations as part of a constricted model of Western liberal democracy does not always fit reality. Far from reflexively emphasizing elections, Western powers often prefer to "wait for elections" far more than local populations. Frequently, Western governments are anxious about the effect that free elections might produce and how they can generate uncertainty. Hence, Western governments commonly prioritize long-term, generic capacity building, which is relatively neutral in terms of the possible models of democracy, as a substitute for insisting on free and fair elections. The United States works positively with many states whose elections are patently not free and fair, cooperating with them on grassroots civic projects. Contrary to the normal critique, in recent years it has often been local populations protesting for free elections, while Western governments ally with regimes in extolling the virtues of more limited forms of accountability and representation.[6]

The empirical evidence suggests that donors are somewhat justified in claiming that they have made more progress than critics realize. Sometimes donors have even moved a little too far. In a small number of cases, donors have been so eager to be seen supporting locally rooted organizational forms that they have been led to back institutions with questionable "democraticness." If analytical debates have become more fluid and varied, so have real-world democracy-support policies. International democracy promoters generally embrace the notion of democratic variation. Several prominent development agencies in particular have become firmly wedded to a mantra of fostering non-Western models. Yet it remains far from clear if and how governments and organizations can reconcile the conceptual tensions this generic aim presents to concrete policy choices.

WESTERN POLICY EXAMPLES OF VARIATION

Democracy promoters have exhibited flexibility at various levels. It is seen in the way they encourage reform through traditional institutions and promote change through civil society organizations. Flexibility is also seen in the way they strengthen socioeconomic rights and support consensual models of democracy.

ENCOURAGING REFORM THROUGH TRADITIONAL INSTITUTIONS

The West's focus on traditional institutions has extended furthest in conflict situations. The United Nations Development Program (UNDP) has engaged with traditional justice institutions in Afghanistan, aiming to link their roles with the formal justice sector.[7] In South Sudan, UNDP has worked extensively with chiefs and supported traditional authorities to promote a better understanding of human rights and women's justice issues.[8] In 2012, a broader UNDP initiative looked at ways in which customary justice systems should be supported more systematically by development aid.[9] In Somalia, the UNDP made a choice to work with customary authorities after failing successfully to support formal rule-of-law institutions.[10] In addition to the efforts of the UNDP, UN officials in South Sudan have supported traditional mechanisms, even though the organization's formal strategies still follow the liberal peace-building template. This support has involved defining rebel fighters as "traditional community leaders" and engaging with them on that basis.[11]

Similar concerns are evident in many of the projects funded by the U.S. government. As part of a Kenya Justice Project in 2012, USAID organized a workshop in Nairobi that brought together Kenyan High Court judges and traditional leaders (chiefs and elders) to discuss how Kenya's customary justice system could help implement the reforms envisioned in the 2010 constitution, particularly with regard to gender discrimination, property rights, land tenure, and equitable access to land.[12] In Afghanistan, USAID's Rule of Law Stabilization Program has an Informal Justice Sector Component, which since 2012 has supported the traditional justice sector; it works directly with traditional dispute-resolution elders and local government and religious stakeholders to foster linkages between the traditional and formal justice systems. The aim is to strengthen Afghanistan's traditional-justice sector and align it with the Afghan constitution, sharia principles, and individual rights.[13] USAID has sponsored hundreds of events that involve thousands of participants from various communities, tribes, and government institutions—events that aim to bridge the gap between Afghanistan's informal and formal justice systems.[14] USAID also supported the creation of a regional conflict resolution initiative that relies on experienced elders to act as "neutral agents" in conflict resolution processes.[15] U.S. projects have also been run to enhance the role of female elders and wise women (*spinsari*).

In such conflict-ridden environments, the United States Institute of Peace and others have undertaken projects that strengthen traditional bodies and, at the same time, ensure they accept rules to limit human rights abuses. In the justice sector, the aim has been to develop customary procedures for minor cases, combined with recourse to state courts for more serious offences. Some professional NGOs have even criticized the United States for being too favorable toward traditional bodies and leaders.[16]

In similar vein, the European Union (EU) has developed a model of conflict analysis that is used to assess local political processes. This model of analysis assumes that variation is necessary for tempering conflict and one part of a broader "political economy" approach to providing development aid.[17] The EU has introduced the concept of a "state-building contract." This is formally based on all-inclusive dialogue with various sides of local conflicts. This dialogue aims at producing a consensual "compact" that defines the use of EU funds—that is an agreement among local actors and factions over the reform priorities to be supported.

The contracts are highly relevant to the Sahel, especially Mali and Mauritania, as well as to South Sudan. EU officials defend state-building contracts as a means of engaging more systematically with the locally specific, traditional institutions that might help bring stability to situations of acute fragility.[18] The aim is to marry the principle of local ownership to a long-term reform and institution-building agenda that local regimes often resist.

PROMOTING CHANGE THROUGH CIVIL SOCIETY ORGANIZATIONS

Developing countries have come to place greater stress on "authenticity" in civil society than was originally the case when interest in civil society support mushroomed in the 1990s. Various UN bodies have therefore gradually pushed their exploration of "traditional" forms of political representation. The head of the United Nations Democracy Fund (UNDEF) framed his organization's approach in a balanced fashion: "It is not for us to ponder on models of democracy but to fund those who can have those debates." Indeed, UNDEF has favored initiatives aimed at bringing together various types of local civic bodies into broad-based reform coalitions.

To some extent, donors' search for locally rooted organizations makes a virtue out of necessity. The United States and other donors have been pushed to search for locally rooted organizations by regimes' clampdowns on professional democracy and human-rights NGOs. More than fifty non-Western governments, including those of Egypt and Russia, have imposed restrictions on the external funding of domestic NGOs. In some cases, this has involved high-profile and dramatic expulsions of Western democracy organizations.

The side effect of authoritarian regimes' determination to constrict externally funded democracy and human rights NGOs is that the United States and other donors are looking more closely at how to support looser forms of civic awareness through organizations other than professional NGOs—given that the latter are now targeted for replicating the adversarial politics typical of Western liberal democracy. Although neither the United States nor other Western powers have advanced far in determining precisely how this can be done, it is an additional factor that has changed the terms of debate.[19]

The 2012 EU democracy and human-rights strategy, which was accompanied by a detailed 36-point Action Plan, focused one of its three core pillars on "the enabling environment." This was devised as a means of getting the framework right for societies to develop their own models and choices of civic activism. Diplomats in Brussels and other national European capitals insist that, in recent years, they have reacted to the long-standing complaint that Western funders favor particular types of civil society organizations that replicate a Western model.

The European Endowment for Democracy has also moved policies in this direction with its leitmotif of "supporting the unsupported"—aiding reformers who do not operate within Western-style civic organizations that fit neatly into the liberal model of politics. Its new grantee-protection system favors a search for organizations that are not necessarily formally registered, liberal-style advocacy NGOs. A recent European Parliament report registers the commitment to push EU funding more toward "nontraditional" civil society organizations.[20]

Many aspects of European democracy support are often inflexibly linked to EU rules and templates: local civil-society leaders in recipient countries without fail complain that technical capacity building provided through large-scale EU institutional and twinning programs can effectively suffocate indigenous organizational forms. However, some dimensions of European strategies incorporate different models. The EU works to a formally eclectic set of principles. Policymakers stress that there is a conspicuous absence of any tightly defined definition of democracy around which they are expected to mold their projects.

EU delegations in a number of countries have drawn up Democracy Profiles, with the idea of uncovering specificities in power dynamics and models of democracy. Up to now, the EU has prepared detailed assessments of each recipient's human-rights situation using standard universal measurements that do not incorporate variations in how power structures actually operate. The new profiles are designed to correct this. The group of pilot countries for this exercise was expanded in 2014. Democracy Action Plans have also been drawn up for each country ostensibly to mold policy tools around local institutional variations. And EU officials who are designing the post-2015 follow-on to the Millennium Development Goals insist that development policy is not about "north to south" influence but about joint partnership. Policymakers also stress that in order to work around difficult regimes, their priority is to support more community-level citizenship initiatives molded to local conditions.

STRENGTHENING SOCIOECONOMIC RIGHTS

Asked how they define their model of democracy support, the most common response from EU officials is that socioeconomic rights are a more important element of EU policies than formal, liberal political rights. European aid figures do indeed show that EU donors spend many times more on social development, social rights, and building state capacity than on promoting the core political dimensions of liberal democracy.

The EU supports an increasing number of projects on trade unions and labor standards and insists this reflects its concept of "deep," or social, democracy.[21] A number of initiatives provide funding to social insurance schemes in many recipient countries. Other programs deepen civic input through "social cohesion laboratories." Rule-of-law initiatives focus more on legal aid and mobile legal clinics to improve access to justice for poor, rural communities concerned with social rights.[22] European governments spend vastly more on social development than on elections or Western-style party building through their aid programs. Officials insist that EU democracy support reflects a more utilitarian than liberal approach, because the priority is strengthening the articulation of collective economic and social interests. One ministry reports that European initiatives have tilted strongly toward "vernacular" understandings of democracy that are built on informal and patronage-based distributions of power.[23]

European funds in Bolivia go toward projects of indigenous social movements that center around notions of distinctive local forms of democracy. The European Instrument for Democracy and Human Rights (EIDHR) has supported a wide range of projects at the intersection of labor and socioeconomic and indigenous rights, particularly in South America.[24] Under the Chávez government, the EU supported cooperation in Venezuela to strengthen local conceptions of cultural and socioeconomic rights. Other projects in Central America funded local groups to lobby for the protection of communal land rights. In Chile, EIDHR has supported the Observatory for the Rights of Indigenous Peoples to combat the social and economic discrimination against indigenous peoples and to strengthen traditional community-leadership structures.[25]

In other regions, the European Commission has supported the social inclusion of marginalized social groups and grassroots democracy. Examples include community mediation in Kashmir,[26] "opportunities for 'direct democracy' through the development and consolidation of participatory media in Russia,[27] secular-religious dialogue on local political models in Tajikistan,[28] grassroots democracy in Fiji,[29] indigenous rights in the Philippines, and union rights in Georgia, the Pacific Islands, and Tunisia.[30]

Germany insists that its democracy policies eschew the imposition of any single German, European, or liberal model. The acceptance of variation is seen as an integral part of the country's vaunted "civilian power" identity. German policy is based on the concept of the Rechtsstaat, constitutionally enshrined rules on the most basic of democratic principles. Germany has been warmly cooperative with Evo Morales's government in Bolivia, fostering dialogue with the president to explore how his reform aims could be channeled toward a distinctive and genuine form of democracy that is able to give prominence to social and economic rights.[31] Representatives of the influential German Stiftungen insist categorically that they do not support a Western model.

SUPPORTING CONSENSUAL MODELS

The EU has generally favored consensual models of democracy over majoritarian ones. Policymakers say this reflects a preference for democracy that is not based on the more adversarial versions of liberal democracy. Some observers argue that if anything, the EU's preference for consensual models is almost too pronounced, in that it precludes debate over fundamental questions at an early stage of democratization.[32]

In the Balkans, the EU has set accession preconditions that give priority to maintaining consensual pacts. Many local civic groups are critical of this approach, because such pacts are built around old-guard nationalist elites. Protests erupted in Bosnia in 2013 among younger sectors of society that were pressing for an open form of competitive democratic politics. These protesters accused the EU of keeping insalubrious elites in power because of its assumption that consensual stability must be maintained through power-sharing quotas. The demonstrators complained that this had actually hindered a more dynamic model of politics and foreclosed the possibility of moderation emerging from a majoritarian system of national politics. The Balkans has given the EU a lesson in the drawbacks of "illiberal consociationalism." Twenty years after the end of the Bosnian war, peace and democracy are both still extremely fragile across the Balkans.

The Belgian government, the International Institute for Democracy and Electoral Assistance, and the United Nations Economic Commission for Africa have together funded a rolling initiative looking at how customary governance can be harnessed to deepen consensus. This had the theme of "democratizing the customary and customizing the democratic."[33]

The EU supports the Association of Southeast Asian Nations (ASEAN) Intergovernmental Commission on Human Rights, which follows a consensus-oriented approach to rights questions—indeed, to the extent that critics dismiss it as a soft rubber stamp for regimes' human-rights policies. A very senior EU ambassador, closely engaged in democracy support, insists the core of the EU's approach to democracy building is mediating for consensus, building confidence among factions and minorities, and creating trust between government and opposition groups.

The EU's rule of law programs have been relatively flexible, working around local structures. These programs have in fact avoided any strict, singular model of the rule of law. In part, this is because the EU itself is so complex. In part, it is because the rule of law is seen in an instrumental sense of aiming to equip third states to handle aspects of the EU acquis and regulatory convergence. Some education projects aimed at generating political awareness and learning in rule of law have begun, even if these remain much less developed than the formal institutional areas of reform support.

TENSIONS OVER WESTERN AID

Despite the significant forms of variation that are supported by Western democracy aid, non-Westerners have complaints. Perhaps the most serious tensions have emerged concerning the issue of liberal rights.

Western governments have frequently pushed against the illiberal provisions of traditional mechanisms. In Afghanistan and Pakistan, for example, Western donors have pressed to remove traditional rules that prevent witnesses from testifying against family members in cases involving assaults on women. Western governments have taken this tack even when it meant clashing with democratic majority opinion. In Mali, popular protests got a democratically elected government to withdraw a more liberal family code—a code that was strongly backed by donors. Libyans say that Western donors have failed to build tribal power into their initiatives, compounding the country's struggle to embed any kind of stable democratic reform and accelerating Libya's descent into civil war.

The converse criticism is also voiced—that Western governments are now almost overdoing the focus on variation and that they sometimes use a discourse of "flexibility of political models" as a pretext for inaction in strategically important authoritarian states.[34] Although pledging strong support for democratic variation, the Dutch government argues that the UN's "cultural diversity" and "traditional values" language is increasingly being used as a means of diluting human rights commitments.[35]

The Middle East illustrates these tensions. Western governments have launched many initiatives exploring various concepts of rights with Islamists. Indeed, secularists accuse donors of moving too far toward Islamist-heavy forms of political reform. This criticism is heard especially from liberal human-rights activists who have received Western support for many years and who remain hostile to moderate Islamist inclusion. Liberal secularists commonly accuse Western governments of "abandoning their own values" and of being too tolerant and positive toward organizations such as the Muslim Brotherhood and its various affiliates across the region.

In 2012, the EU and the United States unsuccessfully pressed liberals not to withdraw from Egypt's constitutional committee in response to proposals for new religious clauses. Diplomats—who see the future of the region primarily through a prism of religious tensions—say they have focused on trying to mediate the divisions between Islamists and secularists far more than they have sought to rein in the guardians of the "deep state," as they have regrouped against reformists of all persuasions, most notably in Egypt but also elsewhere. The focus on generating some modicum of consensus has been particularly evident in Western policies since the July 2013 coup in Egypt.

The picture of Islamist parties striving for a completely distinctive model of democracy against an intolerant and uncomprehending international community caricatures what is in fact a very nuanced situation. While briefly in power in Egypt, the Muslim Brotherhood grappled not so much with inventing a new form of democracy but rather with how to mobilize state institutions to implement policy decisions and deliver better services and economic policy. Western powers were in fact largely supportive long after domestic opinion had turned against then president Mohamed Morsi.

There were tensions between the EU and Ennahdha in Tunisia over proposed illiberal clauses on minority rights (those concerning women, Jews, and homosexuals). A delicate balance was struck. Western governments threatened a reduction in funding levels if highly illiberal clauses that were included in early drafts of the country's new democratic constitutions were not removed. Yet, ultimately Western governments accepted and actively supported the final version of this constitution that leaves considerable potential for state-backed religious edicts to trump liberal rights.

Although tensions have surfaced, in general there is little evidence of Islamist parties pressing for wholesale new models that Western governments actively oppose. Debates and tensions are of a different order in today's tumultuous Middle East.

Sometimes, external powers do push against the grain of local opinion. In August 2014, the EU and the United States pressed Iraq to adopt a government in which sectarian factions share power. They leaned heavily on the Iraqi president to replace Prime Minister Nouri al-Maliki, who had just won democratic elections as the head of his al-Dawa party. More recently, and controversially, French president François Hollande has made assertive speeches on the need to support minority group rights as a means to protect Christians in the Middle East. This is not quite the form of communitarianism that people in the region necessarily prioritize. In a confusing twist to standard debates, many now berate Western donors for wanting to "impose" a nonmajoritarian, non-Western form of democracy in order to favor Christians.

In sum, support for democratic variation is not entirely absent from Western and international democracy support policies. It may so far be patchy and of insufficient magnitude. But the empirical detail on democracy support reveals an incipient conceptual shift.

Western powers insist that they have firmly exited the era of ebullient "offensive liberalism." This was an era when the internal and external sides of liberalism appeared to work in harmony with each other. Today, liberalism endeavors to preserve itself in a more self-protective mode. A more "defensive liberalism" has taken shape that is less inclined to see external proselytizing as integral to its very coherence and essence.[36] The supposed correlation between domestic liberalism and external liberalism is today more critically interrogated. Liberalism domestically is not always assumed to be the same as liberalism internationally.

NON-WESTERN SUPPORT FOR VARIATION

In recent years, there has been much debate over the increasingly active foreign policies of rising non-Western democracies, such as Brazil, Chile, India, Indonesia, Japan, Nigeria, South Africa, South Korea, and Turkey. Specifically, they have all begun to address the issue of democracy support. Their participation is part of a much wider "global marketplace" of influences and ideas that has come to condition national-level politics. Sometimes this marketplace can even involve nondemocratic states supporting democracy—Iran in Iraq, Saudi Arabia in Yemen, and Qatar in Libya—often as a means of favoring particular parties or groups. In Africa, states have become more involved in each other's internal politics. In Latin America, Venezuela not only tests definitions of liberal democracy but also has influenced regional politics in taking its Bolvarian revolution across the continent. Today, non-Western states are sources of international influence, not simply recipients.[37]

Much hope abounds that the rising democracies can lend vitality to global democracy support by adding to the efforts of Western democracy promoters—and that they can make such policies far more legitimate, to the extent that they decouple democracy support from purely Western agendas. Skeptics—in rising democracies and in the West—argue that these states still do more to hinder than to help, given that they adhere to sovereigntist templates of international relations and are usually reluctant to be associated with the aims of Western democracy promotion. Many non-Western democracies are also still struggling to consolidate their own democratic transitions and suffering from economic problems that restrict their foreign policy ambitions.[38]

The role—incipient and potential—of these rising democracies is highly pertinent to the subject matter of this book. It might be surmised that these countries are better positioned to support non-Western variation in democracy than are Western states. Several rising non-Western democracies followed paths of democratic transition that were somewhat different from those charted by advanced Western democracies. Many have social and ethnic structures similar to those of the developing or industrializing countries where calls for non-Western democracy are frequently heard. Rising democracies also share similar kinds of economic problems and, in some cases, have similar strands of social conservatism woven through popular opinion. If the world is indeed set on a path toward more democratic variation, then it would seem intuitively convincing to suggest that the rising democracies will play a more influential role.

But how well positioned are the rising democracies to contribute to fostering greater democratic variation? When compared with Western supporters, do non-Western democracies indeed know more about furthering different forms of democratic representation and accountability?

The record so far suggests that the rising democracies certainly have a number of advantages in encouraging different forms of political reform—forms that cannot be dismissed as unsuitably Western. Several African, Arab, and Asian states in (tentative) transition have in recent years looked to these countries for advice, best practices, and capacity building. In the months after Hosni Mubarak's fall, for example, Egyptian reformers reached out to Indonesian and Turkish officials for their transition experiences, which resonated more than Western lessons. Civil society organizations struggling to make an impact in authoritarian states increasingly turn for support and advice to the rising democracies and not merely to Western countries. However, the jury is out on the question of whether the rising democracies do indeed have distinctive, replicable, and entirely successful models of democracy to convey to the rest of the world.

The foreign policies of rising democracies have much in common—and this in some measure differentiates their perspectives on democracy from those of Western politicians and policymakers. Specifically, these policies include a focus on support for reform that respects national sovereignty and can be construed as noninterventionist. Additionally, this focus is interwoven with peace building as well as mediation and derives from a concern with social justice, rather than subordinating the latter to political reform. These features are sufficient to imbue rising democracies' policies with a distinctive tinge. To some extent, it is possible to detect the very faint contours of an emerging non-Western approach to democracy support—and there are certainly reasons to believe that this both reflects and stands to further democratic variation across different regions.

However, caveats apply. There are also significant differences among rising democracies. These differences are meaningful enough to cast doubt on whether rising democracies are in fact well set to advance a particular non-Western model of democracy or indeed a series of non-Western models. Some rising democracies deviate from Western policies and models more clearly than do others.

BRAZIL

Brazil has shown the political will to defend democracy against coups. It has promoted formal democracy clauses within various Latin American regional charters. And the government has viewed the protection of democracy as integral to its attempts to lead a process of regional integration. At the same time, Brazilian leaders have had some sympathy for leftist populists who claim to be furthering a legitimate form of socially oriented governance. When one talks to officials in Brazil, it is indeed striking how much sympathy they have for the view that Venezuela today represents a variation of democracy and not a form of authoritarianism. They see policy in places such as Venezuela driven by economic interests as much as by any deep-rooted conviction in different systems of governance. Leaders say that their differences with Western governments are more about *tactics* in democracy support.

Another distinctive aspect of Brazilian foreign policy is the link between democracy and conflict resolution. Brazil approaches the democracy agenda through the prism of conflict resolution. The contribution of troops to operations in places such as Haiti has been a significant part of the country's emerging foreign policy identity. This connection with peace building serves to reinforce the government's focus on consensus-oriented models of political reform.

Brazil has been reluctant to support civic protesters mobilizing against autocratic regimes. Its preference for elite-led democratization is not one shared by many repressed democrats struggling to protect basic rights. Activists often raise questions about Brazil's tendency to see the democracy agenda as a means to position itself as a regional power in Latin America.

By way of comparison, Chile's approach is quite different. Mirroring its transition experience, Chile exhibits a strong belief in human rights activism in its international positions. Overall, Brazilian NGOs and analysts complain that the country's ambitions in supporting democracy have diminished dramatically since 2012. Moreover, with growing economic problems, protests, internal human-rights problems, and an increasingly ensconced dominant party, Brazil's soft power is suffering.

TURKEY

Turkey's foreign policies are different from Brazil's in crucial respects. During the latter part of the past decade, Turkey began to embrace democracy support on the back of the country's democratic transition led by the Justice and Development Party (AKP). That transition imbued Turkey with significant credibility in engaging with democratic reformers after the Arab Spring erupted in 2011. Many felt that Turkey was better positioned than Western states to reflect the desire across the Middle East for a non-Western model of democracy. Many Arab reformers saw the AKP as having successfully piloted a democratic transition while retaining its Islamist identity and while fashioning a political system that was not only pluralist but also Islamic in its cultural outlook. Turkey supported democratic transition across the Middle East and North Africa with enthusiasm—albeit more on the part of the AKP than Turkish state institutions. The AKP saw that transitions in Arab states could bring to power Muslim Brotherhood parties that shared much of its own ideology.

However, the shortcomings of this approach have increasingly become evident. First, although the AKP is a nominally Islamist party, it functions in the context of the secular Kemalist heritage. This is not a model that most Arab Islamist parties aspire to, as discussed in chapter 3. Therefore, Turkey has provided some useful lessons to Arab reformers in specific areas, such as financial reform, rather than as a wholesale model. Second, many Turkish experts observe that although the country has been highly active diplomatically, it has limited resources to support democracy in other countries in any tangible manner.

Third, since 2013, Turkey's own democratic credentials have been increasingly in question. Mounting opposition against Prime Minister Recep Tayyip Erdoğan and his increasing centralization of power, restriction of core rights, and brutal repression of civic mobilization have all tarnished Turkey's image as a beacon of Islamist democracy. Today, if Turkey provides a model for anything, it is of a hybrid mix of democracy and an authoritarian-oriented presidential and supermajoritarian system. And many skeptics would say that rather than show a successful model for the Muslim world, recent events in the country demonstrate how difficult it is in practice to combine democracy with a dominant state-guided Islamic culture.

ASIAN DEMOCRACIES

Both Japan and South Korea have significantly increased their politically oriented development aid. In formal terms, both of these countries have strengthened their commitments to democracy support. Both lay claim to a particular model of democratic transition. This perspective sees democracy as integral to state-led economic modernization. Japanese and South Korean aid is strongly oriented toward helping states embed better governance standards in the delivery of economic development programs. This focus certainly speaks to developing states' concern that Western democracy support tends to separate out the twin challenges of economic and political modernization. These successful Asian economies certainly cannot be accused of using democracy support to undercut the role of the state as part of an unhealthy neoliberal agenda.

Of course, this model of democratic transition presupposes a certain level of state capability and a certain type of state ethos. In countries suffering from state institutions captured by vested interests, many would argue that more civic-led processes of change are more appropriate and necessary. It is unclear whether Japan and South Korea have been flexible donors, willing to use their considerable resources to support such local demands for less modernization-oriented policies. Moreover, there is growing concern that Japan's current Abe government sees democracy support as an offshoot of its geopolitical worries, given China's rise; many hold Japan to be as guilty as the United States of "securitizing" democracy promotion.

Indonesia and India both make much of the democratic way in which they manage diverse societies. Both countries argue that their view of democracy is less adversarial than that which predominates in Western liberal democracy. The protection of group rights for minorities is seen as particularly important in both countries' broader regional policies. Indonesia's foreign policies are influenced by peace-building concerns and the unique regional profile of the Bali Democracy Forum. In the country's external support policies, it emphasizes projects on decentralization, the local management of natural resources through traditional community structures, and peace mediation—although Indonesian and ASEAN officials say the new government that took office in late 2014 shows less enthusiasm for democracy support.

India projects its unique experience in managing complex elections and interethnic diversity. India's main democracy-support actions have been in relation to Sri Lanka, where the country's own Tamil minority has pressed the government strongly for active engagement in the controversy surrounding the Sri Lankan government's human-rights abuses against Tamils in the closing stages of the civil war.

***

Overall, rising non-Western democracies' focus on democracy support is no more than embryonic. Their potential should not be dismissed, though. Many nations in the West, and especially the United States, often show impatience with how weak these countries' commitment to international democracy is; Western diplomats and analysts tend to see these states' talk of different models of democracy and democracy support as a disingenuous cloak to cover realpolitik self-interest. It is certainly the case that rising democracies' interest in challenging the current configuration of global power so far outweighs their desire to see a more democratic world order.

Yet, the focus of rising democracies on democracy support will bring variation to the international democracy agenda, which is necessary and of potentially positive value. This is not to say that rising democracies hold to different well-worked-out models of democracy in their foreign policies. The variation they offer is often about new kinds of *tactics* in democracy support rather than completely different models of democracy. Considering critics' complaint that Western democracy is too fixated on elections, it is striking that non-Western democracies' support policies are most active precisely in the area of elections observation. But interesting avenues of variation are certainly being opened up as these new actors engage, albeit tentatively, in democracy support.

Criticizing rising democracies' foreign policies simply for not measuring up to an imagined ideal-type of Western support for pristine liberal democracy is unduly short-sighted. Western democracy promoters in fact show a tendency to disparage rising democracies for shortcomings of which they themselves are equally guilty—after all, realpolitik security alliances still trump democracy promotion in most Western foreign policies just as much as they do in non-Western states' foreign policies. Indeed, some argue that Western powers would do better to limit themselves to cooperating on issues of international order with rising powers rather than seeking to cajole them into dialogue on democracy promotion.[39]

A more nuanced perspective on rising democracies' normative policies is warranted. An issue of central concern in this book is whether rising democracies have developed a coherently distinctive approach to democratic variation and democracy support. On the evidence so far, this must be questioned. Rising democracies certainly feel that in a loose sense they are working with understandings of democratic reform that are different from those that inform Western policies. The notion of having a different approach to democracy is indeed central to the way in which their nascent democracy-support strategies are justified internally. Yet, what such distinctiveness amounts to is invariably not fully worked through into any kind of coherent non-Western model.

Rising democracies emphasize different aspects of democracy support, compared with some Western countries; these aspects include mediation, consensus, economic modernization, and social justice. These are all welcome dimensions to democracy support. The fact that they are emphasized by rising democracies that increasingly have the resources and diplomatic muscle to make a difference is an extremely positive development—and one that should not be easily dismissed by Western powers looking hurriedly for "normative allies" to temper the effects of their own decline. Whether such elements add up to a distinctive, wholesale model of democracy support is doubtful, however. The aspects often presented as being distinctive to rising democracies are not entirely absent from Western policies. It is important to avoid caricatures of both non-Western and Western policies.

The rise of non-Western democracies with more active foreign policies could become a driving force toward the spread of varied models of democracy. At present, such a situation remains a distant prospect. Rising democracies' challenge to the West on questions of sovereignty and intervention is, so far, greater than on models of democracy. They are strongly critical of Western democracies for replicating the model of liberal democracy, but rising democracies also tend to see political change narrowly through the lens of their own experiences of democratic transition. In some senses, this tendency is a strong and welcomed aspect of rising democracies' foreign policies; it is certainly the case that their more recent transitions to democracy, often undertaken at various stages of economic underdevelopment, resonate more with those countries still struggling with authoritarianism than do the more distant experiences of industrialized Western states. However, this perspective can also be a weakness if rising democracies fail to see that other states' conditions may be very different from their own and therefore require foreign policy interventions that go beyond simply sharing the virtues of their own democratic transition.

In short, the democratic variation that rising democracies have so far brought to the table is of a particular kind: they make generalized claims regarding the lessons of their own models and make astute criticisms of Western policies, but these nations still fail to delineate a 360-degree, locally driven view on proper democratic variation. We need to distinguish between aspects of non-Western policies that are distinctive in the sense of helpfully correcting weaknesses in Western policies and aspects that undercut domestic and external efforts to further democracy.

IMPROVING SUPPORT FOR VARIATION ALONG FIVE AXES

Donors acknowledge that more needs to be done to understand the challenge of democratic variation and to strike the right balance between universal values and legitimate divergence. The question is how donors can do so in a way that is more organized and structured. The previous chapter suggested five axes along which the search for democratic variation is most legitimate, necessary, and promising. It is argued here that these conceptual arenas—related to individual rights, economic justice, communitarian identity, participation and representation, and legal norms—offer useful pointers for turning conceptual debates into policy imperatives and international democracy-promotion strategies.

INDIVIDUAL RIGHTS

International democracy supporters should pursue variation in understandings of individual rights in an expansive—not restrictive—fashion. Being tolerant of democratic variation does not imply supporting governments that restrict individual freedoms. Rather, variation should be advanced by positive initiatives that help empower communities effectively to support the exercise of individual democratic rights.

The defense of liberal rights is especially challenging in the Middle East. A form of democracy suited to all shades of citizenship is surely not achievable by the international community supporting regimes that curtail personal rights in the name of religious precepts. Liberal rights are attainable through building the capacity for religious parties and other parts of the community to engage in inclusive debate aimed at tolerance and shared objectives.

The West is often criticized for adhering to an overly passive and individual-based concept of citizenship. There is much the international community can do to address this *without* buying into the evisceration of individuals' basic rights—although it will be a long and difficult task. It calls for initiatives that try to work through how the protection of rights can enhance community-level moral identities—rather than fuse with amoral individualism. This is not to say that tension between the individual and community, between the liberal and religious outlooks, can be made to disappear. But there must be scope for looking at how liberal rights can be framed in way that is more sensitive to religious values and communal cohesion.

Some experts argue that recent cases show it is counterproductive for the EU and the United States to focus explicitly on liberal personal rights—or to cut aid in response to restrictions in this domain, as some European donors did in Uganda after it enacted new laws targeting homosexuals. Non-Western regimes now resist such pressure and turn to antigay and other legislation almost as a badge of honor to show their ability to stand up to the West. Rather, donors should focus on strengthening the institutional checks and balances within other societies to help a more tolerant liberal climate emerge.[40] This may entail a degree of rebalancing in current Western foreign policies with more stress on systemic-level democracy alongside liberal rights.

ECONOMIC JUSTICE

Support for civil society organizations keen on exploring various economic models should be more normal than is currently the case. Indeed, such support should be part of a genuine plurality of engagement with non-Western civil societies. Providing aid for this purpose would help rebut the charge that Western governments support democracy primarily as a means to further their economic interest in free markets. This tactic would also help lessen the confusion over what at times seems to be support for liberal politics, and, at other times, support for a particular type of economic policy.

European democracy supporters already back many projects that facilitate a dialogue among social partners (through initiatives that include trades unions, businesses, and state bodies). These projects are valuable and reflect a willingness to go beyond models based purely on the narrowly liberal concept of limited government. However, still common in most parts of the world is the view that the external economic policies of Western nations often undermine social justice and that this outweighs any positive impact of democracy assistance projects. Western diplomats may feel this unfairly caricatures their policies, but the perception exists, and it breeds much discontent with the liberal model.

Many Western states are themselves struggling to manage economic crisis democratically and in a way that retains social entitlements. This is a potential problem, as it is a factor that strengthens the appeal of highly illiberal populism. But it could also be harnessed as an opportunity. New democracy-support projects could explore the joint challenges that both Western and non-Western governments today face in designing more effective forms of democratic representation as they respond to economic difficulties.

Democracy promoters should not accept the inverse and equally simplistic charge that any support for free markets is intrinsically bad for democracy and is somehow appropriate only to the West. Some kind of balance is required: economic and political freedom can still be mutually reinforcing, in the right measure and circumstances. As a complement to this, it must be recognized that the de facto structures of economic power affect those of political power. Western donors should not be afraid to support new initiatives that explore the relationship between economic and political liberalization, particularly at a time when this relationship is under the spotlight within and outside the West.

POWER QUOTAS AND CONSENSUS

The international community should build on its incipient attempts to meet the concern with consensus in many developing countries. More work should be supported that shares the West's own experiences in quotas and all-inclusive deliberation. At the same time, Western initiatives in conflict situations should not be overly reliant on power sharing among factions. Communitarianism should be embraced, but not as shorthand for projects that risk freezing antagonistic ethnic or other identities. The value attached to consensus in many non-Western societies should not sanction international measures that emasculate open, pluralistic debate. Western democracy supporters should tilt their policies toward more liberal forms of communitarianism.

Although Western democracies are sometimes wary of communitarianism, in practice, donors on the ground sponsor communitarian-based unity deals as a necessary means of crisis management. Donors often find that these deals consolidate the position of highly oligarchic communal leaders who allow little open debate within their own communities. It is right that Western and international organizations address the problem that many people perceive liberal democracy to be harmful to community identity. Democracy support initiatives must work harder to foster arrangements capable of showing the opposite: that healthy democratic accountability and rights-protection is the best way to allow such community identities to be openly expressed and debated. But these identities must themselves be open to deliberation and adaptation, not ring-fenced as the preserve of networks of oligarchic elites.

PARTICIPATION AND REPRESENTATION

It is widely accepted that democracy around the world needs to be enhanced through stronger participatory and deliberative dynamics. Wider participation requires support for movements engaged in vibrant contestation and protest. Better democratic deliberation suggests a higher-quality civic debate that is rationalized in terms of general interests rather than particular ones. A related question is how to support a healthy degree of direct democracy, as technological trends push toward this form of accountability.

Western democracy promoters would say these are hardly new observations and that most of their programs are based on fomenting precisely these kinds of dynamics. Whether these models of democracy are best seen as complements to or in tension with liberal democracy is moot. The operational question is how the international community can offer better support to new forms of participation—and how donors can do so in a way that does not subvert standard representational dynamics. The challenge within and beyond the West is how to engineer a mutually reinforcing interlinkage of representative and participatory dynamics—a combination that can be thought of as "a theory of combined democracy."[41] International democracy promoters need not only to support participation—as is frequently advocated—but also to do more to dovetail their assistance with efforts to make representative channels more responsive. Politics that completely circumvent the legislature risk a return to the concept of delegative democracy described in chapter 3.

Donors must strike a difficult balance: they must do more to draw out the positive potential of new social movements, while also correcting their negative features. Western governments must understand the new trends in civil society as being not only a means of galvanizing democratic quality but also a possible danger to the foundations of smooth-running representative institutions. To help support new forms of association and social nonmovements, donors need to be more flexible regarding the structural and organizational rules with which they insist recipients comply.

The challenge is to foster a concept of democratic civil society that is more liberal and less liberal at the same time. Donors must widen their net of support to include new actors that are more confrontational toward the state and established concepts of political order. But donors must also support more consensual routes to political influence. Democracy support should look to tighten the linkages between civil society and the state—not an idea that is at the forefront of liberalism, which sees civil society's function as restraining more than empowering the state.

Donors should not think that information and communications technology (ICT) is a panacea that negates the need to support the traditional representative institutions of liberal democracy. Many democracy-support projects and initiatives now aim to link new mobilization efforts with traditional representative institutions. However, more work is required in this direction. Social movements need advice and guidance on how to move from contestation to building broad governing platforms. They need assistance in elaborating on positive manifestos and striking trade-offs with a wider range of democratic actors. Initiatives to build crowdsourcing into the writing of party platforms and proposals for new legislation take some steps in this direction. Many current projects help existing aid recipients adopt ICT rather than broaden participatory dynamics to other countries.

Western policymakers complain that the squeeze on financial resources means they are increasingly obliged to demonstrate tangible impact from their projects. This requirement militates against experimentation in exploring diverse democratic models, reinforcing a tendency for donors to seek out conventional projects rather than novel ways to help mold effective accountability. Donors should set aside at least a part of their funding for initiatives that move away from the "box ticking" logic that is common to much of civic society's consultation and support.

NON-WESTERN LEGAL NORMS

Democracy promoters are generally aware of the need to build on their existing work in the area of legal pluralism. Western governments and private foundations have understandably been cautious about supporting forms of customary or informal justice that sit uneasily with universal human-rights commitments. Several donors have been badly burned when they have supported traditional dispute-resolution mechanisms, discovering that these were locally contested and often the source of tension rather than a broadly acceptable and benign form of ensuring greater access to and legitimacy of justice.

The solution is not entirely to shift back to minimizing the potential of such informal systems. Rather, initiatives could most usefully explore the interplay between formal and informal justice and the need for unitary legal standards to combine with local variation in dispute settlement mechanisms. Far greater effort is required to work with local, customary structures in a way that strengthens their potential to provide more effective and consensual justice while bringing them under the rubric of core human-rights norms.

Although donors say they are committed to supporting informal justice, in practice, they still channel the overwhelming share of their rule-of-law support to the hardware of national institutional templates. Their projects pump millions into building courthouses and advising on the adoption of formal institutional patterns that underpin democratic control of the judiciary in Western states. A much higher share should go toward exploring the role of non-Western legal forms, addressing the delicate question of how they can provide greater variation in the delivery of justice without undercutting the need for unified legal systems that strengthen the protection of human rights.

CONCLUSION

This chapter has attempted to bring conceptual debates over democracy's future down to the level of real-life policy challenges that face those nations committed to supporting democratic reform internationally. It has recorded the ways in which Western governments and international organizations have begun to incorporate the search for democratic variation into their foreign policies. The criticism that Western powers seek to impose uniform templates of narrow, liberal democracy no longer holds to quite the same degree as it did a decade ago. Donors undoubtedly need to advance further, however. Non-Western democracies, in particular, have much potential if they extend their nascent democracy-support policies.

Many debates lie within the broad field of liberal democracy rather than being neatly divided along Western and non-Western lines. This implies that democracy support should be based on a mutual exploration of new approaches among Western and non-Western countries. This would be a more propitious way forward than thinking that Western democracy supporters should now switch from liberal democratic templates to some imagined non-Western model. After twenty-five years of practice, democracy aid has still not evolved toward a broader search for democratic renovation in *all* democracies.[42]

This chapter has suggested guidelines for how the five axes of variation proposed in chapter 6 can be incorporated into democracy support policies. Foreign policy must do more along these five axes—related to individual rights, economic justice, communitarian identity, participation and representation, and legal norms. Donors must avoid tipping toward forms of variation that merely subvert democracy. These guidelines do not provide detailed or easy solutions; they are offered rather as a potential bridge between conceptual and policy debates. I offer them here as a way of framing future policy considerations, as donors move forward with their formal commitments to support more varied forms of democracy.

CHAPTER 8

THE FUTURE OF DEMOCRATIC VARIATION

D emocracy's global future is uncertain. Modern politics are pulled and stretched in conflicting directions. There are grounds for both democratic pessimism and democratic optimism. The potential for democratic advance is greater than ever before. But doubts about democracy's health are also more far-reaching.

This book has examined democracy's future "beyond the West"—both literally and figuratively. My focus on political trends and debates in non-Western countries was, in part, because I wished to connect these to the challenges facing the international community's democracy-support strategies. But I also looked "beyond the West" in the more conceptual sense of exploring possible innovations to the current forms of Western democracy.

It is frequently argued today that democracy is in crisis all around the world. In its twenty-fifth anniversary edition published in January 2015, the *Journal of Democracy* reflects on the way in which debates have shifted: it focuses principally on the question of whether democracy is or is not in recession. Steven Levitsky and Lucan Way insist that the commonly assumed democratic recession is a myth—largely because analysts overstated the extent of democratic advance in the 1990s, mistakenly assuming that collapsed autocratic regimes were democratizing. In contrast, Larry Diamond points to the broad erosion of the quality of democracy, regardless of whether various regimes are strictly defined as democratic or not. Whatever one's view on this question, it is sobering to see how a debate about the scale of democratic recession has effaced previous expectations that the community of democratic nations would incrementally expand in number.[1]

Although the turmoil and malaise are palpable in many countries, it must surely be an exaggeration to say that democracy is in irredeemable free fall. The pressure for democratic improvement is not unprecedented. Many of the difficult questions now being asked—from Asia to Latin America and from the Middle East to sub-Saharan Africa—have been asked before. The quest for renovation is integral to democracy's very core, part of its Falstaffian dissenting essence. Democracy has always required and thrived on competition over new ideas and the fluid adaptation to new political circumstances.

Yet some aspects of today's uncertainty are new. The current historical juncture is distinctive in its comparatively high degree of indeterminacy. Conflicting trends coexist. There is no one clear dynamic that structures and drives today's global order. Some trends point in democracy's favor; others do not. Still other dynamics invite a more profound discussion about how we need to redefine what effective democratic accountability looks like.

This age of protest has seen popular mobilizations in many nations around the world—from Brazil and Venezuela to Egypt, Ukraine, Turkey, and Thailand. Citizens are more active, more critical, more interconnected, and less fearful of authority. Global opinion polls show increased support for democratic norms. At the same time, several large authoritarian regimes seem to have inoculated themselves effectively from any new democratic wave. Other states languish in a condition of democratic torpor. Formal democracy exists, but falls dramatically short of its emancipatory promise. Still other countries have enjoyed a stirring democratic breakthrough only to suffer a reversion to authoritarianism.

Conflicting maladies threaten to haunt the future: fragmented discord on the one hand, stifling governmental power and control on the other hand. Incipient trends are pregnant with both possibilities. Either could dominate the future. Will the coming global order be rocked by an active discontent that morphs into "mere anarchy . . . loosed upon the world," as W. B. Yeats warned?[2] Or will the future be afflicted by "the disease of over-organization," as Aldous Huxley famously predicted?[3]

That is, will democracy drift toward formless chaos or ever-more restrictive elitism? The paradox is that both of these possibilities have become greater given how democracy has evolved in recent years. Politicians and analysts warn about both of these dangers. Proponents of non-Western democracy call for both types of reform: more civic loosening and more republican state solidity.

The implication of all this is that democracy's future should not be debated in terms of black and white absolutes. The issue is not merely one of metrics: the number of democratic states compared with the number of autocracies. Democracy's future equally depends on the evolution of its meaning, the various understandings of why it is important, and its contrasting forms of institutional expression—in Western and non-Western regions.

BENIGN VARIATION

The search for forms of democracy that differ from prevailing Western norms is legitimate. The development of democratic variation is likely to become more necessary in the reshaped international order. The global importance of this issue is still not fully acknowledged. This book has made the case that much can be gained by a cooperative search for new forms of democratic quality. It has made that case against skeptical voices that dismiss such a pursuit as merely a disingenuous façade for illiberalism and shades of authoritarianism. I have argued that this general goal can be furthered through innovation along five axes of democratic politics. In doing so, I have sought to contribute ideas on how democratic variation can be given more concrete form—at domestic and international levels. Although the agenda of democratic variation requires serious conceptual rethinking, inquiries in this direction need to be better rooted in the world of realistic and concrete policy implications than they have been to date.

At the same time as exploring this as-yet untapped positive potential, the book has cautioned that there is a need to draw boundaries for the concept of non-Western democracy. It has unpacked a series of debates about democratic quality that apply not only beyond but also within the West. In mapping democracy's future, a judicious balance will be required between common principles and divergence.

The challenge for democratic variation is best understood as one of reimagining and revitalizing the popular ownership of democracy—that is, the ways of giving citizens themselves more input into determining how forms of democratic politics evolve. This would be a more fruitful way forward than starting from the assumption that certain values belong to a particular region or country and never change. The right debate is about the fuller and differentiated expression of liberal values, not about what is culturally unique to a particular region.

The agenda for democratic variation bespeaks a need to reimagine democracy. Yet that effort should not transmute into a challenge to universal aspirations that ends up legitimizing illiberalism or semiauthoritarianism. Liberal democracy should be enriched, not bowdlerized. The emphasis should be on democracy as a system that facilitates plurality. Democracy needs to be portrayed less as a definitive set of institutional templates and more as an arena for exploring authentic preferences. It should not be framed as one value that competes with "local values," but rather a framework that allows those other values and local specificities to flourish.[4]

VARIATION IN DEMOCRACY SUPPORT

These conceptual shifts should feed into international democracy-support policies. Democracy assistance needs fine-tuning. Donors need to allow non-Western states to make choices that do not fit the current templates of democracy support. Although Western governments say they support the development of different democratic models, they have not thought enough about the full implications of this commitment. Donors need to anticipate that democratic variation is likely to extend beyond the limited tweaks to existing policy templates that policymakers invariably expect. Democracy support must incorporate elements of deeper variation that currently do not resonate fully with donors' approaches to political reform in non-Western countries.

For a long time, international democracy promoters were in denial about alternative forms. The evidence presented in this book suggests that most are still hesitant to embrace variation. Democracy supporters have unquestionably begun to take the case for variation in democratic models more seriously. At least in some contexts, donors have even moved to the other extreme of placing arguably too much stock in divergent authenticity. But in general, international democracy supporters still need to show a greater willingness to experiment and explore new options in their funding initiatives.

This book has offered guidelines for such innovation across five thematic axes of democracy building. The recommendations suggest that international democracy supporters should explore

- how individual rights can be better nested within a sense of community identity;

- mechanisms allowing wider participation in economic decision-making;

- power sharing that balances inclusiveness with bottom-up civic vibrancy;

- the potential for new social movements to revive, not circumvent, representative institutions; and

- forms of traditional justice that help burnish both local legitimacy and core human-rights standards.

Much progress has been made in recognizing the quasi-permanent durability of hybrid regimes that do not fit the picture of countries heading inexorably toward a natural end point of Western-style liberal democracy. Donors confidently state that they have moved beyond an easy belief in the transition paradigm. However, little progress is evident on what this means in practical terms for international supporters trying to nudge non-Western regimes in a more democratic direction.

Current democracy-support policies exhibit two types of shortcomings. One problem is that donors still operate on the basis of supporting individual sectors of reform in the rather heroic hope that these will meld together into a broader process of democratic transition. While it is widely accepted today that the breakdown of authoritarianism should not be conflated with democratization, in practice policymakers often seem bereft of ideas for moving from authoritarian collapse to democratic consolidation.

The other problem is that donors focus on "working with hybridity" and that this becomes a coda for mere containment—for accepting illiberal regimes as a legitimate and stable resting place between autocracy and liberal democracy. As this approach comes close to presuming that "hybridity" is somehow a natural state of affairs for non-Western societies, it pushes policy to the opposite extreme of blind faith in uniform Western, liberal democracy—an extreme that is equally illusory.

Both approaches cloud the search for healthy forms of democratic variation. The former takes a building-block approach that neglects the question of how the different components of democratic variation knit together at a systemic level. The latter confuses democratic variety for democratic shortfall. Systematic effort is needed to distinguish the benign aspects of hybrid regimes from the malign aspects.

In short, a difficult balance must be achieved. In the future, variation must be accorded more importance than it currently garners. Liberalism sees argumentation as positive in the striving for betterment. But this must not draw oxygen away from other values. Many societies may legitimately want to offset adversarial competition with some sense of harmony, equilibrium, and consensus. International democracy support must work harder to break the assumption that liberalism is synonymous with a Western way of life and conflictive politics.

While variation is much needed, clearer boundaries or redlines will also be necessary in order to determine "indigenous" forms that are positively antidemocratic. To help the healthy emergence of democratic variation, it will be important to prevent bogus practices that parade themselves disingenuously as "authentic democracy." Indulging what are in truth authoritarian dynamics under the guise of supporting non-Western representation is likely to do this agenda little service. Indeed, it risks delegitimizing the quest for pluralism in democratic forms.

RELEGITIMIZING INTERNATIONAL DEMOCRACY POLICIES

Throughout the book, my contention has been that support for democratic variation outside the West is important for the future legitimacy of democracy promotion. This legitimacy has ebbed in recent years. Governments, civic leaders, and thinkers from Asia, the post-Soviet states, the Arab world, and Latin America have questioned both the premises and effectiveness of international democracy support. Although reformers around the world still seek support, they also express a growing skepticism about the role played by the international community.

Drawing the right conceptual boundaries is essential if global democracy support is to be relegitimized. The international community must be far more flexible in the democratic channels it supports, while being confident enough to reject false claims of authenticity. Critics are right that donors are still too hesitant to look beyond the standard features of liberal democracy. Organizations involved in democracy support need to rectify this shortcoming, yet without moving too far in the other direction as they seek quick solutions to the flagging momentum of their democracy-support strategies.

Definitional overstretch is a risk. This is especially so in many places in Africa, Asia, and the Middle East that are strategically important to the West. In the case of strategic allies, Western powers have been tempted to accept autocratic regimes' highly questionable claims to be advancing locally specific forms of democracy—when in fact autocracies have simply reinforced their own hold on power. There is a risk that Western powers will increasingly claim to be supporting non-Western democratic forms simply as a politically correct veneer for their pursuit of strategic interests.

Erasing at least the most egregious double standards from foreign policies would give Western powers more credibility in distinguishing between what they see as legitimate and unacceptable variation in political systems. Eliminating glaring double standards would also help rebut those conservative skeptics who think the case for non-Western democracy is entirely unfounded and who insist that democracy is Western liberal democracy or it is nothing. Separating democratic variation from geopolitics can help give credibility back to international democracy support.

Indeed, one of the main warnings to emerge from the book is that the international community must avoid instrumentalism. Variation must be supported in the spirit of allowing more local choice, rather than replacing a liberal model with support for other templates now seen as in the West's interest. The irony of those advocating, for example, republican or social democracy is that these are still models that originated in the West—even though they are distinct from much maligned neoliberalism. Non-Western states complain a lot about the West's fixation with majoritarianism, but these states also charge Western powers with becoming keener on minority rights only now as the balance of opinion in many states shifts against

Western interests. Such instrumentalism has done much harm to the image of global democracy policies.

Some firmer principles are needed to rebut charges of instrumentalism. Donors must show they are not keen to support non-Western democracy only as and when it suits their own interests. They should be wary of jumping from the frying pan into the fire—of moving to another paradigm that becomes just as skewed as the current one. Specifically, proponents of non-Western democracy should not oppose those reformers bravely seeking to resist some of the more noxious elements of cultural relativism and intolerant "authenticity."

From their perspective, Western donors feel that the support they give to core liberal rights has been twisted and misrepresented as an ethnocentric insistence on a wholesale model. Even if they are partially justified in this complaint, the misperception means at the very least that the logic behind democracy support has been badly conveyed around the world.

The questions raised by this book are of profound importance for the future development of democracy and for existing democracies' efforts to support political reforms abroad. Some analysts doubt the very notion of external international actors encouraging the right degree of democratic variety in other societies. These debates have raised questions about the very essence and legitimacy of democracy promotion.

Critics argue that although support for limited areas of institutional reform is justified, when societies aspire to a deeper sense of autonomy and self-determination, then the whole notion of these values' being promoted from outside is problematic. Skeptics do not believe that the narrative of "local ownership" is an adequate means of restoring legitimacy to the enterprise of democracy promotion. After all, how can a decision about the kind of local variation that is merited be made on a democratic basis when international actors are involved in designing policies? Liberal internationalism seeks to reconcile two aims that increasingly collide: the struggle against authoritarianism and the struggle against Western-arbitrated uniformity.[5]

This book adopts a less damning position. It has argued that the conceptual debates that have become so vibrant in the search for different forms of democracy can find an echo in the world of practical democracy support. The widespread call for "less Western democracy" does not render international democracy support by definition contradictory on its own terms. Yet it is right to point out that these calls will require democracy promoters to walk a series of much thinner lines in the way they carry out their work.

As global power continues to shift, the calls for non-Western forms of democracy will only become stronger. Western democracy promoters will be increasingly criticized for trying to "export" their own political systems in a world less inclined to believe that such systems are the only or the best "game in town." Organizations concerned with international democracy support will need to respond—indeed, responding adequately to the calls for different forms of democracy is likely to be essential for their own long-term survival.

Donors' challenge will be to determine where the core features of liberal democracy are compatible with such widened variation and where, in contrast, some of their own long-held assumptions will need radical revising. On this, the future picture is unlikely to be uniform. In relation to some issues, democracy promoters—both Western and, increasingly, non-Western—are likely to be well positioned to encourage and explore forms of democratic variation that give democracy a new lease on life. Indeed, in some ways, non-Western rising democracies are now well set to add their distinctive input to making liberal democracy more effective.

In relation to other issues, tension is likely to prevail over various actors' fundamentally different concepts of rights, freedoms, and competitive politics. In these cases, showing greater respect for other societies' preferences will require greater humility and different modes of thinking—even if donors do not fall into absolute relativism and believe that democracy can mean anything at all or that deviation from Western democracy is automatically good and incontestably desired by other societies.

DEMOCRACY'S ECLECTIC FUTURES

The debates over non-Western democracy and democratic variation have not appeared overnight. They have been simmering for some time. Yet they have now accumulated a more powerful momentum. This is fueled by the fact that global politics are now besieged by a whole battery of changes—positive and negative.

The rebalancing of power among states is accelerating. Fragmentation, conflict, and tensions over political models are all intensifying within regions such as Africa, Asia, Latin America, and the Middle East, as well as in the former Soviet states. Change at the macro level—relations among nations—is accompanied by unprecedented rates of change at the micro level—political dynamics within countries. As technology-driven individual empowerment and modernization advance at dizzying speed, the relationship between citizen and state is being fundamentally reframed. Although today's drivers of change are not entirely new, their multifarious eclecticism is of a different order: particularly striking is how globalism and localism now advance simultaneously, more handmaidens than zero-sum alternatives. It is the unique *range* of change that most defines the current juncture and its multiple layers of both possibility and risk.

Against this background of all-encompassing change, democracy is unlikely to remain the same. It would be strange to think that it could, when all that conditions and surrounds it is in unpredictable flux. The question of democratic variation may be on the political agenda, but it has only been explored in detail and promoted energetically within a limited and rather esoteric circle of debate. In future political trends, it is likely to move to center stage—as indeed it must. The new global order is not only about the rise and decline of nations but also about the rise and decline of various types of politics within nation-states.

And this brings with it the prospect of democratic renewal beyond the West, in both practical and conceptual senses. Non-Western countries will increasingly seek out their own distinctive paths of democratic development. And these countries will help nourish a rethinking of democratic values and practices globally, including within the West itself. A core imperative for the twenty-first century will be to democratize democracy. In a fast-changing global order, competitive debate over divergent points of view and difference will be needed as part of democracy's very essence.

Liberalism has always faced challenges. As now, it has at many junctures been assailed from the progressive left and the conservative right. If one principle has been core to liberalism's checkered journey, it is the spirit of self-criticism and renewal. The current need to explore innovative forms of democratic quality provides an opportunity for liberal democracy to reestablish that spirit of renewal. The costs of passing that opportunity by will be high.

NOTES

CHAPTER 2

1. Jack Donnelly, "Human Rights, Democracy and Development," *Human Rights Quarterly* 21, no. 3 (August 1999): 630–32.

2. J. Moller and S. Skaaning, "Autocracies, Democracies, and the Violation of Civil Liberties," *Democratization* 20, no. 1 (January 2013): 82–106.

3. David Clark, *The Forward March of Democracy Halted: World Politics and the Rise of Authoritarianism* (London: Henry Jackson Society, 2015).

4. Anne Applebaum, "Developing Nations Could Benefit From Trying Southern Democracy," *Washington Post*, May 16, 2014.

5. National Intelligence Council, *Global Trends 2030: Alternative Worlds* (Washington, DC: National Intelligence Council, 2012), iv–13.

6. Niall Ferguson, *Civilization: The West and the Rest* (London: Penguin Books, 2011).

7. Katherine Fierlbeck, *Globalizing Democracy: Power, Legitimacy and the Interpretation of Democratic Ideas* (Manchester: Manchester University Press, 2008), 3.

8. United Nations General Assembly, Resolution 62/7, "Support by the United Nations System of the Efforts of Governments to Promote and Consolidate New or Restored Democracies," December 13, 2007, www.un.org/en/ga/search/view_doc.asp?symbol=A/RES/62/7.

9. Ban Ki-moon, "Secretary-General's Message for 2011," September 15, 2011, www.un.org/en/events/democracyday/2011/sgmessage2011.shtml.

10. Ibid.

11. United Nations, "Guidance Note of the Secretary-General on Democracy," www.un.org/en/globalissues/democracy/pdfs/FINAL%20Guidance%20Note%20on%20Democracy.pdf.

12. Salman Khurshid, "International Interests in Middle East Security and Non-Proliferation," address at the IISS Manama Dialogue, Manama, December 8, 3013, www.mei.org.in/front/cms/publicationsDetail.php?id=ODEz.

13. Ambassador Chan Heng Chee, "Democracy, Globalisation and Competitiveness in Singapore," lecture, Yale Law School, New Haven, March 8, 2012, www.law.yale.edu/documents/pdf/News_&_Events/Singaporeambassadortalk.pdf.

14. Joanna Lillis, "Kazakhstan: Nazarbayev Rails Against Western Cultural Imperialism," Eurasianet.org, April 26, 2012, www.eurasianet.org/node/65317.

15. Christopher Dickey and Mike Giglio, "The Quiet General: What Does Egypt's Ruler Want," *Daily Beast*, August 16, 2013, www.thedailybeast.com/newsweek/2013/08/16/general-al-sisi-the-man-who-now-runs-egypt.html.

16. James M. Dorsey, "Egypt's Third Way: A Blend of Islamism and Militarism," *Huffington Post*, August 4, 2013, www.huffingtonpost.com/james-dorsey/egypts-third-way-a-blend-_b_3689557.html.

17. Margit Feher, "Hungary Puts Priority on National Interests," *Wall Street Journal*, July 26, 2014, http://online.wsj.com/articles/hungary-puts-priority-on-national-interests-1406382469.

18. U.S. Department of State, Secretary Condoleezza Rice's Interview on Al Arabiya with Randa Abu Alawmy, Cairo, Egypt, June 20, 2005, http://2001-2009.state.gov/secretary/rm/2005/48350.htm.

19. Embassy of the United States in Yaounde, Cameroon, remarks by H. E. Mr. Robert P. Jackson, Cours Supérieur Interarmées de Défense, May 29, 2012, http://yaounde.usembassy.gov/sp_05292012.html.

20. Arielle Lasky, "In Conversation, Albright Lays Out Global Challenges Facing the Next President," *Stanford Report*, June 4, 2008, http://news.stanford.edu/news/2008/june4/albright-060408.html.

21. "Obama Speaks Out on Middle East Democracy," *Project on Middle East Democracy*, June 1, 2009, http://pomed.org/blog-post/democracy-promotion/obama-speaks-out-on-middle-east-democracy.

22. White House, "Remarks by the President on the Middle East and North Africa," May 19, 2011, www.whitehouse.gov/the-press-office/2011/05/19/remarks-president-middle-east-and-north-africa%20.

23. Hillary Clinton, "Remarks at the Launch of Strategic Dialogue With Civil Society," Washington, DC, February 16, 2011, www.state.gov/secretary/20092013clinton/rm/2011/02/156681.htm.

24. Hillary Clinton, "America's Pacific Century," *Foreign Policy*, October 11, 2011, www.foreignpolicy.com/articles/2011/10/11/americas_pacific_century.

25. Deputy Secretary of State William Burns, Remarks to the Press, Cairo, Egypt, July 15, 2013, http://statedept.tumblr.com/post/55536448996/deputy-secretary-william-burns-spoke-to-the-press.

26. Michael McFaul, "Interview: Up to Kyrgyz to Decide How to Build Their Democracy, Obama Adviser Says," Radio Free Europe/Radio Liberty, May 6, 2010, www.rferl.

org/content/Interview_Obama_Adviser_Says_Up_To_Kyrgyz_To_Decide_How_
To_Build_Their_Democracy/2034565.html.

27. "Statement by High Representative Catherine Ashton on the Occasion of the International Day of Democracy," Brussels, September 15, 2011, www.consilium.europa.eu/uedocs/cms_Data/docs/pressdata/EN/foraff/124598.pdf.

28. "Remarks by High Representative Catherine Ashton During Her Visit in Egypt," July 30, 2013, www.consilium.europa.eu/uedocs/cms_data/docs/pressdata/EN/foraff/138449.pdf.

29. Office for the Promotion of Parliamentary Democracy, "Strengthening Parliaments Worldwide," European Parliament, www.europarl.europa.eu/pdf/oppd/Page_1/oppd_flyer_en.pdf.

30. "Transcript of the Public Forum on the Substance of EU Democracy Promotion," Center for European Policy Studies, Brussels, July 2, 2012, www.eu-ipods.ugent.be/media/4396/transcriptspublicforum.pdf.

31. Minister of Foreign Affairs Espen Barth Eide, "States in Transition: Ensuring Equal Rights and Participation for All," speech, Trygve Lie Symposium, New York, September 27, 2012, www.regjeringen.no/en/dep/ud/whats-new/Speeches-and-articles/e_speeches/2012/symposium_new_york.html?id=705568.

32. World Value Survey, "Online Data Analysis," www.wvsevsdb.com/wvs/WVSAnalizeQuestion.jsp.

33. Michael Bratton, "Trends in Popular Attitudes to Multiparty Democracy in Africa, 2000–2012," Afrobarometer Briefing Paper no. 105, October 2012, www.afrimap.org/english/images/documents/afrobriefno105a%5B1%5D.pdf; Stephen D. Collins, "Does Democracy Enjoy Popular Support in East Asia?" *Taiwan Journal of Democracy* 6, no. 2 (December 2010), 152–53; Pew Research Center, "Pew Global Attitudes Project Question Database," accessed February 26, 2015, www.pewglobal.org/question-search/?qid=1180&cntIDs=&stdIDs.

34. Edmund Fawcett, *Liberalism: The Life of an Idea* (Princeton, NJ: Princeton University Press, 2014).

35. Oliver Richmond, Annika Bjorkdahl and Stefanie Kappler, "The Emerging EU Peacebuilding Framework: Confirming or Transcending Liberal Peacebuilding?," *Cambridge Review of International Affairs* 24, no. 3 (August 2011): 463.

36. I am grateful to Sarah Chayes for this point, based on her experience in Afghanistan.

37. Allison McCulloch, "Consociational Settlements in Deeply Divided Societies: The Liberal-Corporate Distinction," *Democratization* 21, no. 3 (December 2012): 501–518.

38. Patrick Köllner and Steffan Kailitz, "Comparing Autocracies: Theoretical Issues and Empirical Analyses," *Democratization* 20, no. 1 (January 2013): 1–12.

39. Farid Guliyev, "Personal Rule, Neo-Patrimonialism, and Regime Typologies: Integrating Dahlian and Weberian Approaches to Regime Studies," *Democratization* 18, no. 3 (May 2011): 575–601.

40. United Nations Development Program, "Informal Justice Systems: Charting a Course for Human Rights Based Engagement," September 2012.

CHAPTER 3

1. Bernard Lewis, "Islam and Liberal Democracy: A Historical Overview," *Journal of Democracy*, vol. 7 (April 1996); Ray Takeyh, "The Lineaments of Islamic Democracy," *World Policy Journal* (Winter 2001–2002): 60; Asef Bayat, *Islam and Democracy: What Is the Real Question?* (Amsterdam: Amsterdam University Press, 2007). The three authors offer different arguments of this debate.

2. Nader Hashemi, *Islam, Secularism and Liberal Democracy: Toward a Democratic Theory for Muslim Societies* (Oxford: Oxford University Press, 2009); Mohamed Elhachmi Hamdi, "Islam and Liberal Democracy: The Limits of the Western Model," *Journal of Democracy* 7, no. 2 (1996): 81–85.

3. Larbi Sadiki, *The Search for Arab Democracy: Discourses and Counter-Discourses* (New York: Columbia University Press, 2004).

4. Khaled Abou El Fadl, *Islam and the Challenge of Democracy* (Princeton, NJ: Princeton University Press, 2004), 5.

5. Takeyh, "The Lineaments of Islamic Democracy," 62.

6. Ibid.

7. Justice Tassaduq Hussain Jillani, "Democracy and Islam: An Odyssey in Braving the Twenty-First Century," *Brigham Young University Law Review*, no. 3 (September 2006).

8. Tauseef Ahmad Parray, "'Islamic Democracy' or Democracy in Islam," *World Journal of Islamic History and Civilization* 2, no. 2 (2012): 67.

9. Omar Ashour, "Democratic Islam? Assessing the Bases of Democracy in Islamic Political Thought," *McGill Journal of Middle East Studies* 9, no. 1 (2008): 14–16.

10. Ibid., 9.

11. Mahmoud Sadri and Ahmad Sadri, trans. and ed., *Reason, Freedom and Democracy in Islam: Essential Writings of Abdolkarim Soroush* (New York: Oxford University Press, 2000), 148–51.

12. Parray, "'Islamic Democracy' or Democracy in Islam"; Fred Dallmayr, "Islam and Democracy: Reflections on Abdolkarim Soroush," University of Notre Dame, April 2011, www.drsoroush.com/English/On_DrSoroush/E-CMO-20010407-Islam_And_Democracy-Reflections_On_Abdolkarim_Soroush.html.

13. Raja Bahlul, "Toward an Islamic Conception of Democracy: Islam and the Notion of Public Reason," *Critique: Critical Middle Eastern Studies* 12, no. 1 (Spring 2003).

14. Ahmad Yousif, "Islam, Minorities and Religious Freedom: A Challenge to Modern Theory of Pluralism," *Journal of Muslim Minority Affairs* 20, no. 1 (2000): 30.

15. Binnaz Toprak, "Islam and Democracy in Turkey," *Turkish Studies* 6, no. 2 (June 2005): 168.

16. Martin Beck and Simone Hüser, *Political Change in the Middle East: An Attempt to Analyse the Arab Spring*, German Institute of Global and Area Studies Working Papers, 2012.

17. Ashour, "Democratic Islam?," 8.

18. Jan Claudius Völkel, *Middle East and North Africa: Regional Trends 2000–2015 and Scenarios 2015–2030*, Track 1—People and Communities, Bertelsmann Stiftung and Club of Madrid report for the Next Generation Democracy Project, 2014, www.bti-project.org/uploads/tx_itao_download/NGD_MENA_03.pdf.

19. Shadi Hamid, *Temptations of Power: Islamists and Illiberal Democracy in a New Middle East* (Oxford: Oxford University Press, 2014).

20. Alfred Stepan and Juan Linz, "Democratization Theory and the Arab Spring," *Journal of Democracy* 24, no. 2 (2013): 19.

21. Frédéric Volpi, "Explaining (and Re-Explaining) Political Change in the Middle East During the Arab Spring: Trajectories of Democratization and of Authoritarianism in the Maghreb," *Democratization* 20, no. 6 (April 2012): 969–90.

22. Olivier Roy, "The Transformation of the Arab World," *Journal of Democracy* 23, no. 3 (2012): 8.

23. Dalia Mogahed, "Islam and Democracy," *Gallup World Poll Special Report: Muslim World* (Princeton, NJ: Gallup Organization, 2006).

24. Asef Bayat, "Arab Revolutions and the Study of Middle Eastern Societies," *International Journal of the Middle East* 43, no. 3 (2011).

25. Parray, "'Islamic Democracy' or Democracy in Islam," 79.

26. Ronald L. Nettler, "Islam, Politics and Democracy: Mohamed Talbi and Islamic Modernism," *Political Quarterly* 71, no. 1 (2000): 55.

27. Ziya Onis, "Sharing Power: Turkey's Democratization Challenge in the Age of AKP Hegemony," *Insight Turkey* 15, no. 2 (2013): 103–122.

28. Orhan Pamuk, *Snow* (New York: Vintage, 2005), 247.

29. Laurence Whitehead, "Alternative Models of Democracy in Latin America," *Brown Journal of World Affairs* 17, no. 1 (Fall/Winter 2010): 75.

30. Ibid., 77.

31. Koen Abts and Stefan Rummens, "Populism Versus Democracy," *Political Studies* 55 (2007); Francisco Panizza and Romina Miorelli, "Populism and Democracy in Latin America," *Ethics and International Affairs* 42; Kurt Weyland, "Latin America's Four Political Models," *Journal of Democracy* 4, no. 6 (1995): 125–39.

32. Evelina Dagnino, Alberto Olvera, and Aldo Panfichi, *Democratic Innovation in the South: Participation and Representation in Asia, Africa and Latin America* (Buenos Aires: Clacso, 2008).

33. Monica Barczak, "Representation by Consultation? The Rise of Direct Democracy in Latin America," *Latin American Politics and Society* 43, no. 3 (Autumn 2011): 37–59.

34. Anita Breuer, "The Problematic Relation Between Direct Democracy and Accountability in Latin America: Evidence From the Bolivian Case," *Bulletin of Latin American Research* 27, no. 1 (2008).

35. Whitehead, "Alternative Models of Democracy in Latin America," 81–82.

36. Abts and Rummens, "Populism Versus Democracy."

37. Whitehead, "Alternative Models of Democracy in Latin America," 81.

38. Panizza and Miorelli, "Populism and Democracy in Latin America," 39–45.

39. Luis A. Costa Pinto, "Populism in Latin America," Woodrow Wilson International Center for Scholars, 2002.

40. Barczak, "Representation by Consultation? The Rise of Direct Democracy in Latin America," 43.

41. Abts and Rummens, "Populism Versus Democracy," 409.

42. Ibid., 414.

43. Panizza and Miorelli, "Populism and Democracy in Latin America," 44.

44. Whitehead, "Alternative Models of Democracy in Latin America," 82.

45. Dagnino, Olvera, and Panfichi, *Democratic Innovation in the South.*

46. Barczak, "Representation by Consultation? The Rise of Direct Democracy in Latin America," 38.

47. Breuer, "The Problematic Relation Between Direct Democracy and Accountability in Latin America: Evidence From the Bolivian Case."

48. Dagnino, Olvera, and Panfichi, *Democratic Innovation in the South.*

49. Matthew Todd Bradley, "'The Other': Precursory African Conceptions of Democracy," *International Studies Review* 7 (2005).

50. Ibid., 418.

51. Claude Ake, *Is Africa Democratizing?* (Lagos: Malthouse Press, 1996), 6.

52. Claude Ake, "Unique Case for African Democracy," *International Affairs* 69, no. 2 (1993): 242–43.

53. Claude Ake, "Rethinking Democracy in Africa," *Journal of Democracy* 2, no. 1 (1991): 34.

54. Bradley, "'The Other': Precursory African Conceptions of Democracy," 419–20.

55. Ezeanyika S. Ezeanyika, "Can Western Democracy Models Be Institutionalized in Africa? Reviewing Contemporary Problems and Prospects," *Ufahamu: A Journal of African Studies* 36, no. 2 (2011): 8–9.

56. Bradley, "'The Other': Precursory African Conceptions of Democracy," 409.

57. Ibid.

58. Ibid., 421; Olusegun Oladipo, "Tradition and the Quest for Democracy in Africa," 2001, *Polylog: Forum for Intercultural Philosophy*, vol. 2 (2000).

59. Bradley, "The Other': Precursory African Conceptions of Democracy," 411.

60. Ibid.

61. Kwasi Wiredu, "Democracy and Consensus in African Traditional Politics: A Plea for a Non-Party Polity," *Centennial Review* 39, no. 1 (1995).

62. Bradley, "'The Other': Precursory African Conceptions of Democracy," 412.

63. Maxwell Owuso, "Democracy and Africa: A View From the Village," *Journal of Modern African Studies* 30, no. 3 (1992): 372.

64. Michael Bratton and Richard Houessau, "Demand for Democracy Is Rising in Africa, but Most Political Leaders Fail to Deliver," Afrobarometer Policy Paper no. 11, April 2014, 16.

65. Wiredu, "Democracy and Consensus in African Traditional Politics."

66. Jacques M. Nzouankeu, "The African Attitude to Democracy," *International Social Science Journal* 128 (1991): 373.

67. Surain Subramaniam, "The Asian Values Debate: Implications for the Spread of Liberal Democracy," *Asian Affairs* 27, no. 1 (Spring 2000).

68. Daniel A. Bell, "A Communitarian Critique of Liberalism," *Analyse & Kritik* 25 (2005): 219.

69. Joseph Chan, "An Alternative View," *Journal of Democracy* 8, no. 3 (April 1997).

70. Yung-Myung Kim, "'Asian-Style Democracy': A Critique From East Asia," *Asian Survey* 37, no. 12 (1997).

71. Subramaniam, "The Asian Values Debate," 21.

72. Mark R. Thompson, "Whatever Happened to 'Asian Values'?," *Journal of Democracy* 12, no. 4 (October 2011).

73. Subramaniam, "The Asian Values Debate," 24.

74. Stephen J. Hood, "The Myth of Asian-Style Democracy," *Asian Survey* 38, no. 9 (September 1998).

75. Ibid., 857.

76. Clark D. Neher, "Asian-Style Democracy," *Asian Survey* 34, no. 11 (November 1994).

77. Takashi Inoguchi, "Asian-Style Democracy?" in *The Changing Nature of Democracy*, ed. Takashi Inoguchi, Edward Newman, and John Keane (Tokyo: United Nations University Press, 1998), 181.

78. Daniel Bell, *Beyond Liberal Democracy: Political Thinking in the East Asian Context* (Princeton, NJ: Princeton University Press, 2006).

79. Inoguchi, "Asian-Style Democracy?," 176.

80. Subramaniam, "The Asian Values Debate," 25.

81. Daniel Bell, *The East Asian Challenge for Democracy* (Cambridge: Cambridge University Press, 2013).

82. Fareed Zakaria, "Culture Is Destiny: A Conversation With Lee Kuan Yew," *Foreign Affairs* 73 (March–April 1994), 110.

83. Ibid.

84. Thompson, "Whatever Happened to 'Asian Values'?," 156.

85. Ibid.

86. Hood, "The Myth of Asian-Style Democracy," 861.

87. Inoguchi, "Asian-Style Democracy?"

88. Alexi Voskressenski, "Alternative Votes: 'Non-Western' Democracies and Asian Political Systems," *Global Asia* 8, no. 3 (2013): 79–83.

89. Y. Chu Chang and B. Welsh, "South East Asia: Source of Regime Support," *Journal of Democracy* 24, no. 2 (2013): 161.

90. Hood, "The Myth of Asian-Style Democracy," 858.

91. Doowon Suh, "The Challenges to Democracy in Korea," in *A New Context for EU-Korea Relations*, ed. Richard Youngs (Madrid: FRIDE, 2013), 74.

92. I am grateful to Roland Rich for these examples.

93. Francis Fukuyama, "The Illusion of Exceptionalism," *Journal of Democracy* 8, no. 3 (July 1997): 148.

94. Neher, "Asian-Style Democracy," 959–60.

95. Sungmoon Kim, *Confucian Democracy in East Asia: Theory and Practice* (Cambridge: Cambridge University Press, 2014).

96. Subramaniam, "The Asian Values Debate," 26.

97. Inoguchi, "Asian-Style Democracy?," 181.

98. Subramaniam, "The Asian Values Debate," 24.

99. Mark Leonard, ed., *China 3.0* (London: European Council on Foreign Relations, 2012).

100. Ethan Scheiner, *Democracy Without Competition in Japan: Opposition Failure in a One-Party Dominant State* (New York: Cambridge University Press, 2005); J. A. A. Stockwin, "Reshaping of Japanese Politics and the Question of Democracy," *Asia-Pacific Review* 9, no. 1 (2002): 56.

101. Bradley Richardson and Dennis Patterson, "Political Traditions and Political Change: The Significance of Postwar Japanese Politics for Political Science," *Annual Review of Political Science*, vol. 4 (2001).

102. Ibid., 103–104.

103. Stockwin, "Reshaping of Japanese Politics," 47.

104. Ibid., 47.

105. Arend Lijphart, "The Puzzle of Indian Democracy: A Reinterpretation," RGICS Paper no. 18, Rajiv Gandhi Institute for Contemporary Studies, 1994; Teresita Schaffer and Hermani Saigal-Arora, "India: A Fragmented Democracy," *Washington Quarterly* 22, no. 4 (Autumn 1999): 141–50.

106. Atul Kohli, "Introduction," in *The Success of India's Democracy*, ed. Atul Kohli (Cambridge: Cambridge University Press, 2001), 4–5, 11.

107. Ashutosh Varshney, "Why Democracy Survives," *Journal of Democracy* 9, no. 3 (1998): 36–50.

108. Lijphart, "The Puzzle of Indian Democracy: A Reinterpretation."

109. Schaffer and Saigal-Arora, "India: A Fragmented Democracy," 141–50; Ahrar Ahmad, "The State, Participation, and Constitutionalism: Political Crises and Democracy in India," *Asian Affairs: An American Review* 26, no. 3 (1999): 123–36.

110. Kohli, "Introduction," 2.

111. James Manor, "India Defies the Odds: Making Federalism Work," *Journal of Democracy* 9, no. 3 (July 1998).

112. Ibid.

113. Kripa Ananth Pur and Mick Moore, "Ambiguous Institutions: Traditional Governance and Local Democracy in Rural South India," *Journal of Development Studies* 46, no. 4 (April 2010): 603–623.

114. Subrata K. Mitra, "Democracy's Resilience: Tradition, Modernity and Hybridity in India," *Harvard International Review* 32, no. 4 (Winter 2011); David Gilmartin, "Rule of Law, Rule of Life: Caste, Democracy, and the Courts in India," *American Historical Review* 115, no. 2 (April 2010): 413.

115. Ashutosh Varshney, "India's Democratic Challenge," *Foreign Affairs* 86, no. 2 (March/ April 2007).

116. Gilmartin, "Rule of Law, Rule of Life," 424; Kohli, "Introduction," 16.

117. Mukulika Banerjee, "India: The Next Superpower?: Democracy," *IDEAS Reports— Special Reports*, ed. Nicholas Kitchen (London: London School of Economics and Political Science, LSE IDEAS, 2012), www.lse.ac.uk/IDEAS/publications/reports/pdf/ SR010/banerjee.pdf.

118. Francis Fukuyama, *Political Order and Political Decay: From the Industrial Revolution to the Globalization of Democracy* (London: Profile Books, 2014).

119. Daniel Bochsler, Hanspeter Kriesi, et al., *Democracy in the Age of Globalization and Mediatisation* (London: Palgrave Macmillan, 2013).

120. Inoguchi, "Asian-Style Democracy?," 181.

CHAPTER 4

1. Kishore Mahbubani, *The Great Convergence: Asia, the West and the Logic of One World* (New York: PublicAffairs, 2014).

2. Daniel A. Bell, "A Communitarian Critique of Liberalism," *Analyse & Kritik* 25 (2005).

3. Paul Ginsborg, *Democracy: Crisis and Renewal* (London: Profile Books, 2008), 42.

4. Francis Fukuyama, *Political Order and Political Decay: From the Industrial Revolution to the Globalization of Democracy* (New York: Farrar, Straus, and Giroux, 2014), 333.

5. Milja Kurki, "Democracy and Conceptual Contestability: Reconsidering Conceptions of Democracy in Democracy Promotion," *International Studies Review* 12, no. 3 (September 2010).

6. Katherine Fierlbeck, *Globalizing Democracy: Power, Legitimacy and the Interpretation of Democratic Ideas* (Manchester: Manchester University Press, October 2008), 95.

7. Francis Fukuyama, *The Origins of Political Order: From Prehuman Times to the French Revolution* (New York: Farrar, Straus, and Giroux, 2012).

8. Michael Saward, *Democracy* (London: Polity, 2003), vii, 46, and 114.

9. Fukuyama, *The Origins of Political Order*, 7, 224.

10. David Chandler, "Promoting Democratic Norms? Social Constructivism and the 'Subjective' Limits to Liberalism," *Democratization* 20, no. 2 (2013): 215–39.

11. Donald Horowitz, "Ethnic Power Sharing: Three Big Problems," *Journal of Democracy* 25, no. 2 (2014).

12. Cristobal Rovira Kaltwasser, "The Ambivalence of Populism: Threat and Corrective for Democracy," *Democratization* 19, no. 2 (2012): 184–208.

CHAPTER 5

1. Michael Saward, *Democracy* (Cambridge: Polity, 2003), vii and 46.

2. Michael Crozier, Samuel Huntington, and Joji Watanuki, *The Crisis of Democracy: Report on the Governability of Democracies to the Trilateral Commission* (New York: New York University Press, 1973), 161.

3. Paul Ginsborg, *Democracy: Crisis and Renewal* (London: Profile Books, 2009).

4. Tony Judt, *Reappraisals: Reflections on the Forgotten Twentieth Century* (New York: Penguin Books, 2008), 89.

5. Donatella Della Porta, *Can Democracy Be Saved? Participation, Deliberation, and Social Movements* (Cambridge: Polity Press, 2013).

6. David Priestland, *Merchant, Soldier, Sage: A New History of Power* (London: Penguin Books, 2012).

7. For overviews, see C. B. Macpherson, *The Real World of Democracy* (Oxford: Clarendon Press, 1966); or David Held, *Models of Democracy*, 2nd edition (Cambridge: Polity Press, 1996). For a book examining the nature of liberal democracy in different regional contexts, see Frederick C. Schaffer, *Democracy in Translation* (Ithaca, NY: Cornell University Press, 1998); Larbi Sadiki, *The Search for Arab Democracy: Discourses and Counter-Discourses* (New York: Columbia University Press, 2004); Boaventura de Sousa Santos, *Democratizing Democracy: Beyond the Liberal Democratic Canon* (London: Verso, 2005); and Daniel Bell, *Beyond Liberal Democracy: Political Thinking for an East Asian Context* (Princeton, NJ: Princeton University Press, 2006).

8. John Keane, *The Life and Death of Democracy* (New York: Simon and Schuster, 2009).

9. Moises Naím, *The End of Power* (New York: Basic Books, 2013).

10. Mark Chou, *Theorising Democide: Why and How Democracies Fail* (London: Palgrave, 2013), 49.

11. Beate Jahn, *Liberal Internationalism: Theory, History, and Practice* (London: Palgrave, 2013).

12. Alan Ryan, *The Making of Modern Liberalism* (Princeton, NJ: Princeton University Press, 2012), 11.

13. Mark Mazower, "Has Democracy Had Its Day?" *Prospect Magazine*, May 2013, www.prospectmagazine.co.uk/features/has-democracy-had-its-day.

14. Richard Beardsworth, *Cosmopolitanism and International Relations Theory* (Cambridge: Polity, 2011); Robert Fine, *Cosmopolitanism* (London: Routledge, 2007); Andrew Linklater, *The Transformation of Political Community* (Cambridge: Cambridge University Press, 1998).

15. Daniel Bell, *Beyond Liberal Democracy: Political Thinking in the East Asian Context* (Princeton, NJ: Princeton University Press, 2006).

16. Ryan, *The Making of Modern Liberalism*, 31.

17. Christopher Hobson, "Liberal Democracy and Beyond: Extending the Sequencing Debate," *International Political Science Review* 33, no. 4 (2012): 441.

18. Devin Joshi, "The Protective and Development Varieties of Liberal Democracy: A Difference in Kind or Degree?," *Democratization* 20, no. 2 (2013): 187–214.

19. Slavoj Zizek, *Living in the End Times* (London: Verso, 2010), 5, 37, 157, and 200.

20. Slavoj Zizek, *The Year of Dreaming Dangerously* (London: Verso, 2012), 87.

21. Pankaj Mishra, "The Western Model is Broken," *Guardian*, October 14, 2014.

22. Joao Carlos Espada, "The Sources of Extremism," *Journal of Democracy* 23, no. 4 (2012): 16–23.

23. Wolfgang Streeck, "The Crises of Democratic Capitalism," *New Left Review* 71 (September–October 2011); Wolfgang Streeck, "Markets and Peoples: Democratic Capitalism and European Integration," *New Left Review* 73 (January–February 2012); Colin Crouch, *The Strange Non-Death of Neo-Liberalism* (London: Polity Press, 2011).

24. Zizek, *Living in the End Times*, 5, 37, 157, and 200.

25. Steven Webber and Bruce Jentleson, *The End of Arrogance: America in the Global Competition of Ideas* (Boston: Harvard University Press, 2010), 104.

26. Jan Aart Scholte, "Reinventing Global Democracy," *European Journal of International Relations* 20, no. 1 (2014).

27. Tim Dunne and Trine Flockhart, *Liberal World Orders* (Oxford: Oxford University Press, 2013).

28. Ewan Harrison and Sara McLaughlin Mitchell, *The Triumph of Democracy and the Eclipse of the West* (London: Palgrave Macmillan, 2014).

29. Eric Li, "The Life of the Party," *Foreign Affairs* 92, no. 1 (2013): 34–46.

30. John Gaventa, "Triumph, Deficit or Contestation? Deepening the 'Deepening Democracy' Debate," IDS Working Paper no. 264 (July 2006).

31. Della Porta, *Can Democracy Be Saved?*

32. Manuel Castells, *Networks of Outrage and Hope: Social Movements in the Internet Age* (London: Polity Press, 2012).

33. Paul Mason, *Why It's Kicking Off Everywhere: The New Global Revolutions* (New York: Verso Books, 2012).

34. Mary Kaldor and Sabine Selchow, *The Bubbling up of Subterranean Politics in Europe*, (London: LSE Civil Society and Human Security Unit, 2012), 18–19 and 24.

35. Zygmunt Bauman, *Liquid Times: Living in an Age of Uncertainty* (Oxford: Polity, 2007).

36. F. Miszlivetz, "'Lost in Transformation': The Crisis of Democracy and Civil Society," in *Global Civil Society 2012: Ten Years of Critical Reflection* (London: Palgrave, 2012), 62–64.

37. Helmut Anheier, Mary Kaldor, and Marlies Glasius, The Global Civil Society Yearbook: Lessons and Insights 2001–2011," in *Global Civil Society 2012: Ten Years of Critical Reflection*, ed. Mary Kaldor, Henrietta L. Moore, and Sabine Selchow (London: Palgrave Macmillan, 2012).

38. Pierre Rosanvallon, *Counter-Democracy: Politics in an Age of Distrust* (Cambridge: Cambridge University Press, 2009).

39. Charles Tilly, *Democracy* (Cambridge: Cambridge University Press, 2007), 23.

40. Pippa Norris, *Critical Citizens: Global Support for Democratic Governance* (Oxford: Oxford University Press, 1999).

41. David Held, *Models of Democracy* (Redwood City: Stanford University Press, 2006), 263–71 and 307.

42. James Bohman, *Democracy Across Borders: From Demos to Demoi* (Cambridge, MA: MIT Press, 2007); John Dryzek, *Deliberative Global Politics: Discourse and Democracy in a Divided World* (Cambridge: Polity Press, 2006); Ulrich Beck and E. Grande, "Cosmopolitanism: Europe's Way Out of Crisis," *European Journal of Social Theory* 10, no. 1 (2007): 67–85; Larry Siedentop, *Democracy in Europe* (London: Penguin, 2000).

43. Della Porta, *Can Democracy Be Saved?*

44. Ivan Krastev, *In Mistrust We Trust: Can Democracy Survive When We Don't Trust Our Leaders* (TED Conferences, 2013), 44.

45. Ivan Krastev, *Democracy Disrupted* (Philadelphia: University of Pennsylvania Press, 2014); Rosanvallon, *Counter-Democracy: Politics in an Age of Distrust*.

46. Andre Bachtiger and Dominik Hangartner, "When Deliberative Theory Meets Empirical Political Science: Theoretical and Methodological Challenges in Political Deliberation," *Political Studies* 58, no. 4, 609–629.

47. Edmund Fawcett, *Liberalism: The Life of an Idea* (Princeton, NJ: Princeton University Press, 2014).

48. Thomas M. Franck, "Is Personal Freedom a Western Value?" *American Society of International Law* 91, no. 4 (October 1997): 594–627.

49. Quentin Skinner, *Liberty Before Liberalism* (Cambridge: Cambridge University Press, 2012).

50. Ryan, *The Making of Modern Liberalism*, 8 and 71.

51. Luc Ferry, *A Brief History of Thought: A Philosophical Guide to Living* (New York: Harper Perennial, 2010), 266.

52. Arend Lijphart, *Democracies: Patterns of Majoritarian and Consensus Government in Twenty-Nine Countries* (New Haven: Yale University Press, 1984), 30.

53. Ryan, *The Making of Modern Liberalism*, 39.

54. Judt, *Reappraisals: Reflections on the Forgotten Twentieth Century*, 10.

55. John Kampfner, *Freedom for Sale: Why the World Is Trading Democracy for Security* (London: Simon and Schuster, 2009), ch. 7.

56. Jan-Werner Muller, *Contesting Democracy: Political Ideas in Twentieth-Century Europe,* (New Haven, CT: Yale University Press, 2011).

57. Philip Pettit, "Depoliticizing Democracy," *Ratio Juris* 17, no. 1 (2004): 52–65.

58. Michael Coppedge, John Gerring, and Staffan Lindberg, "Global Standards, Local Knowledge: The Varieties of Democracy," V-Dem Institute, 2012, 17–18.

59. Ibid., 26.

60. Matthijs Bogaards, "Where to Draw the Line? From Degree to Dichotomy in Measures of Democracy," *Democratization* 19, no. 2 (2012): 690–712.

61. Michael Coppedge and John Gerring, "Conceptualising and Measuring Democracy: A New Approach," *Perspectives in Politics* 9, no. 2 (2011).

62. Amy Alexander and Christian Welzel, "Measuring Effective Democracy: The Human Empowerment Approach," *Comparative Politics* 33, no. 3 (2011).

CHAPTER 6

1. Larry Diamond, *The Spirit of Democracy: The Struggle to Build Free Societies Throughout the World* (New York: St. Martin's Griffin, 2009).

2. Michael Saward, *Democracy* (Cambridge: Polity Press, 2003), 113.

3. Milja Kurki, "Democracy and Conceptual Contestability: Reconsidering Conceptions of Democracy in Democracy Promotion," *International Studies Review* 12, no. 3 (September 2010).

4. Laurence Whitehead, "Alternative Models of Democracy in Latin America," *Brown Journal of World Affairs* 17, no. 1 (Fall/Winter 2010).

5. T. H. Marshall, *Citizenship and Social Class and Other Essays* (Cambridge: Cambridge University Press, 1950).

6. David Collier and Steven Levitsky, "Democracy With Adjectives: Conceptual Innovation in Comparative Research," *World Politics* 48, no. 3 (April 1997).

7. Kate Nash, "Human Rights, Markets, States, and Movements," *Open Democracy*, July 18, 2014.

8. Tony Judt, *Reappraisals: Reflections on the Forgotten Twentieth Century* (London: Random House, 2009), 429.

9. Marc F. Plattner, "Liberalism and Democracy: Can't Have One Without the Other," *Foreign Affairs* (March–April 1998).

10. Michael Coppedge, John Gerring, and Staffan Lindberg, "Codebook Version 1.0," V-Dem Institute, March 2014.

11. Staffan Lindberg, Michael Coppedge, John Gerring, and Jan Teorell, "V-Dem: A New Way to Measure Democracy," *Journal of Democracy* 25, no. 3 (July 2014): 159–69.

12. Daniel A. Bell, "Which Rights Are Universal?," *Political Theory* 27, no. 6 (December 1999).

13. David Elstein, "Mou Zongsan's New Confucian Democracy," *Contemporary Political Theory* 11, no. 2 (May 2012): 192–210.

14. P. Ben-Nun Bloom, "Globalisation Has Contributed to Declining Levels of Religious Freedom Across the World," LSE *EUROPP* (blog), July 14, 2014, http://blogs.lse.ac.uk/europpblog/2014/07/14/globalisation-has-contributed-to-declining-levels-of-religious-freedom-across-the-world.

15. For a discussion of this, see Alan Wolfe, *The Future of Liberalism* (New York: Knopf, 2009).

16. Cairo Institute for Human Rights Studies, *Citizenship in Egyptian Political Discourse*, EUSpring project report, 2015, http://www2.warwick.ac.uk/fac/soc/pais/research/clusters/irs/euspring.

17. Pankaj Mishra, "After Paris: It's Time for a New Enlightenment," *Guardian*, January 20, 2015.

18. Thomas Piketty, *Capital in the Twenty-First Century* (Cambridge, MA: Belknap Press, 2014).

19. Beate Jahn, "Interventions in Foreign Countries to Promote Liberal Objectives Are Bound to Fail Due to the Internal Contradictions Within Liberalism Itself," LSE *EUROPP* (blog), June 16, 2014, http://blogs.lse.ac.uk/politicsandpolicy/interventions-in-foreign-countries-to-promote-liberal-objectives-are-bound-to-fail.

20. Katherine Fierlbeck, *Globalizing Democracy: Power, Legitimacy and the Interpretation of Democratic Ideas* (Manchester: Manchester University Press, 2008), 110.

21. Daniel A. Bell, "A Communitarian Critique of Liberalism," *Analyse & Kritik* 25 (2005): 221.

22. See special edition of *Journal of European Public Policy* 20, no. 2 (2013), especially the opening essay, S. Kröger and D. Friedrich, "Introduction: The Representative Turn in EU Studies," 155–70.

23. Carne Ross, *The Leaderless Revolution: How Ordinary People Will Take Power and Change Politics in the 21st Century* (New York: Plume, 2011).

24. Y. Sintomer, R. Traub-Merz, and J. Zhang, eds., *Participatory Budgeting in Asia and Europe: Key Challenges of Participation* (Basingstoke: Palgrave, 2013).

25. For a review of the literature of the variation in customary systems, see Anne Helium, "Human Rights and Gender Relations in Postcolonial Africa: Options and Limits for the Subjects of Legal Pluralism," *Law and Social Inquiry* 25, no. 2 (2000): 635–55.

26. United Nations, "Informal Justice Systems: Charting a Course for Human Rights-Based Engagement" (New York: United Nations, n.d.), www.unwomen.org/-/media/

headquarters/attachments/sections/library/publications/2013/1/informal-justice-systems-charting-a-course-for-human-rights-based-engagement.pdf.

CHAPTER 7

1. Donatella Della Porta, *Can Democracy Be Saved?* (Cambridge: Polity, 2013), 188; Milja Kurki, "Democracy and Conceptual Contestability: Reconsidering Conceptions of Democracy in Democracy Promotion," *International Studies Review* 12, no. 3 (September 2010).

2. Armine Ishkanian, "Engineered Civil Society: The Impact of 20 Years of Democracy Promotion on Civil Society Development in Former Soviet Countries," in *Civil Society and Democracy Promotion*, ed. Timm Beichelt, Irene Hahn, Frank Schimmelfennig, and Susann Worschech (London: Palgrave Macmillan, 2014).

3. Della Porta, *Can Democracy Be Saved?*

4. Irene Hahn-Fuhr and Susan Worschech, "Introduction," in *Civil Society and Democracy Promotion*.

5. An exception is Kurki, "Democracy and Conceptual Contestability."

6. Michael McFaul, *Advancing Democracy Abroad: Why We Should and How We Can* (Lanham, MD: Rowman and Littlefield, 2009), 66.

7. UNDP Afghanistan, "Traditional Justice in Afghanistan," United Nations Development Program, Justice and Human Rights in Afghanistan, May 2010, www.undp.org.af/Projects/Justice/FactSheetTraditional%20Justice.pdf.

8. "UNDP Helps Traditional Leaders Build Stronger Local Justice Systems in South Sudan," United Nations Development Program, July 27, 2011, www.no.undp.org/content/undp/en/home/presscenter/pressreleases/2011/07/27/traditional-leaders-build-stronger-local-justice-systems.

9. UNDP, UNICEF, and UN Women, "Informal Justice: Charting a Course for Human Rights-Based Engagement," n.d., www.undp.org/content/dam/undp/library/Democratic%20Governance/Access%20to%20Justice%20and%20Rule%20of%20Law/Informal-Justice-Systems-Charting-a-Course-for-Human-Rights-Based-Engagement.pdf.

10. UNDP, "Development Programmes Must Engage Informal Justice Systems, UN Study Says," United Nations Development Program, September 26, 2012, www.undp.org/content/undp/en/home/presscenter/pressreleases/2012/09/26/development-programmes-must-engage-informal-justice-systems-un-study-says.

11. Diana Felix da Costa and John Karlsrud, "Contextualising Liberal Peacebuilding for Local Circumstances: UNMISS and Local Peacebuilding in South Sudan," *Journal of Peacebuilding and Development* 7, no. 2 (2013): 53–66.

12. USAID, "Projects: Kenya," USAID Land Tenure and Property Rights Portal, http://usaidlandtenure.net/projects/kenya.

13. USAID Afghanistan, "Rule of Law Stabilization Program—Informal Component," www.usaid.gov/node/50356.

14. USAID Afghanistan, "Two Justice Systems Work Together," July 24, 2011, http://afghanistan.usaid.gov/en/USAID/Article/2311/Two_Justice_Systems_Work_Together.

15. USAID Afghanistan, "Elders Combat Conflict in Arghandab," http://afghanistan.usaid.gov/en/USAID/Article/2086/Elders_Combat_Conflict_in_Arghandab.

16. Ali Wardak and Humayun Hamidzada, "The Search for Legitimate Rule, Justice and a Durable Peace: Hybrid Models of Governance in Afghanistan," *Journal of Peacebuilding and Development* 7, no. 2 (2013): 79–88.

17. EAS and European Commission, "Guidance Note on the Use of Conflict Analysis in External Action," 2013, http://capacity4dev.ec.europa.eu/sites/default/files/file/13/11/2013_-_1900/guidance_note_on_conflict_analysis_in_support_of_eu_external_action.pdf.

18. Volker Hauck, Greta Galeazzi, and Jan Vanheukelom, "The EU's State-Building Contracts," ECDPM Briefing Note 60, European Center for Development Policy Management, December 2013.

19. Thomas Carothers and Saskia Brechenmacher, *Closing Space: Democracy and Human Rights Support Under Fire* (Washington, DC: Carnegie Endowment for International Peace, 2014).

20. European Parliament, "Improving the EU's Support for Civil Society in Its Neighbourhood: Rethinking Procedures, Ensuring That Practices Evolve," European Parliament study, July 2012.

21. European Union, *Annual Report on Human Rights and Democracy in the World 2012* (2013), 69–70, http://register.consilium.europa.eu/pdf/en/13/st09/st09431.en13.pdf.

22. European Commission, *Social Protection in EU Development Cooperation*, COM (2012), 446.

23. ODI-Netherlands Ministry of Foreign Affairs, *Development, Security and Transitions in Fragile States*, meeting report, February 2010, 17.

24. EIDHR, "Apoyo a la Promoción de la Democracia y de los Derechos Humanos en America Latina: Compendido 2007–2009," September 2010.

25. Observatorio Cuidadano, "Proyecto: La Discriminacion en Chile en un Contexto de Globalizacion Economica. Una Propuesta de Trabajo Desde Los Derechos Humanos y la Interculturalidad," www.observatorio.cl/proyectos.

26. See the Center for Dialogue and Reconciliation website, www.cdr-india.org.

27. EIDHR, "Promoting Democracy and Human Rights in the European Neighbourhood and Partnership Countries and in Kazakhstan and Tajikistan," European Instrument for Democracy and Human Rights, June 2010, 11, http://ec.europa.eu/europeaid/what/human-rights/documents/enpi_compedium_2007_2009_en.pdf.

28. Ibid., 24.

29. Live & Learn Environmental Education, "Building Grassroots Democracy in Fiji," www.livelearn.org/projects/building-grassroots-democracy-fiji.

30. EuropeAid, "Delivering on Democracy: Highlight of the Semester," European Instrument for Human Rights and Democracy, January–June 2011, 23, www.eidhr.eu/files/dmfile/EIDHR_DemocracyReport2.pdf.

31. Jonas Wolff, "Democracy Promotion and Civilian Power: The Example of Germany's 'Value-Oriented' Foreign Policy," *German Politics* 22, no. 4 (2013): 477–93.

32. Katrine Haukenes and Annette Freyberg-Inan, "Enforcing Consensus? The Hidden Bias in EU Democracy Promotion in Central and Eastern Europe," *Democratization* 20, no. 7 (2013): 1268–96.

33. International IDEA, "Customary Governance and Democracy-Building: Executive Summary," Addis Ababa Conference, September 15–16, 2010, www.idea.int/resources/analysis/upload/Executive-summary.pdf.

34. Anne Wetzel and Jan Orbie, "The EU's Promotion of External Democracy: In Search of the Plot," CEPS Policy Brief 281, 2012, 3.

35. Netherlands Foreign Ministry, "Responsible for Freedom: Human Rights in Foreign Policy," 2011, 30, www.government.nl/documents-and-publications/notes/2011/08/17/human-rights-memorandum-responsible-for-freedom-2011.html.

36. For the basic presentation of these concepts of offensive and defensive liberalism, see Benjamin Miller, "Democracy Promotion: Offensive Liberalism Versus the Rest (of IR Theory)," *Millennium* 38, no. 3 (2010): 561–91.

37. Thomas Carothers and Oren Samet-Marram, "The New Global Marketplace of Political Change," Carnegie Paper, Carnegie Endowment for International Peace, April 2014.

38. This section draws on extensive material published as part of the Carnegie Rising Democracies Network. See http://carnegieendowment.org/specialprojects/RisingDemocraciesNetwork.

39. Trine Flockhart, Charles A. Kupchan, Christina Lin, Bartlomiej E. Nowak, Patrick W. Quirk, and Lanxin Xiang, *Liberal Order in a Post-Western World* (Washington, DC: German Marshall Fund/Transatlantic Academy, 2014), 149, www.gmfus.org/publications/liberal-order-post-western-world.

40. Omar Encarnacion, "The West Should Rethink Its Approach for Promoting Gay Rights Abroad and Instead Focus on Strengthening Democracy and Civil Society," LSE *EUROPP* (blog), August 5, 2014.

41. Paul Ginsborg, *Democracy: Crisis and Renewal* (London: Profile Books, 2008), 53 and 117.

42. Thomas Carothers, "Democracy Aid at 25: Time to Choose," *Journal of Democracy* 26, no. 1 (January 2015).

CHAPTER 8

1. Steven Levitsky and Lucan Way, "The Myth of Democratic Recession," *Journal of Democracy* 26, no. 1 (January 2015); Larry Diamond, "Facing Up to the Democratic Recession, *Journal of Democracy* 26, no. 1 (January 2015).

2. See William Butler Yeats, "The Second Coming," 1919.

3. Aldous Huxley, *Brave New World Revisited* (New York: Harper Perennial Modern Classics, 2005), 119.

4. David Held, *Models of Democracy*, 3rd edition (Oxford: Wiley-Blackwell, 2006), 261.

5. Hans Agné, "Is Successful Democracy Promotion Possible? The Conceptual Problem," *Democratization* 21, no. 1 (2014): 49–71.

SELECTED BIBLIOGRAPHY

Abou El Fadl, Khaled. *Islam and the Challenge of Democracy*. Princeton, NJ: Princeton University Press, 2004.

Abts, Koen, and Stefan Rummens. "Populism Versus Democracy." *Political Studies* 55, no. 2 (2007): 405–424.

Agné, Hans. "Is Successful Democracy Promotion Possible? The Conceptual Problem." *Democratization* 21, no. 1 (2014): 49–71.

Ahmad, Ahrar. "The State, Participation, and Constitutionalism: Political Crises and Democracy in India." *Asian Affairs: An American Review* 26, no. 3 (1999): 123–36.

Ake, Claude. *Is Africa Democratizing?* Lagos: Malthouse Press, 1996.

———. "Rethinking Democracy in Africa." *Journal of Democracy* 2, no. 1 (1991): 32–44.

———. "The Unique Case for African Democracy." *International Affairs* 69, no. 2 (1993): 239–44.

Alexander, Amy, and Christian Welzel. "Measuring Effective Democracy: The Human Empowerment Approach." *Comparative Politics* 33, no. 3 (2011): 271–89.

Ananth Pur, Kripa, and Mick Moore. "Ambiguous Institutions: Traditional Governance and Local Democracy in Rural South India." *Journal of Development Studies* 46, no. 4 (April 2010): 603–623.

Ashour, Omar. "Democratic Islam? Assessing the Bases of Democracy in Islamic Political Thought." *McGill Journal of Middle East Studies* 9, no. 1 (2008): 7–27.

Bachtiger, Andre, and Dominik Hangartner. "When Deliberative Theory Meets Empirical Political Science: Theoretical and Methodological Challenges in Political Deliberation." *Political Studies* 58, no. 4 (2010): 609–629.

Barczak, Monica. "Representation by Consultation? The Rise of Direct Democracy in Latin America." *Latin American Politics and Society* 43, no. 3 (Autumn 2011): 37–59.

Bauman, Zygmunt. *Liquid Times: Living in an Age of Uncertainty*. Oxford: Blackwell's, 2007.

Bayat, Asef. "Arab Revolutions and the Study of Middle Eastern Societies." *International Journal of the Middle East* 43, no. 3 (August 2011): 319–329.

———. *Islam and Democracy: What Is the Real Question?* Amsterdam: Amsterdam University Press, 2007.

Beardsworth, Richard. *Cosmopolitanism and International Relations Theory*. Cambridge: Polity, 2011.

Beck, Martin, and Simone Hüser. *Political Change in the Middle East: An Attempt to Analyse the Arab Spring*. German Institute of Global and Area Studies Working Papers, 2012.

Beck, Ulrich, and E. Grande. "Cosmopolitanism: Europe's Way Out of Crisis." *European Journal of Social Theory* 10, no. 1 (2007): 67–85.

Beichelt, Timm, Irene Hahn, Frank Schimmelfennig, and Susann Worschech, eds. *Civil Society and Democracy Promotion*. London: Palgrave Macmillan, 2014.

Bell, Daniel A. "A Communitarian Critique of Liberalism." *Analyse & Kritik* 25 (2005): 215–38.

———. *Beyond Liberal Democracy: Political Thinking in the East Asian Context*. Princeton, NJ: Princeton University Press, 2006.

———. *The East Asian Challenge for Democracy*. Cambridge: Cambridge University Press, 2013.

———. "Which Rights Are Universal?" *Political Theory* 27, no. 6 (December 1999): 849–56.

Bochsler, Daniel, Hanspeter Kriesi, et al. *Democracy in the Age of Globalization and Mediatisation*. London: Palgrave Macmillan, 2013.

Bogaards, Matthijs. "Where to Draw the Line? From Degree to Dichotomy in Measures of Democracy." *Democratization* 19, no. 2 (2012): 690–712.

Bohman, James. *Democracy Across Borders: From Demos to Demoi*. Cambridge, MA: MIT Press, 2007.

Bratton, Michael, and Richard Houessau. "Demand for Democracy Is Rising in Africa, but Most Political Leaders Fail to Deliver." Afrobarometer Policy Paper no. 11 (2014).

Breuer, Anita. "The Problematic Relation Between Direct Democracy and Accountability in Latin America: Evidence From the Bolivian Case." *Bulletin of Latin American Research* 27, no. 1 (2008): 1–23.

Carothers, Thomas, and Saskia Brechenmacher. *Closing Space: Democracy and Human Rights Support Under Fire.* Washington, DC: Carnegie Endowment for International Peace, 2014.

Carothers, Thomas. "Democracy Aid at 25: Time to Choose." *Journal of Democracy* 26, no. 1 (January 2015): 59–73.

Carothers, Thomas, and Oren Samet-Marram. "The New Global Marketplace of Political Change." Carnegie Paper. Washington, DC: Carnegie Endowment for International Peace, 2015.

Castells, Manuel. *Networks of Outrage and Hope: Social Movements in the Internet Age.* London: Polity Press, 2012.

Chan, Joseph. "An Alternative View." *Journal of Democracy* 8, no. 3 (April 1997): 35–48.

Chandler, David. "Promoting Democratic Norms? Social Constructivism and the 'Subjective' Limits to Liberalism." *Democratization* 20, no. 2 (2013): 215–39.

Chang, Alex, Yun-han Chu, and Bridget Welsh. "South East Asia: Source of Regime Support."·*Journal of Democracy* 24, no. 2 (2013): 150–64.

Chou, Mark. *Theorising Democide: Why and How Democracies Fail.* London: Palgrave, 2013.

Clark, David. *The Forward March of Democracy Halted: World Politics and the Rise of Authoritarianism.* London: Henry Jackson Society, 2015.

Collier, David, and Steven Levitsky. "Democracy With Adjectives: Conceptual Innovation in Comparative Research." *World Politics* 48, no. 3 (April 1997): 430–51.

Collins, Stephen D. "Does Democracy Enjoy Popular Support in East Asia?" *Taiwan Journal of Democracy* 6, no. 2 (December 2010): 151–55.

Coppedge, Michael, and John Gerring. "Conceptualising and Measuring Democracy: A New Approach." *Perspectives in Politics* 9, no. 2 (2011): 247–67.

Coppedge, Michael, John Gerring, and Staffan Lindberg. "Global Standards, Local Knowledge: The Varieties of Democracy." V-Dem Institute, 2012.

Crouch, Colin. *The Strange Non-Death of Neo-Liberalism.* London: Polity, 2011.

Crozier, Michael, Samuel Huntington, and Joji Watanuki. *The Crisis of Democracy: Report on the Governability of Democracies to the Trilateral Commission.* New York: New York University Press, 1973.

Dagnino, Kurt, Alberto Olvera, and Aldo Panfichi. *Democratic Innovation in the South: Participation and Representation in Asia, Africa and Latin America.* Buenos Aires: Clacso, 2008.

Diamond, Larry. "Facing Up to the Democratic Recession." *Journal of Democracy* 26, no. 1 (January 2015): 141–55.

———. *The Spirit of Democracy: The Struggle to Build Free Societies Throughout the World.* New York: St. Martin's Griffin, 2009.

Donnelly, Jack. "Human Rights, Democracy and Development." *Human Rights Quarterly* 21, no. 3 (August 1999): 608–32.

Dryzek, John. *Deliberative Global Politics: Discourse and Democracy in a Divided World.* Cambridge: Polity Press, 2006.

Dunne, Tim, and Trine Flockhart. *Liberal World Orders.* Oxford: Oxford University Press, 2013.

Elstein, David. "Mou Zongsan's New Confucian Democracy." *Contemporary Political Theory* 11, no. 2 (May 2012): 192–210.

Espada, Joao Carlos. "The Sources of Extremism." *Journal of Democracy* 23, no. 4 (2012): 16–23.

Ezeanyika, Ezeanyika S. "Can Western Democracy Models Be Institutionalized in Africa? Reviewing Contemporary Problems and Prospects." *Ufahamu: A Journal of African Studies* 36, no. 2 (2011): 1–21.

Fawcett, Edmund. *Liberalism: The Life of an Idea.* Princeton, NJ: Princeton University Press, 2014.

Felix da Costa, Diana, and John Karlsrud. "Contextualising Liberal Peacebuilding for Local Circumstances: UNMISS and Local Peacebuilding in South Sudan." *Journal of Peacebuilding and Development* 7, no. 2 (2013): 53–66.

Ferguson, Niall. *Civilization: The West and the Rest.* London: Penguin Books, 2011.

Ferry, Luc. *A Brief History of Thought: A Philosophical Guide to Living.* New York: Harper Perennial, 2010.

Fierlbeck, Katherine. *Globalizing Democracy: Power, Legitimacy and the Interpretation of Democratic Ideas.* Manchester: Manchester University Press, 2008.

Fine, Robert. *Cosmopolitanism.* London: Routledge, 2007.

Franck, Thomas M. "Is Personal Freedom a Western Value?" *American Society of International Law* 91, no. 4 (October 1997): 594–627.

Fukuyama, Francis. "The Illusion of Exceptionalism." *Journal of Democracy* 8, no. 3 (July 1997): 146–49.

———. *The Origins of Political Order: From Prehuman Times to the French Revolution*. New York: Farrar, Straus, and Giroux, 2012.

———. *Political Order and Political Decay: From the Industrial Revolution to the Globalization of Democracy*. London: Profile Books, 2014.

Gaventa, John. "Triumph, Deficit or Contestation? Deepening the 'Deepening Democracy' Debate." IDS Working Paper no. 264 (July 2006).

Gilmartin, David. "Rule of Law, Rule of Life: Caste, Democracy, and the Courts in India." *American Historical Review* 115, no. 2 (April 2010): 406–27.

Ginsborg, Paul. *Democracy: Crisis and Renewal*. London: Profile Books, 2008.

Guliyev, Farid. "Personal Rule, Neo-Patrimonialism, and Regime Typologies: Integrating Dahlian and Weberian Approaches to Regime Studies." *Democratization* 18, no. 3 (May 2011): 575–601.

Hamdi, Mohamed Elhachmi. "Islam and Liberal Democracy: The Limits of the Western Model." *Journal of Democracy* 7, no. 2 (April 1996): 81–85.

Hamid, Shadi. *Temptations of Power: Islamists and Illiberal Democracy in a New Middle East*. Oxford: Oxford University Press, 2014.

Harrison, Ewan, and Sara McLaughlin Mitchell. *The Triumph of Democracy and the Eclipse of the West*. London: Palgrave Macmillan, 2014.

Hashemi, Nader. *Islam, Secularism and Liberal Democracy: Toward a Democratic Theory for Muslim Societies*. Oxford: Oxford University Press, 2009.

Haukenes, Katrine, and Annette Freyberg-Inan. "Enforcing Consensus? The Hidden Bias in EU Democracy Promotion in Central and Eastern Europe." *Democratization* 20, no. 7 (2013): 1268–96.

Held, David. *Models of Democracy*, 3rd edition. Redwood City: Stanford University Press, 2006.

Helium, Anne. "Human Rights and Gender Relations in Postcolonial Africa: Options and Limits for the Subjects of Legal Pluralism." *Law and Social Inquiry* 25, no. 2 (2000): 635–55.

Hobson, Christopher. "Liberal Democracy and Beyond: Extending the Sequencing Debate." *International Political Science Review* 33, no. 4 (2012): 441–54.

Hood, Stephen J. "The Myth of Asian-Style Democracy." *Asian Survey* 38, no. 9 (September 1998): 853–66.

Horowitz, Donald. "Ethnic Power Sharing: Three Big Problems." *Journal of Democracy* 25, no. 2 (2014): 5–20.

Huxley, Aldous. *Brave New World Revisited*. New York: Harper Perennial Modern Classics, 2005.

Inoguchi, Takashi, Edward Newman, and John Keane, eds. *The Changing Nature of Democracy*. Tokyo: United Nations University Press, 1998.

Jahn, Beate. *Liberal Internationalism: Theory, History, and Practice*. London: Palgrave, 2013.

Jillani, Tassaduq Hussain. "Democracy and Islam: An Odyssey in Braving the Twenty-First Century." *Brigham Young University Law Review*, no. 3 (September 2006): 727–54.

Joshi, Devin. "The Protective and Development Varieties of Liberal Democracy: A Difference in Kind or Degree?" *Democratization* 20, no. 2 (2013): 187–214.

Judt, Tony. *Reappraisals: Reflections on the Forgotten Twentieth Century*. New York: Penguin Books, 2008.

Kaldor, Mary, Sabine Selchow, and Henrietta L. Moore, eds. *Global Civil Society 2012: Ten Years of Critical Reflection*. London: Palgrave, 2012.

Kaltwasser, Cristobal Rovira. "The Ambivalence of Populism: Threat and Corrective for Democracy." *Democratization* 19, no. 2 (2012): 184–208.

Kampfner, John. *Freedom for Sale: Why the World Is Trading Democracy for Security*. London: Simon and Schuster, 2009.

Keane, John. *The Life and Death of Democracy*. New York: Simon and Schuster, 2009.

Kim, Yung-Myung. "'Asian-Style Democracy': A Critique From East Asia." *Asian Survey* 37, no. 12 (1997): 1119–34.

Kohli, Atul, ed. *The Success of India's Democracy*. Cambridge: Cambridge University Press, 2001.

Köllner, Patrick, and Steffan Kailitz. "Comparing Autocracies: Theoretical Issues and Empirical Analyses." *Democratization* 20, no. 1 (January 2013): 1–12.

Krastev, Ivan. *Democracy Disrupted*. Philadelphia: University of Pennsylvania Press, 2014.

Kröger, Sandra, and Dawid Friedrich. "Introduction: The Representative Turn in EU Studies." *Journal of European Public Policy* 20, no. 2 (2013): 155–70.

Kurki, Milja. "Democracy and Conceptual Contestability: Reconsidering Conceptions of Democracy in Democracy Promotion." *International Studies Review* 12, no. 3 (September 2010): 362–86.

Levitsky, Steven, and Lucan Way. "The Myth of Democratic Recession." *Journal of Democracy* 26, no. 1 (January 2015): 45–58.

Lijphart, Arend. *Democracies: Patterns of Majoritarian and Consensus Government in Twenty-Nine Countries.* New Haven, CT: Yale University Press, 1984.

———. "The Puzzle of Indian Democracy: A Reinterpretation." RGICS Paper no. 18. Rajiv Gandhi Institute for Contemporary Studies, 1994.

Lindberg, Staffan I., Michael Coppedge, John Gerring, and Jan Teorell. "V-Dem: A New Way to Measure Democracy." *Journal of Democracy* 25, no. 3 (July 2014): 159–69.

Linklater, Andrew. *The Transformation of Political Community.* Cambridge: Cambridge University Press, 1998.

Macpherson, C. B. *The Real World of Democracy.* Oxford: Clarendon Press, 1966.

Mahbubani, Kishore. *The Great Convergence: Asia, the West and the Logic of One World.* New York: PublicAffairs, 2014.

Manor, James. "India Defies the Odds: Making Federalism Work." *Journal of Democracy* 9, no. 3 (July 1998): 21–35.

Marshall, T. H. *Citizenship and Social Class and Other Essays.* Cambridge: Cambridge University Press, 1950.

Mason, Paul. *Why It's Kicking Off Everywhere: The New Global Revolutions.* New York: Verso Books, 2012.

McCulloch, Allison. "Consociational Settlements in Deeply Divided Societies: The Liberal-Corporate Distinction." *Democratization* 21, no. 3 (December 2012): 501–518.

McFaul, Michael. *Advancing Democracy Abroad: Why We Should and How We Can.* Lanham, MD: Rowman and Littlefield, 2009.

Miller, Benjamin. "Democracy Promotion: Offensive Liberalism Versus the Rest (of IR Theory)." *Millennium* 38, no. 3 (2010): 561–91.

Mitra, Subrata K. "Democracy's Resilience: Tradition, Modernity and Hybridity in India." *Harvard International Review* 32, no. 4 (Winter 2011).

Mogahed, Dalia. "Islam and Democracy." *Gallup World Poll Special Report: Muslim World.* Princeton, NJ: Gallup Organization, 2006.

Moller, Jorgen, and Svend-Erik Skaaning. "Autocracies, Democracies, and the Violation of Civil Liberties." *Democratization* 20, no. 1 (January 2013): 82–106.

Muller, Jan-Werner. *Contesting Democracy: Political Ideas in Twentieth Century Europe.* New Haven, CT: Yale University Press, 2011.

Naím, Moises. *The End of Power.* New York: Basic Books, 2013.

Neher, Clark D. "Asian-Style Democracy." *Asian Survey* 34, no. 11 (November 1994): 949–61.

Nettler, Ronald L. "Islam, Politics and Democracy: Mohamed Talbi and Islamic Modernism." *Political Quarterly* 71, no. 1 (2000): 50–59.

Norris, Pippa. *Critical Citizens: Global Support for Democratic Governance.* Oxford: Oxford University Press, 1999.

Nzouankeu, Jacques M. "The African Attitude to Democracy." *International Social Science Journal* 128 (1991).

Oladipo, Olusegun. "Tradition and the Quest for Democracy in Africa." *Polylog: Forum for Intercultural Philosophy* 2 (2000).

Onis, Ziya. "Sharing Power: Turkey's Democratization Challenge in the Age of AKP Hegemony." *Insight Turkey* 15, no. 2 (2013): 103–122.

Owusu, Maxwell. "Democracy and Africa: A View From the Village." *Journal of Modern African Studies* 30, no. 3 (1992): 369–96.

Panizza, Francisco, and Romina Miorelli. "Populism and Democracy in Latin America." *Ethics and International Affairs* 23, no. 1 (2009): 39–46.

Parray, Tauseef Ahmad. "'Islamic Democracy' or Democracy in Islam." *World Journal of Islamic History and Civilization* 2, no. 2 (2012): 66–86.

Pettit, Philip. "Depoliticizing Democracy." *Ratio Juris* 17, no. 1 (March 2004): 52–65.

Piketty, Thomas. *Capital in the Twenty-First Century.* Cambridge, MA: Belknap Press, 2014.

Plattner, Marc F. "Liberalism and Democracy: Can't Have One Without the Other." *Foreign Affairs* (March–April 1998).

Della Porta, Donatella. *Can Democracy Be Saved? Participation, Deliberation, and Social Movements.* Cambridge: Polity Press, 2013.

Priestland, David. *Merchant, Soldier, Sage: A New History of Power.* London: Penguin Books, 2012.

Richardson, Bradley, and Dennis Patterson. "Political Traditions and Political Change: The Significance of Postwar Japanese Politics for Political Science." *Annual Review of Political Science* 4 (2001).

Richmond, Oliver, Annika Bjorkdahl, and Stefanie Kappler. "The Emerging EU Peacebuilding Framework: Confirming or Transcending Liberal Peacebuilding?" *Cambridge Review of International Affairs* 24, no. 3 (August 2011): 449–69.

Rosanvallon, Pierre. *Counter-Democracy: Politics in an Age of Distrust.* Cambridge: Cambridge University Press, 2009.

Ross, Carne. *The Leaderless Revolution: How Ordinary People Will Take Power and Change Politics in the 21st Century.* New York: Plume, 2011.

Roy, Olivier. "The Transformation of the Arab World." *Journal of Democracy* 23, no. 3 (2012): 5–18.

Ryan, Alan. *The Making of Modern Liberalism.* Princeton, NJ: Princeton University Press, 2012.

Sadiki, Larbi. *The Search for Arab Democracy: Discourses and Counter-Discourses.* New York: Columbia University Press, 2004.

Sadri, Mahmoud, and Ahmad Sadri, trans. and ed. *Reason, Freedom and Democracy in Islam: Essential Writings of Abdolkarim Soroush.* New York: Oxford University Press, 2000.

Santos, Boaventura de Sousa. *Democratizing Democracy: Beyond the Liberal Democratic Canon.* London: Verso, 2005.

Saward, Michael. *Democracy.* London: Polity, 2003.

Schaffer, Frederick C. *Democracy in Translation.* Ithaca, NY: Cornell University Press, 1998.

Schaffer, Teresita, and Hermani Saigal-Arora. "India: A Fragmented Democracy." *Washington Quarterly* 22, no. 4 (Autumn 1999): 141–50.

Scheiner, Ethan. *Democracy Without Competition in Japan: Opposition Failure in a One-Party Dominant State.* New York: Cambridge University Press, 2005.

Scholte, Jan Aart. "Reinventing Global Democracy." *European Journal of International Relations* 20, no. 1 (2014): 3–29.

Siedentop, Larry. *Democracy in Europe.* London: Penguin, 2000.

Sintomer, Yves, Rudolf Traub-Merz, and Junhua Zhang, eds. *Participatory Budgeting in Asia and Europe: Key Challenges of Participation.* Basingstoke: Palgrave, 2013.

Skinner, Quentin. *Liberty Before Liberalism.* Cambridge: Cambridge University Press, 2012.

Stepan, Alfred, and Juan Linz. "Democratization Theory and the Arab Spring." *Journal of Democracy* 24, no. 2 (2013): 15–30.

Stockwin, J. A. A. "Reshaping of Japanese Politics and the Question of Democracy." *Asia-Pacific Review* 9, no. 1 (2002): 45–59.

Streeck, Wolfgang. "The Crises of Democratic Capitalism." *New Left Review* 71 (September–October 2011): 5–29.

———. "Markets and Peoples: Democratic Capitalism and European Integration." *New Left Review* 73 (January–February 2012): 63–71.

Subramaniam, Surain. "The Asian Values Debate: Implications for the Spread of Liberal Democracy." *Asian Affairs* 27, no. 1 (Spring 2000): 19–35.

Takeyh, Ray. "The Lineaments of Islamic Democracy." *World Policy Journal* 18, no. 4 (Winter 2001/2002): 59–67.

Thompson, Mark R. "Whatever Happened to 'Asian Values'?" *Journal of Democracy* 12, no. 4 (October 2011): 154–65.

Tilly, Charles. *Democracy.* Cambridge: Cambridge University Press, 2007.

Toprak, Binnaz. "Islam and Democracy in Turkey." *Turkish Studies* 6, no. 2 (June 2005): 167–86.

Varshney, Ashutosh. "Why Democracy Survives." *Journal of Democracy* 9, no. 3 (1998): 36–50.

Volpi, Frédéric. "Explaining (and Re-Explaining) Political Change in the Middle East During the Arab Spring: Trajectories of Democratization and of Authoritarianism in the Maghreb." *Democratization* 20, no. 6 (April 2012): 969–90.

Voskressenski, Alexi. "Alternative Votes: 'Non-Western' Democracies and Asian Political Systems." *Global Asia* 8 no. 3 (2013): 79–83.

Wardak, Ali, and Humayun Hamidzada. "The Search for Legitimate Rule, Justice and a Durable Peace: Hybrid Models of Governance in Afghanistan." *Journal of Peacebuilding and Development* 7, no. 2 (2013): 79–88.

Webber, Steven, and Bruce Jentleson. *The End of Arrogance: America in the Global Competition of Ideas.* Boston: Harvard University Press, 2010.

Weyland, Kurt. "Latin America's Four Political Models." *Journal of Democracy* 4, no. 6 (1995): 125–39.

Whitehead, Laurence. "Alternative Models of Democracy in Latin America." *Brown Journal of World Affairs* 17, no. 1 (Fall/Winter 2010): 75–88.

Wiredu, Kwasi. "Democracy and Consensus in African Traditional Politics: A Plea for a Non-Party Polity." *Centennial Review* 39, no. 1 (1995).

Wolfe, Alan. *The Future of Liberalism.* New York: Knopf, 2009.

Wolff, Jonas. "Democracy Promotion and Civilian Power: The Example of Germany's 'Value-Oriented' Foreign Policy." *German Politics* 22, no. 4 (2013): 477–93.

Youngs, Richard, ed. *A New Context for EU-Korea Relations.* Madrid: FRIDE, 2013.

Yousif, Ahmad. "Islam, Minorities and Religious Freedom: A Challenge to Modern Theory of Pluralism." *Journal of Muslim Minority Affairs* 20, no. 2 (2000): 29–41.

Zizek, Slavoj. *Living in the End Times.* London: Verso, 2010.

———. *The Year of Dreaming Dangerously.* London: Verso, 2012.

INDEX

Tables and figures are indicated by "t" and "f."

A

active citizenship, Western ideas of, 57
activism, alternative forms of, 122–124
administrative bureaucracy, power of in Japan, 65
Afghanistan, 24, 64, 133, 134, 139
Africa, 12, 49–56, 68, 126
AKP. *See* Justice and Development Party (AKP)
alternative models, 14, 106
Arab awakening, reform produced, 32
Arab Spring, 29, 36
Ashton, Catherine, 18–19
Asia, 56–64, 68, 124, 146–147
AsiaBarometer, 61
Asian model, 12, 56–57
Asian view, of Singaporean representatives, 16
Association of Southeast Asian Nations (ASEAN) Intergovernmental Commission on Human Rights, 139
associative democracy, 97
authoritarian regimes, 33t
"authentic democracy," 129
authenticity, 81, 135, 163
authoritarian dynamics, 55t, 79–81, 161, 162
authoritarian regimes, 12, 60t, 158

authoritarianism
    in Africa, 53
    covert support for, 6, 79
    Egypt reverted to, 38
    reform toward a more open form of, 32
    struggle against, 164
"autonomy," 92
axes. *See* democratic variation, axes for

B

Bali Democratic Forum, 147
Bangkok declaration (1993), 57
benign variation, 159–160
Bharatiya Janata Party (BJP), in India, 66
Bolivia, 137, 138
Bolsa Família welfare program, 48
Brazil, 43–45, 48, 49, 144–145
Burma, 21, 61

C

capacity building, prioritizing, 132
Charlie Hebdo journalists, killings of, 114
chauvinistic populism, 104
Chávez, Hugo, 48, 80
Chavista Revolution, 49
chieftaincy, in Africa, 52
Chile, 137, 145

China, 63, 90, 124
Christians, in the Middle East, 141
citizen-initiated procedures, in Latin
    America, 48
citizens
    demands in the Middle East, 35
    feeling disenfranchised, 85
    less fearful of authority, 158
    monitoring bodies, 97
citizenship
    campaigns for more active, 96
    debates over the notion of, 35
    passive and individual-based, 150
civic activism, 124
civic awareness, 135
civic debate, 79
civic movements, 93
civic protesters, younger generation of, 94
civic rights, in the Middle East, 34
civic watchdogs, monitoring public policy,
    92
civil society, 130, 131
civil society organizations, 135–137, 143
"civil state" model, 34
"civilian power" identity, of German policy,
    138
"clash of democratizations," 90
Clinton, Hillary, 17–18
collective identity rights, 112
collective public sphere, 46
colonialism, in Africa, 49–50
combined democracy, theory of, 153
communal institutional forms, 78
communalism, in Africa, 51
communalist democracy, 51
Communist Party, 63
communitarian liberalism, 95
communitarian philosophers, 88
communitarian thinkers, 74
communitarianism, 118–122, 152
community
    appropriate forms of, 119
    consensus or collective judgment of,
        30

control over individuals, 32
empowerment, 110, 111
    identity, 161
    moral identities, 150
"compensatory alleviation," providing, 108
conceptual boundaries, drawing, 163
conceptual debates, 150
"concrete universality," 102
confessional system, in Lebanon, 42
conflict interventions, recent failures of, 23
conflict resolution models, 24
Confucianism, 57, 119
Congress Party, in India, 66
consensual "compact," for use of EU funds,
    134–135
consensual democracy, 39, 52, 69, 99, 119
consensual models, 40, 138–139
consensus, 79, 119, 152
consensus building, African tradition of, 50
consensus model, of democracy, 97
consociational democracy, 24
constitutionalized liberal rights, 112
contestation, new movements about, 131
context-legitimate democracy, 111
context-specific democracy, 122
"contextual legitimacy," 23
core freedoms, 35, 106
core non-Western values, waiting to take
    root, 21
core principles, speaking out for, 17
core values, changing over time, 77
"corporate consociationalism," 24
cosmopolitanism, 87–88
"counter democracy," protest politics as, 92
"critical citizenship," 92
crowdsourcing, 117, 154
Cuban model, influential in Latin America,
    12
"cultural diversity," 140
cultural nationalism, emergence of, 57
customary governance, harnessing, 139
customary justice system, in Kenya, 134
customary systems, dismissive attitude
    toward, 126

D

debt, easy provision of, 89
decentralization, 51, 59
decisionmaking, 116, 117
"deep," or social democracy, EU's concept
    of, 137
"deep state," guardians of, 140
"defensive liberalism," 142
"definitional fallacy," defining democracy,
    84–85
"definitional gerrymandering," avoiding,
    106
definitional points, assuming political
    meaning, 9
delegative democracy (*caesarismo
    democratico*), 47
deliberative democracy, 92–93, 94, 122
democracy
    with abridged liberal rights, 8
    associative, 97
    authentic, 20, 129
    categorizing, 109
    classifying, 98
    combined, 153
    communalist, 51
    consensual, 39, 52, 99
    consensus-oriented and consultative
        forms of, 50
    consociational, 24
    context-legitimate, 111
    context-specific, 122
    counter, 92
    curtailing personal and civil liberties,
        13
    deepening, 116
    deliberative, 92–93, 94, 122
    demand for across Africa, 56
    different approach to, 148
    direct, 46, 48, 94
    economic, 116, 153
    economic policies, compatibility with,
        117
    electoral, 99
    equalitarian, 99

exploring authentic preferences, 160
forms of, 159
in free fall, 158
future of, 102, 157, 159, 165–167
illiberal, 8, 34
in Latin America, 45
liberal, 8, 14, 15, 22, 23, 24, 49, 75,
    76, 85, 86, 99, 108, 113, 149, 152,
    160
liquid, 91
majoritarian, 99
making choices, 69
managed, 80
meaning of, 84–85
measuring, 98–100
in the Middle East, 41–43
models, 79, 109
monitory, 85
moral principles, 31
movement, 51
Muslim, 41
non-Western, 1, 3, 5, 8, 11–27,
    71–81, 112, 159
in North Africa and the Middle East,
    29–43
older more liberal than younger, 69
participative, 91–94
participatory, deliberative, 99
principles of, 9
problems with in U.S. and Europe, 86
pro-protest, equating with, 16
protective, 61
quality, erosion of, 157
reduced to balance among power
    blocs, 120
reimagining, 84, 159
relegitimizing, 92
revitalizing, 3
rising, 142, 147
social, 88, 118
spirit of, 102–105
unlikely to remain the same, 166
variations in, 3, 99, 109
Western, 11, 13, 21, 23, 51, 77,

84–88, 103, 130, 146, 148, 157, 165
Democracy Action Plans, 136–137
democracy agenda, 144
democracy assistance, 160
democracy index 2014
    African countries, 54t–55t
    Asian countries, 60t
    Latin America, 44t
    North Africa and the Middle East, 33t
Democracy Profiles, drawn up by EU delegations, 136
democracy promotion, 162, 164, 165
democracy support, 146, 151, 155, 160–162
democratic advance, potential for, 157
democratic civil society, concept of, 153
democratic concepts, abuse of, 56
democratic control, over economic processes, 75
democratic credentials, of Turkey, 145
democratic deliberation, 153
democratic forms, 1, 5–6, 15
democratic government, no single model for, 18
democratic Islamists, 32, 35
democratic outcomes, in India, 67
"democratic participatory project," 48
democratic processes and values, abridging core, 21
"democratic products," design of, 36
democratic quality, 8, 159
democratic recession, as a myth, 157
democratic representation and accountability, in Africa, 50
democratic track record, in India, 66–67
democratic values, 7, 51
democratic variation
    advanced by positive initiatives, 150
    axes for, 6, 102, 110–127, 149–155, 161
    benign, 159–160
    beyond Western practices, 103
    challenge for, 159

as a cover for undemocratic behavior, 102
crucial vectors of, 105
currently supported, 129–133
debate on, 83–100
in democracy support, 160–162
existing within regions, 69
flowing from exploratory openness, 4
forms of, 103
framework for, 101–128
framing a search for, 84
future of, 157–167
importance of, 162
legitimate forms of, 127
models of, 64–67
moderate, 2–4
moving center stage, 166
in non-Western countries, 112
non-Western support for, 142–149
potential African, 50
pursued through innovations, 6
quest for, 7
reimagining democracy, 160
from rising democracies, 149
search for, 102, 162
separating from geopolitics, 163
support for, 141, 163
democratization, 30, 40, 90
developing nations, worse inequality, 115
developmental model, 88
"different democracy," calls for, 79
"differentiated democracy" discourse, 14
"differentiated universalism," 87
digital activists, challenging "tradition," 36
Dilma Rousseff government, 49
direct democracy, 46, 48, 94, 153
dispute resolution, 26, 125
dispute-settlement mechanisms, at a local level, 25
disruption, as an end in itself, 93
diverse social groups, forced homogenization of, 47
donors
    channeling rule-of-law support, 155

embracing variation, 132–133, 165
failing to focus on community
   development, 131
focusing on "working with hybridity,"
   161–162
method of finding civil society, 130
support to core liberal rights
   misrepresented, 164
supporting traditional dispute
   resolution, 154
double standards, eliminating, 163

E

Eastern European states, 19, 69
economic and political freedom, 152
economic change, models of justified, 107
economic choices, reassessing the processes
   of, 118
economic crisis, 88, 89, 91
economic decisionmaking, 161
"economic democracy," 116
economic elites, power of, 114
economic freedom, married to managed
   political control, 108
economic gains, in Latin America, 48
economic inequality, in Western countries,
   114–115
economic injustices, 88
economic institutions, 118
economic justice
   civil society organizations exploring,
      151–152
   espousing non-Western models on, 22
   liberalism as, 114–118
   needing strong state capacity, 75
   pursuit of, 103
economic liberalism, injustices of, 107
economic performance, across regime types,
   75
economic policies
   concerns over, 115
   pursuit of fairer, 76
   of Western nations, 151
economic power, structures of, 152

economic reform, inimical to democracy,
   116
economic success, in the Asian model, 58
economic variation, need for, 107
Economist Intelligence Unit, 73
egalitarian democracy, 99
Egypt, 33, 37–38, 113, 143
elections
   free, 107
   as increasingly meaningless, 93
   in Nigeria, 56
   non-Western support policies for, 147
   Western governments promoting, 130,
      132
Electoral Commission, in India, 67
electoral democracy, 99
elite-led democratization, preference for,
   144
elites, quotas flowing to, 119
"emancipatory promise," fulfilling
   democracy's, 46
"engineered civil society," 130
Ennahdha party, in Tunisia, 39, 40, 141
Erdoğan, Recep Tayyip, 40, 145–146
European Commission, supported social
   inclusion, 138
European Endowment for Democracy, 136
European External Action Service diplomat,
   19
European governments, spending on social
   development, 137
European Instrument for Democracy and
   Human Rights (EIDHR), 137
European Union (EU)
   consensual models of democracy,
      138–139
   democracy and human-rights strategy,
      136
   focus on homosexual rights, 150
   frustration with elite consensus, 86–87
   model of conflict analysis, 134
   participatory budgeting, 124
   policies, 98, 137
   pressing Iraq to allow sectarian
      factions, 141

exclusionary illiberalism, 86

F

federal structures, in Ukraine, 120
Fiji, 62, 138
flawed democracies, 33t, 44t, 54t, 60t
flexible and empowering rights, 110–114
"floating but anchored" democracy, 106
frameworks
    Asian institutional, 57
    democratic variation, 101–128
    Islam democracy, 30, 31
"free" countries, in Africa, 53
free market economic doctrine, 115
free market liberalism, 108
free markets, 117, 151
Freedom House, rankings, 98
full democracies, 44t, 54t, 60t

G

general will, liberal concept of, 95
generations, differences over democracy, 94
Ghannouchi, Rached, 38, 39
Gini coefficient, political models and, 75
global civil society activity, 92
"global marketplace," 142
global opinion polls, on democratic norms,
    158
global power, shifting, 165
globalism, advancing with localism, 166
globalization, 88, 121
globalized capitalism, 96
grantee-protection system, 136
"Greek ethos," spirit of, 92
group identities, democratic institutions
    and, 122
group rights, protection for minorities, 147
"guardian institutions," 80
Gulf Cooperation Council, 43

H

Hezbollah, in Lebanon, 42

High Peace Council, in Afghanistan, 64
horizontal accountability, in Latin America,
    45
human-rights situation, EU assessments of,
    136
hybrid regimes, 33t, 44t, 54t, 60t
    claiming divergence from liberal
        democracy, 106
    distinguishing benign aspects from
        malign, 162
    as a distortion of local demands, 14
    incorporating illiberal features, 23
    indices exhibiting discrepancies in, 99
    lack of liberalism of, 25
    quasi-permanent durability of, 161
hyperlibertarian protesters, 93

I

ICT. See information and communications
    technology (ICT)
identity formation, internal processes of, 78
ijma, principle of, 30
ijtehad, principle of, 30–31
illiberal clauses, on minority rights, 141
"illiberal consociationalism," drawbacks of,
    139
illiberal democracy
    defined, 8
    distinguishing from nonconsolidated,
        77
    support for in the Middle East, 34
illiberal forces, increasingly empowered, 14
illiberal populism, 108, 151
illiberal practice, 106
illiberal regimes, 13, 161
illiberal restrictions, on rights, 59
illiberal state, 16, 86
illiberal values, 77
illiberal views, defending the Brotherhood,
    37
illiberalism, 8
inclusiveness, 80, 128
income inequality, measure of, 75
India, 66–67, 146–147

indices, comparing forms of democracy, 99
"indigenized" forms of democracy, 77
"indigenous" forms, determining
    antidemocratic, 162
Indignados movement, 91
individual rights
    alongside consensus and social
        harmony, 119
    versus collective concerns, 88
    nesting within a sense of community
        identity, 161
    prioritization of, 111
    protection of basic, 107
    pursuing variation in understandings
        of, 150–151
individualism, in Western democracies, 22
Indonesia, 59, 62, 146–147
industrial societies, 77
inequality, 46
informal justice, 26, 126
Informal Justice Sector Component, of
    USAID in Afghanistan, 134
information and communications
    technology (ICT), 36–37, 122, 154
innovation, 103, 161
institutional forms, values expressed
    through, 22
institutional frameworks, Asian, 57
institutional gridlock, in the West, 104
institutional impartiality, core principle of,
    116
institutional options, available for
    reformers, 105
institutionalized communitarianism, 120
institutionalized self-rule, forms of, 104
institutions
    adapting to local cultural and social
        contexts, 58
    encouraging reform through
        traditional, 133–135
instrumentalism, 163, 164
interest group corporatism, 97
intergroup consensus, 119
international community, supporting
    participation, 153

International Democracy Day, message for,
    15
international democracy policies,
    relegitimizing, 162–165
international democracy promoters, 133,
    160
international democracy support, 129–156,
    162
International Institute for Democracy and
    Electoral Assistance (IDEA), 15
internationalization, 89
Iraq, 24, 120
Islam
    compatibility with democracy, 29–35
    democracy frameworks for, 30, 31
    factors beyond, 35–37
    principles serving "as a bridge," 39
Islamist concepts
    of democracy, 21
    of rights, 113
Islamist parties
    distinctive model of democracy, 140
    restrictions on human rights, 112
Islamist principles, political system and, 38

J

Japan, 65–66, 146
Jordan, 41, 42
Journal of Democracy, 157
justice, 155, 161. *See also* economic justice;
    informal justice; social justice
Justice and Development Party (AKP), in
    Turkey, 40, 145
justice systems, customary or traditional, 25

K

Kenya Justice Project, 134
Khurshid, Salman, 15–16
kleptocracy, 50

L

Latin America, 12, 43–49, 68, 124
leaders

focus on controversial, 47–48
functioning without, 91
Lebanon, 42, 120
Lee Kuan Yew, 57
leftist populist regimes, core debate about,
   45
leftist populists, Brazilian leaders' sympathy
   for, 144
legal norms, non-Western, 154–155
legal pluralism
   in Afghanistan, 64
   built on calls for non-Western rule of
      law, 23
   demand for, 25–26
   recent trends in, 125
legal systems, 125, 127
legalism, in East Asia, 58
legislatures, in Latin America, 45
"liberal consociationalism," 24
liberal democracy
   in African conditions, 51
   assault on, 76
   based on rule of law, 99
   becoming ungovernable, 85
   beset by a malaise, 103
   in Brazil, 49
   conservative values, 72
   critical scrutiny of, 85
   defending Islamists' freedom to beliefs,
      113
   defined, 8
   enriching, 160
   European, needing to rebalance, 114
   feeding neoliberal economics, 75
   focus on, 14
   as harmful to community identity, 152
   as inherently unstable, 86
   "liberal" component of, 95
   objecting to the "liberal" part of, 23
   "showcase," 45
   as a tool for conflict resolution, 24
   Western democracies replicating the
      model of, 149
   Western democracy as, 22

Liberal Democratic Party (LDP), in Japan,
   65
liberal human-rights architecture, 107
liberal internationalism, colliding aims, 164
liberal market reforms, 115
liberal model, donors still sticking to, 130
liberal order, core of, 90
liberal political systems, 86
liberal procedure, notion of, 111
liberal rights, 34, 113, 139, 150
liberal secularists, in the Middle East, 140
liberal social norms, 72
liberal values, 72, 160
liberalism
   challenges to, 86, 166
   community and, 74, 95
   conflating with secularism, 35
   core of individual innovation and
      questioning, 96
   curtailing democracy to defend, 38
   as economic justice, 114–118
   as an elastic concept, 106
   history of, 94
   individual, emphasizing rights of, 74
   preserving in a more self-protective
      mode, 141–142
   relationship between economic and
      political, 75
   tension with democracy, 89
   toleration, as a philosophy of, 111
"liberalism minus," 105
"liberalism plus," 6, 105–110
liberty
   ancient, participative versus modern,
      private, 79, 87
   negative, 95
   political, 116
Libya, 140
"limited liberal democracies," 61
"liquid democracy," 91
local context, adapting democracy to, 50
local democratic traditions, in Africa, 56
"local ownership," narrative of, 164
local populations, protesting for free

elections, 132
"local values," conforming to, 2
local-community level, Islamist parties
    efforts at, 35
localism, advancing with globalism, 166
"locally credible" model, 106
locally rooted justice, 125
locally rooted organizations, donors' search
    for, 135
loya jirga, form of, 64

M

Maduro government, reaction to revolts,
    48–49
majoritarian democracy, 69, 99
majoritarian Westminster model, in India,
    66
majoritarianism
    insensitive to minority interests, 119
    liberal democracy limiting, 97
    in Turkey, 40
    West's fixation with, 163
majority rule, democracy more than, 19
Malaysia, 59, 61
Mali, 135, 140
Maliki, Nouri al, 121, 141
managed democracy, 80
market economy, 46
"market sovereignty," 88
Mauritania, 135
"merchant class," 85
meritocracy, advancing, 58
Mexico, 43–45
middle class, growing in developing states,
    78
Middle East, 16, 29–43, 140
Millennium Development Goals, of EU,
    137
mobilization
    based on ICT, 122
    in many nations around the world,
        158
models, for democracy, 85
modernity, variety of paths toward, 104

modernization theory, inverse of, 58
"monitory democracy," 85
moral relativism, of Western liberal
    democracy, 31
Morales, Evo, 49, 80, 138
Morocco, 41, 42
Morsi, Mohamed, 37, 141
multiparty systems, not fitting in African
    societies, 52
Museveni, Yoweri, 52, 56
Muslim Brotherhood, 37, 141
Muslim countries
    illiberalism versus rights, 112
    liberal rights imposing non-Islamist
        agenda, 113
Muslim democracy, Erdogan's idea of, 41
Muslim scholars, 30, 31

N

Naím, Moises, 85–86
National Dialogue, in Tunisia, 40
National Intelligence Council (NIC), 14
national interests, versus individual
    freedoms, 98
national-level judicial systems, 125
nation-states, forging viable, 12
negotiated settlements, between warring
    factions, 24
neoliberal economics, 74–76
neopatrimonialism, in Africa, 50
neutrality, between participants in a
    democracy, 116
New Confucian understanding, of
    democracy, 110
"New Liberal," 107
NGOs (nongovernmental organizations),
    123, 130, 135
Nietzsche's will to power, 96
Nigeria, 52, 56
1973 Trilateral Commission, 85
non-Confucian cultures, in Asia, 61
nonelectoral forms of representation, 123
nongovernmental organizations (NGOs),
    123, 130, 135

noninterventionist support for reform, 143
nonliberal democracy, call for wholesale, 77
nonliberal power-sharing, 23–24
nonpartyism, 51
non-Western alternatives, to Western liberal
   democracy, 3
non-Western countries, seeking democratic
   development, 166
non-Western democracies
   commitment to international
      democracy, 147
   in regions, 29
   rising, 142, 165
non-Western democracy
   advocates of, 3
   boundaries for the concept of, 159
   as calling for illiberal democracy, 8
   calls for, 1, 5, 11–27, 71
   compared to nonliberal democracy,
      22–23
   problems with the notion of, 71–81
   restrictions on individual rights, 112
non-Western forms, Varieties of Democracy
   project not pointing toward distinctive,
   109
non-Western illiberal soft authoritarians, 81
non-Western justice, 125–127
non-Western legal norms, 154–155
non-Western political models, 19
non-Western populations, frustrations
   expressed, 26–27
non-Western regimes, antigay legislation,
   150
non-Western societies, 76, 93, 101
non-Western trends, responding to, 23–26
"norms versus institutions" division, 7
norms-versus-values distinction, 112
"not free" countries, in Africa, 53

O
Occupy movement, 91
"offensive liberalism," era of, 141
Office for the Promotion of Parliamentary
   Democracy, 19

On Liberty (Mill), 96
one-party dominance, in Japan, 65
opposition change agents, donors drawn
   to, 131
Orban, Viktor, 16, 86
Orientalism, contemporary form of, 77

P
participative democracy, 91–94
participative processes, 118
participatory, deliberative democracy, 99
participatory and deliberative dynamics,
   153–154
participatory budgeting, 48, 123
parties, among least trusted political
   institutions, 122
"partly free" countries, in Africa, 56
patron-client relations, in Asia, 58
peace building, 23, 143, 144
"the people," banner of, 47
Philippines, 61, 138
Plato, 80–81
pluralism, 102
polarization, 97, 114
policy areas, beyond EU parliamentary
   interference in, 98
political authority, role of, 63
political competition, Western focus on, 50
political conflicts, in India, 67
political development, 21, 75
political elites, disaffection with
   mainstream, 87
political influence, consensual routes to,
   154
political institutional models, regional
   differences, 110
political models, 166
political order, founded on Islam's
   principles, 32
political participation, 119
political parties, in Africa, 51
political principles, versus institutional
   forms, 22
political process, changes to, 115

political reform, rising democracies encouraging, 143

political space, restriction of, 116

political style, choice of, 79

political system
in Asia, 57
economic and operational aspects of, 20

political trends, in Africa, 53

political values, spreading across cultures, 73

politics, changes interacting with cultural values, 77

"politics of presence," focusing on, 123

populism
chauvinistic, 104
defined, 46
democracy and, 47
framing debates, 45
illiberal, 108, 151
rise of, 80

populist democracies, 48

populist parties, in many Western countries, 13

"postmodern global democracies," 89

postparliamentary democracy, 97

power
concentration of, in Latin America, 49
rebalancing among states, 89, 166
sharing, 78, 161
shifting from the West to "the rest," 19

power quotas, 118–122, 152

"predatory modernization," 89

principles, of democracy, 9

"privatization of politics," 87

privatization processes, benefits to elites, 118

pro-democratic voices, in developing states, 77

professional middle classes, in the Middle East, 35

pro-Independence movement, origins of Indian democracy, 66

property rights, de-emphasis of private, 46

protective democracy, in Asia, 61

protests, cutting across democracy's institutions, 93

"public, political" identity, 32

Putin, Vladimir, 21, 72

Q

Qatar, 43

quotas, 118–119, 121, 152

Quran, 31

R

"rampant liberalism," 86

rationalism, Chinese leaders lauding, 90

Rawls, John, 88, 95–96

real-life policy challenges, 155

realpolitik security alliances, 148

rebel fighters, as "traditional community leaders," 133

Rechtsstaat, concept of, 138

"redistributive regulated party rule," 65

reform
paths, 13
respecting national sovereignty, 143
through traditional institutions, 133–135
types of, 159

regime types
in the Middle East, 32
by scale of social values, 73f

regional debates, 68–69

regional models
of democracy, 5
for non-Western democracy, 29

regions, own distinctive form of politics, 29

"rejectionism," spirit of, 93

religion, role in the Middle East, 34

religion-based political activity, banned in Egypt, 38

religious boundaries, limiting openness, 31

religious edicts, trumping liberal rights, 141

religious rights, protecting, 113

renewal, as core to liberalism, 166–167

renovation, quest for, 158
representation, alternative forms of,
122–124
representative and participatory dynamics,
153
republican ethos, of classic democracy, 87
"republican model," 46
Rice, Condoleezza, 16–17
rights. *See also* liberal rights; *other types of
rights*
  consensus-oriented approach to
    questions, 139
  flexible and empowering, 110–114
  infringements in the West, 104
  protective, Lockean understanding
    of, 97
  safeguarding basic, 120
rising democracies
  adding distinctive input, 165
  adding vitality to global democracy
    support, 142
  challenge to the West, 148–149
  differences among, 144
  focus on democracy support, 147
  foreign policies of, 143
rising non-Western democracies, supporting
  democracy beyond their borders, 6
rising powers, bolder assertion of national
  sovereignty, 13
rule of law, 26, 46, 125, 139
Rule of Law Stabilization Program, 134
rural-urban divide, within national polities,
  94
Russia, 21, 120, 138

S

Salafist Nour Party, 37
Saleh family, 41
Saudi Arabia, 43
Schumpeterian definition, 84
sectarianism, 52
"secular state," 34
secular-autocratic forces, restricting rights,
  112

"secular-rational" values, societies adhering
  to, 73
self-criticism, core to liberalism, 166
self-management councils, in Mexico, 48
self-rule, core ethos of, 104
sharia, 35, 37
Shia Houthi rebel campaign, 41
Shia party, in Bahrain, 42–43
shura (consultation), principle of, 30, 31
Singapore, 58, 62
Sisi, Abdel Fattah, 16, 38
"smart authoritarianism," 14
social actors, access to decisionmaking
  processes, 117
social attachments, sustaining, 88
social capital, accumulation of, 131
social change, outstripping institutional
  structures, 78
"social citizenship," Marshall's classic
  concept of, 106
"social cohesion laboratories," 137
social configurations, in Thailand, 61
social decay, Western democracies in, 72
social democracy, 88, 118
social equality, pursuit of, 103
social illiberalism, 74
social injustice, 108
social insurance schemes, 137
social justice, 30, 74, 96, 143
social justifications, role of, 26
social media sites, constrained in China, 63
social movements
  Brotherhood's identity as, 37
  distinction from civil society
    organizations, 131
  moving from contestation to building,
    154
  new in Western and non-Western
    countries, 91
  positive potential of new, 153
  reviving representative institutions,
    161
  single-issue, 93
"social nonmovements," 36, 123

social norms, 62, 72–74

social traditionalism, 61

social values, 73, 73f

societal cleavages, in India, 66

soft authoritarianism, 80

South Africa, 52, 53

South Korea, 62, 124, 146

South Sudan, 133, 135

state action, overcoming collective action problem, 90

state and civil society, as mutually constitutive, 117

state bodies, consulting religious authorities in Arab countries, 34

state capture, pathologies of, 14

"state guidance," developing better, 98

"state-building contract," EU introduced, 134

state-led economic modernization, 146

Stiftungen, representatives of, 138

strategic allies, accepted by Western powers, 163

Sunni jihadist Islamic State, 121

Sunni political societies, in Bahrain, 42

super rich, India's, 67

"supporting the unsupported," 136

Supreme Court, in India, 67

Syrian conflict, overflowed into Lebanon, 42

systemic-level democracy, 151

T

Tamils, human-rights abuses against, 147

technical capacity building, through EU, 136

templates. *See* Western templates

Thailand, 61, 62

theocratic models, for Muslim societies, 50

"a theory of combined democracy," 153

Theory of Justice (Rawls), 95

Third Wave of democracy, 12, 13

totalitarian ideology, rebuttal of, 95

trade-offs, between representation and accountability, 97

traditional mechanisms, illiberal provisions of, 139

traditional systems, reasserting themselves, 126

"traditional values," 73, 140

transitions, hybrid regimes and, 24–26

trends, pushing against political uniformity, 23

"tribal democracy," talk of in Jordan, 42

"trustee model of democracy," 58

Tunisia, 36, 38–40, 113, 138, 141

Turkey, 40, 145–146

U

Uganda, 52, 150

Ukraine, 120, 139

ultramajoritarian democracy, 34

UN secretary-general, policy paper on democracy, 15

United Arab Emirates, 43

United Nations Democracy Fund (UNDEF), 135

United Nations Development Program (UNDP), 133

United Nations (UN) General Assembly, 15

United States

    focus on homosexual rights, 150

    polarization in, 86

    pressing Iraq on sectarian factions, 141

    template of democratic reform, 98

United States Institute of Peace, 134

Universal Declaration of Human Rights, 20

USAID, workshop in Nairobi, 134

V

values

    Asian, 57

    imposing on another country, 17

    universal, 18

values-forms distinction, 22

variation. *See* democratic variation

variation and plurality, motives for the search for, 103

varieties
adding to existing democratic
templates, 106
of liberalism, 114
Varieties of Democracy project, 98–99, 109
Venezuela, 48–49, 137, 142, 144
village councils, in India, 67
village-level forms, of decisionmaking, 53

W

wealth disparity, liberal democracy and, 114
Weibo, use of, 63
"welfare liberalism," 96
welfare states, 98
Western aid, tensions over, 139–142
Western capitalism, 22
Western democracy
basic elements of, 21
call for less, 164–165
challenging the liberal elements of, 23
exploring possible innovations, 157
needing to improve democratic
quality, 84
promoters, 130, 148, 165
push back against, 13
question of alternatives to, 11
reexamining, 84–88
support, 146
underperforming, 19
violence and effort midwife to
modern, 77
Western donors. See donors
Western foreign policies, design of, 129
Western governments
"institutional development," 23
managing economic crisis
democratically, 151
overdoing focus on variation, 140
preferring to "wait for elections," 132
pursuing own economic interests, 116
seeking to encourage democratic
variation, 130
seeking to impose uniform templates,
155

Western liberal state, protecting rights of
religious minorities, 32
Western liberalism, as varied and complex,
100
"the Western order," critics of, 104
Western policy, examples of variation,
133–139
Western policymakers, demonstrating
tangible impact from projects, 154
"Western political package," extending, 103
Western politics
style of, 79
trends within, 104
Western power interests, 90
Western templates
donors channeling rule-of-law support
to, 155
no single, 87
United States spreading, 98
unsuited to non-Western countries, 2
variety of, 106
Western-arbitrated uniformity, struggle
against, 164
Western-versus-non-Western democracy
debate, 8
Western-versus-non-Western division, 101
Whitehead, Laurence, 46, 106
workplace "economic democracy," 75–76
World Values Survey, 20, 73

ABOUT THE AUTHOR

Richard Youngs is a senior associate in the Democracy and Rule of Law Program, based at Carnegie Europe. He works on EU foreign policy and on issues of international democracy.

Youngs is also a professor of international relations at the University of Warwick. Prior to joining Carnegie in July 2013, he was the director of the European think tank FRIDE. He has held positions in the UK Foreign and Commonwealth Office and as an EU Marie Curie fellow. He was a senior fellow at the Transatlantic Academy in Washington, DC, from 2012 to 2013.

His latest books include *The Uncertain Legacy of Crisis* (Carnegie, 2014); *Europe in the New Middle East* (Oxford University Press, 2014); and *Climate Change and European Security* (Routledge, 2014).

CARNEGIE EUROPE

Carnegie Europe was founded in 2007 and has become the go-to source for European foreign policy analysis in Brussels on topics ranging from Turkey to the Middle East and the Eastern neighborhood to security and defense. Carnegie Europe's strong team of scholars provides unparalleled depth of analysis and thoughtful, carefully crafted policy recommendations on the strategic issues facing the European Union and its member states.